Time-Limited, Intermittent Therapy with Children and Families

Time-Limited, Intermittent Therapy with Children and Families

by

Thomas Kreilkamp, Ph.D.

Harvard Community Health Plan
Cambridge, Massachusetts

BRUNNER/MAZEL, *Publishers* • New York

Library of Congress Cataloging-in-Publication Data

Kreilkamp, Thomas, 1941–
    Time-limited, intermittent therapy with children and families / by
Thomas Kreilkamp.
        p.   cm.
    Bibliography: p.
    Includes index.
    ISBN 0-87630-532-X
    1. Psychotherapy, Brief.   2. Family psychotherapy.   3. Parent and
child.   I. Title.
RC480.55.K74 1989
616.89′14—dc19   88-30229
                                                                        CIP

Copyright © 1989 Brunner/Mazel, Inc.

Published by
BRUNNER/MAZEL, INC.
19 Union Square
New York, New York 10003

MANUFACTURED IN THE UNITED STATES OF AMERICA

10 9 8 7 6 5 4 3 2 1

For Ivan and Jacob

There is always a margin between what is asked and what is offered, between the hopes, which are unlimited, and the response, which is necessarily relative. In that always gaping trench, desires proliferate, crazed by false expectations and wild figments of the imagination. That trench is also where the dependent's resentment and, often, the provider's guilt begin to develop. The relationship between a dependent and a provider is a duet, but it is an inharmonious duet.—Albert Memni, *Dependence*, 1984, p. 48.

Contents

Preface

This book has three principal lines of argument, which are
wound together. One presents a detailed analysis of the system
of the Harvard Community Health Plan (HCHP), in particular
the parts relevant for those of us in the mental health de-
partments, in the belief that this system helps support the
form of therapy we do, or perhaps more intimately has by its
existence—its administrative procedures, and its systemic supports for a form of short-term therapy—helped to create the
form of therapy we now practice. Another offers a theory of
therapy, a theory which borrows from various parts of psychology and psychiatry, a theoretical orientation which provides us clinicians assistance in our attempts to help people
in our system. A third gives examples of how this theoretical
approach is applied in practice in our setting. These lines of
argument cannot be entirely separated, because they are all
wound together in our work, but to some degree we will
begin with an analysis of the system within which we work,
and then move to the theoretical underpinnings of our therapy,
offering examples as we go along of how our theoretical
approach is applied in practice.

The work we do is short-term, which is usually construed
as "taking less time" or "involving fewer meetings." Although
this is accurate to some degree, it does not tell the whole
story. Many of the currently prevalent ideas about short-term
therapy (e.g., those of Malan, Mann, Sifneos, and Davanloo)[1]
involve applying traditional psychodynamic notions to work

---

[1] See the bibliography for detailed references to works or authors cited.

done within a shorter time frame (12 or 20 or 50 sessions, typically but not always once weekly). Our approach is somewhat different. We start not from thinking how we can shorten ordinary therapy, or how we can select certain patients for whom a shorter form of treatment would do just as well as a longer form. Rather, we start from thinking that we need to provide help to anyone (everyone) from our membership who asks for it. The numbers who ask for help are large, in part because the price is low ($3 a visit), in part because of the area we are in (Cambridge, where therapy is regarded to some degree as a normal part of life), and for many other reasons, which will be discussed in more detail later. We have never had enough staff to allow us to see everyone weekly, even had we wanted to do that. So our social and experiential situation at HCHP has provided us with an opportunity and challenge: to develop a way of thinking about therapy which would allow us to work with many more patients than most therapists ordinarily would in other settings. How do we do this?

One way to summarize succinctly the differences between our approach and that of others is to say that our approach is not simply an adaptation of traditional, psychoanalytically oriented, long-term therapy to the constraints of a time-limited situation. Such adaptations are very common, using slightly different methods—more activity on the part of the therapist in helping the patient define a focus for the short-term work, for example—but keeping intact much of the vocabulary and conceptual apparatus of traditional analytic work. Our thinking is different. It is not just that we see people for less time, but that we think about the entire process in a different way than someone does who is simply trying to compress what might in one context take a year or more into a couple of months.

Naturally there are certain ways in which most therapists are similar. Most therapists listen, at least at first, to what the patient has to say; most therapists believe that people are complicated, and so forth. But our approach is, I think, very different from that of most of the other prominent short-term therapy proponents, and it is these differences that the book will outline and analyze. To understand how we arrived at our own method of treatment, however, it is helpful to know something about the system within which we all work, and the beginning of the book will be devoted to that topic.

How is our approach different? We rely less on free association than most private therapists or long-term therapists, because we have less time and cannot simply wait to see what unfolds. We rely much more on an active approach. But mainly we try to engage the patient's sense of responsibility for himself in a fundamental way. This attempt has many facets and occurs in a context that provides an active caring therapist who is part of a larger system of care. But responsibility is a fundamental idea, and many details of our approach can best be understood as a way of working toward helping the patient assume responsibility, and avoiding taking it away from the patient. Exactly how this works cannot be said quickly, and there is certainly a sense in which all therapists have this as a goal. So I will attempt to explain in detail how our approach enables us to achieve this goal at least some of the time with some patients.

Our approach is very much embedded within a system; that is, our methods work because they involve not just a therapist with a child or family, but a therapist who works for a *health-care system* which is *providing care* to a family. So one of the central points in this book will be an often-repeated insistence on the importance of the setting within which we practice. As therapists, we are rather consciously oriented toward an appreciation of the family system of the child who is our patient. This book goes further, in trying to make explicit the important role of the therapist's system, the system within which we each are employed and in conjunction with which we each provide care. To put it in another way, our methods of providing treatment could not easily be applied in an individual private practice, since our methods depend on the context within which they are applied. Some of our methods could, of course, be applied by any individual clinician; and most of them could be applied in any group practice setting or clinic. So although we are an HMO, the methods we have developed are not specific to an HMO setting. Rather, they would be pertinent anywhere there are large numbers of people desiring or needing treatment, and limited resources of staff and time to meet those needs. This point will become more clear in the course of the book and will be reiterated in the concluding chapter.

To some degree, insisting on the importance of setting involves applying a social-psychological analysis to a clinical situation. My own view is that such an orientation is vital, not just to thinking about how the context affects the therapy, but to thinking about therapy itself. There is a tradition of applying a social-psychological analysis to therapy which goes back at least to Jerome Frank's influential book *Persuasion and Healing.*[2] I will not be trying to summarize this literature in this book, but one way to understand some of the thinking behind the approach this book will describe is to see it as flowing in part from an attempt to look at clinical processes through a social-psychological lens.

Other important themes in the book will include our awareness of the importance of development not just of a child but of a family, or parents, and of the child in interaction with the parents and family. Additionally, we are aware of the importance of seeing therapy as a developmental process with stages of its own.

Our insistence on the primacy of action (over feeling, over insight, over understanding) is based in the argument that action creates change. Certainly feelings, insight, and understanding are not ignored. No therapist could ignore these important constituents of all action. But the way in which our approach may be distinctive is in the emphasis placed on action, our own action as therapists, and the actions of the patients in their attempts to change their lives. There is a sense in which people create themselves through action, through trying something and observing the consequences. If

---

[2] Two recent publications which discuss this topic and provide abundant bibliographic references are those of Leary and Maddox (1987) and Weary and Mirels (1982).

the therapist believes that, then a certain optimism is possible; insofar as action is always possible, change is always possible.[3]

Although in this book I am presenting my own point of view, I must here acknowledge my general debt to my colleagues who have worked with me over the years. None of us—except our own trainees—learned our approach in any training program; we have been very much engaged in evolving an approach out of our experience, and many of my colleagues have shared this adventure with me. Were they to write a similar book, they might make different points, and would certainly have a different way of making sense of what we do.[4] So there is no party line, no one method that we all acknowledge. And one of the aims of this book, besides to let others outside our system know what we are doing, is to stimulate a discussion of these approaches. Others will have differing ways of doing similar things, and we can all learn from one another.

---

[3] This view is rather typically American in its pragmatic orientation; the debt we owe (albeit it rather unconsciously) to that strand of American philosophy known as pragmatism is considerable. There is also a sense in which this point of view has a deep-seated fundamentally moral aspect; by their deeds shall ye know them.

[4] A volume edited by my colleague Simon Budman contains several examples of analyses done by colleagues of the work we do, and other articles have been published in a variety of contexts over the past few years, although most of these focus on work with adults.

Acknowledgments

This book describes an approach to short-term therapy with children and families that has been developed at a health maintenance organization, the Harvard Community Health Plan (HCHP). The book will present my version of the work we do; although the presentation will be informed by many discussions I have had with my colleagues over the years, the book will remain my own personal view. I have been working in the Cambridge Center of HCHP, and it is mainly my colleagues in this Center to whom I am indebted for my understanding of our approach to patients. I am also grateful, however, to fellow clinicians in other centers who have been interested in trying to make more explicit the constituents of our therapeutic approach. In addition, I appreciate the opportunities I have been given to present these ideas in a variety of contexts, some of them supervisory with residents and fellows from hospitals affiliated with the Harvard Medical School (mainly McLean, and Cambridge Hospital), and some of them more formal teaching or lecture settings. In particular, I appreciate the collegiality of various members of the Cambridge Child Guidance Center, which does work very different from ours but with whom we often share cases and, even more important, ideas; and the support and stimulation of a study group of which I was part for several years, which included a diverse group of faculty members all affiliated with Cambridge Hospital; Sam Braun, Nancy Cotton, Zonda Mercer, Dave Van Buskirk, Ron Siegel, and Connie Tagiuri.

I owe a particular debt to colleagues and friends who read all or portions of this manuscript in draft form and who shared with me their reactions. I would like to thank in particular Gina Arons, Michele Bograd, Jim Harburger, and Dave Van Buskirk. All my colleagues at HCHP deserve thanks, in particular those members of my own child team over the past years.

Time-Limited,
Intermittent Therapy
with Children and
Families

1

The System Within Which We Work

I will begin by describing the setting within which our work is done; and I begin here because the setting within which child therapy occurs is crucial to the question of how the therapy is done. This view, of the importance of setting or context, is perhaps not central in the field, but it needs to become more accepted, and one of the tacit arguments throughout this book will be that context is always important. Many therapists will recognize that context is important in the discussions of symptoms; most therapists will acknowledge that attention needs to be paid to context in considering a patient. Such questions as where the patient lives and what role his symptom plays in the groups he is part of are not unusual. But as clinicians we need also to attend to the importance of our own settings, the contexts provided for us by the workplace in which we do our work.

THE TREATMENT SETTING

Let me briefly describe our setting. We are a growing health maintenance organization in Boston with many centers ranging in size from roughly 10,000 to about 60,000 members.

The one I work in is in Cambridge and has about 40,000 members. Each center has its own mental health department composed of individuals from varying backgrounds, usually including—as ours does—psychiatrists, psychologists, social workers, and psychiatric nurses. There are often trainees as well, from any of a number of disciplines, though our training program is very small.

I will be focusing on the work done by those of us in the child mental health portion of the larger mental health department. There are three or four of us, none full time, although this number may vary somewhat. Referrals come to us usually from the pediatrics department; a pediatrician may initially suggest the referral, or the request may originate with the family, but either way, the pediatrician fills out a form and sends it to us. Most referrals originate around a particular child who is the identified patient, although typically when we initially see a child we see his or her family as well, including particularly the caretakers, whoever they may be.

New patients are assigned by a staff person who books appointments, answers the phone, and handles routine requests for information. Ordinarily she will assign a new patient to the provider who has the next available opening; each provider is assigned some fixed number of new patients each week, the number depending on whether the provider is full time or part time. Typically a half-time person will see two new patients a week, a full-time person four, although this number varies depending on other factors (amount of administrative work, other kinds of clinical work such as running groups, etc.). The flow of new patients is unceasing and requires no intervention on our part; that is, we do not need to recruit new patients. The reasons for this include a generally accepting attitude in Boston about seeing a shrink (as the children will typically refer to the process), but important as well are the ease of access (in our institution), the cost (only $3 for each visit, up to a maximum of 10 in a calendar year),[1]

---

[1] Ten additional visits in a calendar year cost $15 each with some provision for a sliding scale for patients in great need of help who cannot afford to pay that amount.

the convenience (people who belong to our health plan typically do not live very far away, so that getting into our offices is not usually difficult), and the already existing institutional transference (or whatever the patients' relatively favorable views of our system should be called).

In our setting, children are brought in by their caretakers to see pediatricians whenever there is a problem the caretaker wants help with, and thus the children we therapists see are accustomed to coming into our building for medical attention. Very few children come to see a therapist before they have seen a pediatrician (the system is set up so that having a relationship with a primary care provider—a pediatrician or an internist—is a prerequisite for seeing someone in mental health). Occasionally a family joins the health plan and then immediately requires mental health attention before they have had a chance to begin seeing other doctors, but this is uncommon. Thus, most of the children we therapists see have a relationship with other providers in our building, and in a sense they have a relationship with the building, with the setting in which we practice. Similarly, their parents know the building and are accustomed—more than the children, in fact—to coming to our setting for help. Children, certainly, may experience their visits to a pediatrician as painful, especially when they are given a shot! But parents nearly always experience pediatric attention as helpful. (If they consistently do not, they of course may leave the Plan.)

This creates an a priori positive transference, to use language which is conventional in our field. Perhaps it should be called an institutional transference; at any rate, that is the phrase we often use.[2] Thus, even before we begin seeing a child, we have something in our favor. We are seeing people—conventionally, each of us sees a child with his or her family, or at least with the primary caretakers—who are accustomed to coming to our setting for help.

---

[2] I do not want to pretend that there are never cases of negative institutional transference. Not everyone who feels negatively about us leaves the Plan, and this poses problems, but these are a minority of cases.

But there are other factors in our setting which enhance our role. For example, there is the fact that there are few institutional barriers to access to our services. Anyone may see a mental health provider by making a request to a primary care provider. The pediatricians work closely with us and recommend us to their patients, and thus they are influential in helping us start off on the right foot with the patients. We see many children before their problems are very severe, although not every child with obvious problems will be brought to see us by the parents, since parents may resist admitting that there is a problem. But compared with many settings in which child therapists work, our setting brings us a large number of children and families in the early stages of the development of a problem. This makes intervention vastly easier.

Thus, care is provided within a system that involves multiple providers, all of them working in the same organization. This system of care has an impact on the patient whether or not the various providers involved in a given case meet face to face to discuss the case. What constitutes this system from the point of view of the patient?[3]

What seems to be most important is the fact that so much of the patient's health care is organized under one roof. In practical terms, this means that in our Center, which has two floors, a patient may come in to see an eye doctor and run into the child mental health clinician, whom he has not seen for a while. Similarly, a parent who is referred by a pediatrician to child mental health can come to the same building that he and his children are used to coming to; the child is coming to a familiar place; if there are siblings, they can wait in a child care room until the others are finished with their appointment.

The physical organization of our Center also affects the providers. They can run into one another in the hallways and

---

[3] We do not need to be concerned with the system as perceived by the administrators who run the system, since their view is probably not congruent with that of the patient. The patient is the one receiving the care, the one who has a problem and who wants to get better.

touch base, either briefly if the encounter occurs where patients are numerous and conversation must be restricted, or
in a more detailed way if the encounter is in an area where
there are no patients.

But the most important effect of our all being under the
same roof is that it dramatically changes the nature of the
barrier that ordinarily exists between most people and consultation with a child or family therapist. The whole encounter
is made less weighty, less a serious life event; it becomes
more like leaning over the back fence to consult with a
neighbor who happens to be a flower expert about what is
going wrong with the roses. This is an exaggerated comparison.
Families are still worried when they come in to see us; children
are still resistant to the consultation; and a substantial number
of people—we suspect, though we have no data on this—still
avoid coming anywhere near a mental health provider. But
the encounter between us and the patients occurs in a different
context in our setting than it would in most other settings.

To take another example, when a high school student can
walk down the hall to see a guidance counselor, the likelihood
of his doing so is greater than if he has to make an appointment
to go to another part of the city. There still may be substantial
resistance, but the ease of access is improved. And if the
teacher comes to the guidance counselor and reports a concern about a student, the counselor can reach out to the
student in a variety of ways. Similarly, if a pediatrician comes
to us to report a concern, we can reach out by making a
phone call, once the pediatrician has told the family to expect
a call. The patient may still refuse to come in, but the sheer
fact that this kind of arrangement is possible—not common,
not routine, but possible—changes the nature of the system
within which the care is being provided from that which
obtains in the larger private practice sector of the city.

Thus, we have entrée into the family lives of our patients
by virtue of their coming to us for medical care. The pediatrician, after establishing some leverage with the family based
on months or years of providing reliable care, can suggest to
the family that they come to see us; or the pediatric clinician

can call us and ask us to call the family, having alerted the family that this would happen. Of course, ultimately everything is up to the family. We do not see them if they do not want to be seen. They have to get themselves to their appointments. But our group practice and our charting system, which keeps notes on each patient, together provide a degree of knowledge of each family not easily come by in many other settings.

The chart is useful in many ways, since it documents all encounters (including some phone calls made by the patient to our system) that have occurred between this patient and our system. If the patient has seen other providers (doctors, nurses, therapists, etc.), this information is in the chart. So we find out quickly if the person we are seeing has consulted other mental health people at our center in the past. This of course is not an exhaustive record; any contacts the patient has had outside of our system are not in this record unless the patient has asked or allowed the doctor to put them there. Children's charts often have such outside information, from schools, from testing sessions which have occurred, from previous encounters with any of a number of other agencies. But the fact that such information is not there does not mean that it does not exist, and part of any initial evaluation includes inquiring about the other relevant sources of information.

But the principal use of the chart is to allow and encourage consultation among those of us who work at our center. When we see that someone else has known this family, someone besides the pediatrician, we can consult. I am most likely to do this when the patient has seen one of my mental health colleagues, and in those cases, such consultation is usually quite useful.

The chart also provides a convenient way to communicate back to the referring provider. Minimally, the referring provider will know that I have seen a patient and that an evaluation and intervention are happening. More may be learned if there is more detail in the note, and if the provider has time to read it carefully. In either case, if he has particular concerns, he can call or stop me in the hall and inquire further.

Probably the most important aspect of the way in which the system within which we practice influences the care we provide is connected to our knowledge that the patient usually will not vanish. The patient will stop a piece of short-term work with us but will return to the Center to see the pediatrician, and the pediatrician in turn will report to us if things are not going well (or occasionally, will even report when things are going well!). This is not to pretend that no one gets lost in this system. Our system is still mainly set up for families who can manage to get themselves into our Center for appointments, which are scheduled strictly by the clock. We have almost no drop-in capacity, and if a patient mixes up the day of the appointment, that creates problems. When the patient comes late, that creates problems. We cannot usually reschedule a patient tomorrow who does not come for his appointment today, and from the point of view of the patient, that is unfortunate. And we seldom can go after people who do not come in; we can make phone calls, but we do almost no home visits, and no seeking out of people on the streets (as a dedicated teenage counselor working for a citywide program might do). So there are certainly a number of people with difficulties in living who are not served well by our system. But there are a larger number who are served well.

FORMS OF INTERVENTION

Given that each clinician sees new patients each week—whatever the exact number of clinical hours in our week, they soon become filled with patients—how do we proceed? One immense difference between our setting and the ones most of us trained in is our current lack of the sense of leisure we usually felt in training to take our time collecting information about whatever the problem was. Many training settings presuppose a rather relaxed calendar, in which there are always more days and weeks if necessary. Our setting feels more like an emergency room, where the main imperative is prompt action, although most of the patients we see are not in acute crisis, and even the ones who are usually are not in mortal danger. Adapting to this unceasing flow of new patients is not always easy, but there are important stages in the development of attitudes (the clinician's attitudes) that make this adaptation happen.

First, the clinician needs to see that working with a child and a family begins from the very first contact, and that the work is not neatly broken down into a period of evaluation followed by a period of treatment. Furthermore, the treatment—whatever it may be—must be seen as diagnostically relevant. For example, one may elect to focus on some issue in a series of sessions (between two and six, typically) and use the patient's response to that intervention as an index of the appropriateness of more interventions. In our setting, research has shown that the average number of sessions per patient in a calendar year is five. However, some patients only come in once or twice (perhaps because their presenting problem has already improved before their first appointment, perhaps because they are not very eager for treatment in the first place, or for other reasons). Some come in for more than 20 visits in a given year. In my own practice, there are some people I see once a month, some every other week, and many others I see for a brief period of intensive work around a crisis. With some families, such brief interventions may occur more than once in a given year.

Some people and some families use therapy well and some do not, but it is hard to assess this without trying something with them. The fact that the family does not respond now to what I try with them does not mean that they would not respond to some other therapist, or that they would not respond at some later time when they're more ready for whatever intervention I tried. But if they do respond, then that is evidence that further attempts would be useful, on later occasions, when and if other problems arise.

We often refer to doing a short-term piece of work, and what we mean is that we work on some limited problem for a series of sessions and then stop regular meetings, leaving the patient to work through on his own that which has been done in the therapy. Such working through is always imperative, in all forms of therapy, and we have discovered that when they are motivated, patients can do some portion of this internal working-through process without regular meetings with their therapist. Thus, a short-term piece of work is made possible when the patient can assimilate therapy and when he knows he can return for further help when he encounters a problem.

What forms of intervention are possible? The typical distinction made in the field of therapy is between supportive and insight-oriented therapy. This distinction is not totally irrelevant to the work we do, but it is not the most useful one available, because most of what we do, when it is positive, is experienced by the patient as supportive. So any positive contact with a patient is supportive at some level. Furthermore, it remains unclear to what extent insight contributes to change, or how it contributes. There is no question that people change, but there are many questions about the role of insight—as defined within orthodox psychotherapeutic approaches—in that process. Most of our patients come to us wanting some change in their lives, and this often seems appropriate to us. We do not tell them that change is a mere epiphenomenon, not worthy of our attention, merely behavioral, mere surface. Rather, we encourage them to think that this is a realistic expectation and hope, and necessarily our efforts are oriented toward trying to produce some change. (The work of Jay Haley, and his analysis of the work of Milton Erickson, are particularly relevant here.)

THE PEDIATRICIAN'S REFERRAL

Intervention, as I have said, begins at the beginning, and the simplest form perhaps involves the pediatrician agreeing with the parents that something needs to be done. This means that the pediatrician is legitimizing the parents' concern, and agreeing with their point of view, at least to some degree (assuming they requested help). For some parents, this already is helpful; they may experience being sent to a specialist (i.e., the child mental health professional) as a form of being taken seriously. This phenomenon can be a problem in the medical world; the desire of many patients to see a specialist, and their sense that nothing really is happening until they see a specialist, may not be constructive in all cases, but sometimes it works to our advantage. Our setting is a medical setting, our referrals come from medical doctors, and whether we like it or not, patients come to us in a setting where we are seen as specialists. This works to our advantage when the patient feels that help is already occurring just in the very process of referral to a "specialist."

Not all families experience the referral to us in this way. There are some who feel the pediatrician is making too much of what is in their view a trivial problem. They may resist the referral and not come until the pediatrician has suggested it several times, or until the problem has become much worse. Pediatricians often consult with us about such situations, although there is seldom anything we can do directly to encourage such patients to come in and see us. But in our setting, we know when such situations occur. The notes in the chart clarify the process that has led to the presence in our office of a particular person or family. This is often invaluable information.

Some parents come in seeking long-term therapy for their children. But for others, the idea of such therapy is frightening. If the therapy is open-ended, the parents may fear that it will go on forever. There is a part of most parents who bring a child in that hopes that the child will be seen as healthy (no matter how critical they are of the child). So there is a way in which telling the parents that this problem is a real one, but it is not so serious that I need to see your child every week for a year, nor is it serious enough to need hospitalization, helps the parents, since it reinforces their own desire to see the child positively. (There are also cases where this is emphatically *not* true, where the parent wants the child labeled sick and will go to tremendous lengths to obtain that result.)

So the first intervention occurs when the pediatrician either suggests to a family that they come in and see one of us with their child, or agrees with a family that they would do well to come in and see us. Next a support staff person calls the family to arrange the appointment (or the family may call first). The next stage in the process occurs when the family meets one of us. Occasionally this first meeting is preceded by a clinical phone contact, after a family is first called by our area assistant in an attempt to set up this initial appointment. If a parent seems to have more questions about what is going to happen than the area assistant can easily handle, she will give this message to the clinician who is going to see the family, and the clinician will then call the family to see what is happening. Often parents want to inquire about the child and obtain advice immediately about how to handle her behavior. Occasionally a parent wishes to inquire about the orientation and training of the clinician. Sometimes the parent is anxious and it is not clear why, and some period of discussion on the phone may be necessary before the anxiety abates. There may be specific questions about whether both parents need to come, or whether the child should be included in the first meeting; since these are questions the area assistant knows the answer to (both parents should come; the child should come as well), the fact that the parent has not been satisfied by the information provided by the area assistant is in itself noteworthy and usually testifies to the presence of some degree of anxiety about the upcoming encounter with us.

THE DEVELOPING RELATIONSHIP

Specifying what happens next is difficult, since it involves the unfolding of a relationship between one of us and the family in our office. There are different aspects to this process. One important aspect is the acceptance of whatever the family comes in with, as though we are saying, "Oh, that again. Yes, I've seen that before." Perhaps this is an attempt to help the family see that what they are living through is not tragic, is not the end of their family or their child, does not spell disaster. Other people have had similar experiences and lived through them. Underneath this message is a current of optimism; if we have seen this problem before and we don't shudder and quake or run from the room, then probably we think something can be done about the problem. I nearly always admit that this is an occupational disease of mine if the family seems incredulous at my optimism; that is, I say that I have to be optimistic to stay in this business. I believe in change for the better; if I did not, I would not continue doing what I am doing. And saying this is perhaps a strategic maneuver.

What do I mean by this? Voicing negative or critical thoughts which I think a patient is experiencing is a way to make clear that I recognize that the patient is not entirely taken in by my blithe assertion of optimism; it is a way of garnering cooperation in a peculiar sense, since if the patient agrees with me—agrees that I am only optimistic because I'm in this profession—then the patient is in a sense moving toward a position of agreeing with me in other ways. So I try to communicate a sense of understanding what the patient is thinking, of being willing to join with the patient—and expect to have the patient join with me—around a view of me as flawed and imperfect but nonetheless perhaps able to help. And there is in all this as well an attempt to undercut, from the very beginning, whatever tendency toward overvaluation exists. I am a specialist who is supposed to know the answers, according to the unwritten subtext of the whole process which led this patient from a medical provider to my office, but I do not want to occupy that role entirely. I *do* want to be listened to—I want to be able to make suggestions which have some weight, which the patient will attend to—but I do *not* want to be seen as an all-knowing expert who always does the right thing.

Here my general skepticism is pertinent, skepticism I feel about all of us and our behavior. I think we seldom know the right thing to do ahead of time; all we can do is try something and then observe what happens. There are some things that are more likely to be correct than others; similarly, there are some things that are more likely to be mistaken than others; and I want to be taken seriously as a knowledgeable guide to the map that specifies those varied forms of activity. But of certain knowledge there is precious little, and part of any intervention we make involves trying to help

families see that. There are many ways of living, and unfortunately no list of rules. Thus I almost never tell parents that
something they are trying is a mistake. Rather, I say, well
your way has not worked for you, so perhaps it is time to try
something else. If your way had worked, you would not b
telling me about it, you would probably not be here. So no
we know something: this particular technique, the one yo
tried, does not work. So what other possibilities are there

I might say this with regard to how to handle a crying ba
in the middle of the night; if the parents have tried taking
baby to bed with them and that does not help either the b
or the parents sleep, then we know that does not work. (
might say it with regard to whatever particular discipli
measure parents have tried in an effort to get a 16-yea
to improve her grades: so grounding her for a whole sem
does not improve her grades. Well, you have tried a stren
intervention; you have made it clear that you care abou
and her future; I know that is why you have gone to
trouble, but it has not worked. So what can we do ne:

Part of the idea is to move forward from a firm b;
what has already happened in this family. Another air
let the parents know that I can see they are doing wh
are doing because they love their child, because th
devoted parents. This is particularly important for pa
adolescents, who nearly always believe they are going
their various contortions in order to help the child.
a teenager in the house for weeks on end would be
on the parents as on the child; it is a lot of work, an
up with the grief and disappointment this strategy c
in the child also requires a lot of stamina and proba
a lot out of the parents. I acknowledge this because
it and because I have found that doing so helps th
grieve for their failure and then look forward, towa
way of handling the problem. Grief may be too stro
but there is some element of mourning whenev
experience failure with a child. They mourn for the
view of themselves, the one they had during the
of their marriage before they had children. Durir

they talked about having children; they probably hoped that their children would turn out extraordinary, better than the parents and better than any child. They probably had all kinds of ideas about how to raise children, ideas that would improve radically on the ways their own parents used. And now they must admit failure in the sense that their attempt to be good parents has led to unhappiness. Not only is my child not the genius I had hoped for, but he is unhappy; how have I failed?

But this is not a world-class tragedy, since this happens with every family, or so I would insist. I have never met parents who did not wish for more or other than they get from their children. And this process is not necessarily terribly destructive.[4] Rather, it can be seen as human, at least, human in the way we are human at this time in this country. From a cross-cultural and pan-historical point of view, perhaps the current North American tendency to have few children and place large burdens of hope and expectation on their heads is rather peculiar. It certainly is not typical of the way all people have felt about their children through history. But in the current situation, the one which provides the social-cultural background for many of the families I see in my office, this misfortune occurs quite regularly. The misfortune, in short, is that parents expect too much of their children, and children invariably fail to provide everything parents want from them.

Not all families I see fit into this pattern, of course. I see some families from other backgrounds, and their orientation toward their children is usually very different. Often the differences are unclear to me, since in most cases I am far from being an expert in the familial ways of other cultures. So if I am dealing with a family which immigrated recently to America from Haiti, or Portugal, or Greece, or Italy, or India, then I am on much less solid ground. For I do not know what the underlying context is, and the problem is rarely simply a linguistic one, since usually the families speak enough

---

[4] Alice Miller seems to argue along these lines in her thought-provoking, but I think fundamentally mistaken books. I will discuss her arguments in more detail at later point.

English so we can communicate in my native tongue. The problem is more a cultural one, and much of the time I am groping to try to grasp what their ground rules are, what their underlying expectations and hopes and fears are.

THE WORK OF THE PARENTS

So during the initial interview, I am trying to do many things simultaneously. In addition to what I have already discussed, I am usually laying the groundwork for the parents to see that my expectation is that they will have to do most of the work. Their life is their life, and I cannot live it for them. Their child is their child, and the child's behavior is the parents' business in a very fundamental way.

With some families, this point of view is rejected rather strenuously. They come to me with their child in the expectation that I will take the child and cure him, and when they finally understand that I expect them to do most of the work, they stop seeing me. What proportion of my cases is affected severely by this problem I have no way of knowing, but it is substantial. Accepting this is difficult for me; it is one of the misfortunes of life which at times appears tragic, and it is one aspect of my limited powers. I cannot help wishing I had unlimited powers; there is a part of me which would like to agree with these parents, which would like to say, give me your child and I will make him well, but I must constantly acknowledge that this is unrealistic. And there are few therapists who prefer work with children who do not have many rescue fantasies, and there are many people who trigger these rescue fantasies, and chief among them are the families who will not change their ways of handling their child but who want the therapist to change the child for them.

Nearly always these are very unhappy children; nearly always they could use some rescuing. So it is a constant distress of this work to encounter these families, and in truth, the distress is to some degree heightened by our system, since ignoring these families is harder for us than it would be in other systems. For they do not always go away. They may not come to see the therapist, but they continue to see the pediatrician, who will continue to reflect her own sense that something ought to be done, something more than has been done. So pediatricians may be caught up in the parents' wish for someone to take care of their child; after all, that's what pediatricians do (take care of children who are suffering). And our pediatric colleagues, or any of our colleagues who have contact with the family, may come to us and say, can't you do something more, these people are suffering so terribly. Thus we often find it hard to ignore completely those families who come to us and then stop seeing us, finding what we have to offer beside the point, or alien to their own desires.

A CLINICAL EXAMPLE

Perhaps another example will help illustrate. A parent comes in to my office, distressed because she suspects that the terrible marital discord and tension in her home is affecting her eight-year-old son. She wants me to help her child cope with the difficult situation, she says. He must be suffering, she suggests. How could he not be; our home is so disruptive and chaotic and noisy. I watch the child playing happily in my office and I discover, from observation and from talking with the mother and with the teacher, that the child is asymptomatic. There are no vivid signs of distress apparent in the child's sleep, appetite, play, peer relations, or school performance, although inevitably as the mother realizes that I have been gathering this impression, she usually will force my attention toward something she sees as problematic in the child. For example, she says, the child reported a bad dream one morning at breakfast. The dream was like a nightmare, although the child had not awakened in the middle of the night, or at any rate, she said, the child had not come and wakened her, although he may have awakened briefly and then gone back to sleep. Behind this story is the mother's sense that her child should not have nightmares, although if this were said to her she would laugh and say, well, of course, everyone has nightmares sometimes.

Although the child seems to be behaving all right, the mother knows—she wishes to convey this emphatically—that the boy notices that things are not right between the parents, and this distresses her. Again, if I had said to her that she wishes he were less observant, she would probably say no, she enjoys having a curious observant child. And if I had said to her that the boy's life would be easier if his parents did not fight, she would agree but uneasily, since putting the matter in that way seems to imply that there is nothing to be done for the child unless the parents can manage to stop fighting, or can change their way of fighting so it intrudes less on the household.

In this case, after talking with the mother and child, I see the child again alone, talk with the teacher, and then meet again with the mother, after having asked her to bring her husband along with her, although she does not do this, saying that he won't come. I discuss with her a variety of topics, including her own family of origin. How many brothers and sisters did she have, what was her childhood like? These questions are asked out of what I hope appears to be my own interest in her and curiosity about her, for I do not want her to infer that I am asking because I think this information is relevant to her own child and her perception of this boy's problems. I discover that her own family of origin was not perfect: her father was alcoholic, and she remembers her childhood as being less than blissful. She wants so much more for her child than she had, more in the way of family happiness, and now it seems that her child is condemned to grow up in an unhappy family. And her wish had been that she would have a perfect family, or at least a family which was more harmonious.

What can be done? The child does not, in any ordinary sense, need therapy. There are no serious symptoms, there are barely any minor symptoms, the child is not in distress. But the mother is in distress, and the child may also be in some subtle way. Some of the child's distress, of course, may be connected with that of the mother. If the mother could work out some solution to her difficult life situation, that in turn might help the child. Saying this is prosaic. But there are many prosaic realities, and some parents who are quite capable of seeing them once they are pointed out do not see them on their own, or are so bewildered by the complexity of their situation that they have difficulty looking at one topic and bringing it into clear focus. So one way to be useful is perhaps to help her see that part of what she needs is to relieve her own distress.

A problem arises when the parent hears this suggestion as an accusation that she is causing the child's distress, and most parents who come in with this kind of story have enough guilt that it does not take much to trigger more guilt. Thus, part of the work for me here is to manage to convey my suggestion to her in such a way that she hears me as being deeply sympathetic to her own plight and eager to help her feel better. So instead of saying, your child is fine but your marriage needs work and you'd better come in with your husband, I say, your child's suffering is probably connected, as you have suggested, with the turmoil in the household, and the best way for us to help your child is to look more closely at the turmoil in the household. What shall we do about this? Or I say that she is struggling to help her child have a good life and feels that this is not going in the direction she wants it to go; that is, I want to convey to her that I grasp how hard she is trying and how despairing she feels about the failures, but I also want her to heed my suggestion that she come in with her husband to talk more about this. So I stop short of saying, you need to work as a couple in therapy, so come to me with your husband for this needed treatment; instead I say, bring your husband in, I'd like to meet him and hear what he has to say about your son, and I suggest that she give me the phone number so that I can call myself and make this suggestion to her husband. Making such calls is nearly always successful; it is a rare father who will refuse to come in to discuss his child. My hope of course will be to engage him with me in such a way that he will feel that I am on his side as well as his child's side, that I am able to be helpful to his family.

This is an example in which I eventually want to offer a form of therapy. As it happens, the form of therapy I think would be most useful is couples therapy, to address the tension between the husband and wife. Typically, I would see whether they could be engaged together in this process. If so, then I would meet with them several times once a week or every other week, and then usually we would pause for a month or so to give them a chance to try out at home some of the ideas we have been discussing together in my office. This is the juncture at which most of the responsibility for what happens next is placed in their hands. If they wish, I will schedule an appointment one or two months in the future. Or if they prefer, they agree to call to schedule an appointment when they are ready to resume our work. Either way, the time between our appointments can mean that the couple gradually loses track of what we were doing and then do not keep a next appointment. And I am busy enough so that I do not pursue such people, but even if I were not so busy, I think that pursuing them does not make sense, since most people benefit more in the long run by being treated as responsible adults who must take charge of their lives rather than as people in need of watchful care. For this latter stance, in which I as therapist am watching over their progress and checking up on them and reminding them to keep coming in, is appropriate with young children, less so with older children, and inappropriate with adults unless they are either severely damaged or transiently incapable of caring for themselves (because of illness or severe distress).

Here I am making a statement partly about my therapeutic ideology and partly about my values, but I am doing so in the firm belief that my therapeutic stance and values are consistent with those of the larger culture in which we live. And I am doing so in a context which is not remorselessly individualistic and opposed to all human interdependence; I am rather saying, implicitly and sometimes explicitly, that dependence on a professional in matters involving behavior in a marriage or at home should not be a permanent condition. For a man to be dependent on a woman is not a bad thing; for a couple to be dependent on a therapist for more than a brief while is not beneficial. So as a professional therapist, I try to work against increasing the dependence and reliance

of my patients on me, but I support wholeheartedly any movements my patients make toward increased intimacy or interdependence with others. I will make much the same argument
in discussing questions of therapy with children and parents.

The example I have been discussing is one in which I
recommended what amounts to couples counseling around
marital issues. This is one typical form of intervention, but
there are a variety of others, which can include psychological
testing, individual therapy for a child or a parent, family
therapy, consultation with the professionals who are already
involved, consultation with the family (in a way that is often
referred to as child guidance, i.e., offering guidance to parents
about how they handle their children), and group therapy for
child or parents. I would like to discuss each of these, not
exhaustively but in enough detail so that it becomes clear how
we decide which of these modalities to use.

There is a complex network of factors which influences the
decision about which modality to use, or which combinations
of modalities to try, and any choice is both contingent and
temporary. The contingency hinges on our need to pay close
attention to how a child or family reacts to what is offered
to them, for a continuation of the attempt—whatever it may
be—hinges on its being useful. And any choice is designed in
the expectation that it will not be tried for long, so that
switching to another modality, or trying something new, is
not only possible but normal. Rarely do families who come
to us for help and find us helpful stop seeing us after one
brief episode of treatment, whatever form the treatment may
take. They return for other forms of treatment, sometimes
with the same provider, sometimes with other providers, if
they have engaged with our system in a way that feels helpful
to them, or in a way that leads them to expect that we might
be helpful. This knowledge—that a patient will continue in
our system, will return for other forms of help—makes much
easier the task of designing some intervention, for if one does
not have the burden of knowing that failure means the end,
then failure can be integrated into another attempt. If I offer
individual therapy to a child and nothing changes, I can change

to family therapy if there is enough connectedness (or whatever word should be used in this regard) between me and our system on the one hand, and the family on the other.

OUR HOLDING ENVIRONMENT

Behind this fact is our capacity to hold the family in some complex metaphorical sense—that is, independent of how often we see a family, or what happens when we see them, there is some part of a family's involvement with us that is characterized by our sustaining them through our relationship with them. This does not mean that we are always available to see them; it does not mean that we return phone calls within 15 minutes or even within an hour; it does not mean that we offer anything particularly unusual. But we are there in some important sense, and families that benefit from our system know that, and rely on that, and are healthy enough and competent enough to use that without abusing it.

This point is crucial and needs to be stressed. Perhaps an example will help. Peter Sifneos is known now for his writing about one form of short-term therapy with adults. But he wrote an earlier book called *Ascent from Chaos* (1964) about his treatment of a very difficult patient, and the treatment was very different from that elaborated in his later and better-known books: it involved elaborate giving to the patient, giving of time, of food and drink, of attention, and all of it in a relatively ad lib way. Whenever the patient wanted something, he would be given it. This went on for a long time, and was accompanied by vast amounts of talking. What Sifneos was doing with this patient was nurturing the patient in a way that most parents do with young children. His hope was that by his tolerating and fostering a regression into almost complete dependence on the part of the patient, eventually the patient would gather his resources and begin to move forward. According to the account presented in his book, this is what happened.

I think there are a number of patients who would benefit from this form of treatment, but it is quite frankly too expensive

and time consuming for anyone but a family to provide (Sifneos's patient was in a hospital during much of his treatment,
for a variety of physical problems). But I am interested in this
story not because I think it provides a useful method of
treatment—such treatment is impracticable—but because it
offers a model of one form of relationship, a form that is both
healthy and necessary for babies and children, and much less
healthy and necessary for most adults. Adults who need this
form of relationship will prosper only if they succeed in
obtaining it in their own personal lives, for such a relationship
is beyond our professional resources. But few adults can ever
obtain this kind of relationship from others, even when it is
sorely needed because of earlier experiential deficits.

Furthermore, there is a sense in which most relationships
that are important to people offer some quality similar to that
which Sifneos tries to offer his patient, and which parents
routinely offer children. Finding words for this is hard. But
one way of talking about this aspect of relationships has been
to use the phrase *holding environment,* which is awkward and
perhaps farfetched for an ordinary outpatient therapeutic relationship, but which captures some of what we are trying to
talk about here.[5]

There is a sense in which a family provides a holding
environment for a child, a place for the child where there
will be some element of security and caring. But beyond that,
there is a sense in which all human relations provide that
same quality, if they are meaningful connections. This is a big
if, for many of us have relations with others that are not very
deep or important. When Riesman wrote *The Lonely Crowd*
(1955), he drew attention to this aspect of our American life.
And there has always been a strand of critical writing about
psychotherapy which argued that people pay therapists to
provide what their friends ought to provide, that therapy becomes a form of paid friendship.[6] Every since Freud argued
that the most important ingredients of therapy are a person

---

[5] The phrase comes from Winnicott, the well-known child psychiatrist.
[6] See the book by Schofield, *Psychotherapy: The Purchase of Friendship* (1964).

who listens and a person who talks (or sits silent, but in a relationship characterized by transference, by feelings), therapists have been open to the criticism that all they do is talk. And talking seems, on the surface, to be something which all of us do with one another constantly.

But I want to argue that there is a way to do the talking and to provide some of what Sifneos was providing his very disturbed patient without seeing a patient weekly, or even regularly. And the heart of this is the relationship that becomes established between the patient (and family) and us and our system. Most of this is contained in the connection between the family and the individual clinician, but not all of it, although being precise about the rest of it is difficult. But there is a clear sense in which we manage to create and gratify a dependency in our patients, and yet do so in a way that promotes considerable autonomy and independence of functioning.

All therapists try to do this, even though they might not put it in exactly these terms. For the whole profession of therapy is permeated by a tension between the attempt to be professional, to be knowledgeable, to be expert, and the need to avoid doing what so many other experts do, that is, tell the client: "Leave that to us; that's what we're here for." Accountants and lawyers and many doctors and engineers and public relations people and bankers—all these and many other professionals tell their clients that the client should *leave that to us*. The message is: We have a domain of expertise, and in that realm our knowledge is reliable, and you should trust us to take care of things.

This message is very consistent with the role of expert and professional in our culture. But therapists try both to maintain the role of expert, and yet reflect back to the patient the immense importance and even necessity of his doing something himself, taking care of himself. Doing this is in a sense a magical act, since on the face of things it might be hard to imagine why someone would pay hard-earned money for a form of expertise which eventually says, well, it's your problem, you're the one who has to do something about this.

However, many models exist in the professional world that parallel this situation. For example, a ballet coach tells the student how to do it, but it is the student who must eventually do it. There are coaches who are not able to perform the movements but who can still teach, and students often benefit from the teaching even though it is just words. Or an expert in some particular software program may be able to tell someone over the phone what to try when a problem is encountered. Try this: that is the message. Now what if some of what is called therapy with children is like this? This, if true, is only one small part of the whole gamut of modalities that might be offered to a given family, but it is a real and important one. Often this has been called child or parent guidance, but the historical associations of that phrase involve connotations of this being less than real therapy, and I do not wish to imply that. Giving advice is an important part of what we do, but it is done in a way that acknowledges the importance of relationships, of feelings, of personality dynamics, and of familial dynamics, so it is more than just advice. It is advice designed for a particular person or family in a particular situation.

Another part of what is offered is the relationship. It may be attenuated in comparison with important real-world relationships, but it nonetheless offers elements of caring, of reliability, of being available when needed. For some people, such as Sifneos's patient, what we can offer is nowhere near enough. We are not always there: the patient phones in and his provider is not available because she is seeing a patient, or because she is away until two days later. If the frustration of either waiting until the provider is free, or talking to a different provider who is available, is too great, then the patient will not prosper with our system. But most of our patients seem to find our system a pain and a nuisance but good enough so that they do not go elsewhere.[7]

---

[7] We have limited data on those who leave our system because they dislike it. Each year people leave our system and new people join; many of those leaving are going because their job has changed and they now have a different health insurance package, but some of them are leaving because they dislike what they have been experiencing.

So the model I am suggesting here is of a therapist as a professional who does not say, leave it to me, but instead says, let me help you figure out what to do about your problem, someone whose roles include that of consultant and supporter and teacher and guide, as well as therapist. There is no one word which would capture all of this, but all of this must be kept in mind when thinking about what we do in our work.

DEPENDENCY AND RESPONSIBILITY

The delicate balance is between nurturing some degree of dependency on us and our system, and yet insisting in word and tone and deed that the patient must have the ultimate responsibility for his feelings and behavior. Frequent meetings with a therapist may nurture dependency in the patient, just as hospitalization may nurture dependency, and the unfortunate side effects of too great a dependency are numerous. For example, it may make decision making harder. The patient needs to make decisions without feeling that he has to consult with the therapist about every one. Which of us does not have a friend who has been in long-term therapy and who feels that all important decisions must be discussed at length with the therapist before anything definitive is done? Our system and our method attempt to avoid that, although we also want to be available for discussion about decisions and dilemmas when that is essential.

On the other side, when the patient is too dependent, the therapist may become too responsible, and frequent meetings between a therapist and patient (once or twice a week or oftener) can have that effect as well. And if there is an occupational disease of psychiatrists and other mental health professionals, it is feeling too responsible, far more so than is realistic or helpful to the patients. Being responsible and in charge is exciting at times, burdensome at others; but for

---

And furthermore, there are some who stay in our system to use one or another part of it—e.g., to use the pediatrics department—but who do not use other parts of it— e.g., the mental health part. And we have no good data on either of these groups whom we might call dissatisfied users.

a therapist to feel responsible for the patient is probably not helpful for the patient. It probably is not conducive to growth, not conducive to the patient's assuming more control of his own life. Thus, it is ultimately not therapeutic and therefore is to be avoided. Our system has the virtue of providing poor soil for the growth of such intertwined dependency and responsibility.

Our methods of treatment have evolved in a resource-limited setting, but they are probably pertinent to most settings. Resources are always limited, although there may be certain situations in which the limitations seem less glaring. So thinking about how to provide psychotherapy in a context where the limitations are more apparent may lead to an approach that is pertinent even in other settings.

However, the point of view I am describing builds on a sense that thinking in terms of limited resources is not just one way of coping with an economically limited situation, a situation of poverty or scarcity. Instead, I would argue, our way of doing therapy is more responsive to the actual situation of people than other ways—more responsive not because most people are poor and cannot afford the real thing, a full-fledged psychoanalysis, but more responsive because there are better ways to help many people than to sit and listen to them free associate and talk for many, many hours, hoping eventually to provide interpretations that may be correct, that may lead to insight, that may lead to change.[8]

---

[8] The psychoanalytic approach as a theory is invaluable. I have no interest in jettisoning it, nor could I do without it. But the analytic approach as a method of therapy is, I think, often ineffective, appropriate for only a limited pool of people, and surely tremendously wasteful not just of the highly trained analyst's resources (of time and energy), but of the patient's resources (of time and energy). Furthermore, the analytic approach almost surely overrates insight as a vehicle of change. Analysts know this in a sense, as they struggle to formulate the necessary ingredients of true insight, the sort of insight that will lead to change. This attempt to formulate the ingredients of true insight is necessary because all analysts know there are people who seem to have abundant insight who simply do not change. Psychoanalysts would probably also recognize that change occurs frequently in people where there is no insight (there is an obvious sense in which we are all changing constantly, even without having the benefit of psychoanalysis, and usually without having insight into what is fueling the change).

In struggling with these and other issues, we have arrived at a method of treatment that works to produce change in whatever manner seems most effective, although we are severely constrained by numerous factors. To take a trivial example, we cannot hire a babysitter for a distressed parent who would probably feel much better if he could get an hour or two away from his children several times a week. This might be an effective intervention in some cases, one which would reduce the symptomatic distress that brought this particular parent into our office, but it is not one we can make. And there are many effective interventions we cannot make for similar reasons. But once one decides to be more active, there are more interventions possible than one might think. There are definitely people who need more than we can give them, but the more is rarely, I think, a question of more hours of listening and talking in our offices. The more usually has to do with rather fundamental problems in their lives: lack of money, of opportunity, of health, of time. Nothing we can do will redress these significant problems. But often there is much that can be done through therapy.

Eugene Gendlin points out in a recent article that many studies of therapy define a treatment group as "spending time in a room with someone who intends to make therapy happen. The irregular findings show that therapy intention sometimes leads to effects, sometimes not. That finding should be reported to the public, not that therapy happened and was ineffective" (1986, p. 131).

This is a critical point: one cannot provide therapy to someone who does not want it, nor can every therapist provide therapy to every patient who comes his way. We all know this, as therapists. In our system, we use this knowledge, by acknowledging that some people are not ready for therapy (not now, maybe later); by letting or encouraging some patients to see other therapists if nothing is happening with one therapist; by trying different modalities if one is not working. All of this is only possible within a framework involving a large group practice, with many different therapists with different styles and with different preferences for different modalities;

a framework that does not wed the patient to the therapist; where there are many patients so no therapist needs to feel he must hang on to the patient who manages to make it in to a first appointment.[9]

The most convenient way to refer to our methods of treatment is to call them time-limited, intermittent forms of treatment. In other words, our therapeutic interventions are brief, like the ones described by Mann, Malan, Davanloo, and Sifneos (all of them talking, principally, about adult populations), but that is not their distinguishing characteristic. Much more important is the way in which we have discovered that we can offer help without needing to see a given patient weekly and indefinitely. In crucial ways, the resources we offer are not just those techniques or treatments that can be given in a face-to-face setting, but include as well other ways of making contact with a patient and his family, and other ways of helping sustain a family. Knowing what phrase to use to refer to this dimension of our work is hard. The gist of it is that we provide a relationship, not just between a patient and an individual provider, but between a patient and a system, which—when it works—is seen by the patient as a benevolent structure that is there when needed.

Part of my aim here is to make clear how this providing of a relationship works. But I am not talking about public relations, or about advertising that conveys an image of a caring responsive staff; I am talking about the reality of the context within which the care we provide is offered. There is a sense in which our individual clinical skills, exerted with individual patients and their families, function as well as they do only because of the structure within which we work. And the

---

[9] We do run the opposite risk: that therapists want to get rid of patients, either explicitly or tacitly. This is especially true in a system like ours, where one is required to take a certain number of new patients each week. If one stops seeing a new patient, then there is more room in one's schedule. And any process which takes people out of one's schedule is likely to be encouraged, since all therapists—in our understaffed system with so much patient demand for services—feel overburdened much of the time.

maintenance and stability of this structure are important positive forces tending toward health. Or at any rate, that will be a critical portion of my argument.

In the next chapter, we will look at one of the fundamental ideas behind our methods of therapy, the idea of action and activity, carried out by both the therapist and the patients.

2

The Importance of Action

Psychotherapy is mainly talking and listening. This has been true since Freud made what are still rather compelling arguments for the beneficial impact of these activities on certain of the difficulties in which humans find themselves repeatedly. What varies among different therapists is what is said, how it is said, to whom, and on what occasions. Some of this variation is hard to capture in words, since it is related to personality differences among therapists or to nuances of tone and manner. I will be facing time and again in this book the difficulties of putting elusive phenomena into words; this difficulty must be pointed out at the beginning, in part because it is central to the entire therapeutic enterprise, not just to writing about it. We shall have occasion to discuss this at some length later.

The talking and listening we do as therapists are forms of doing, and I will be emphasizing the activity involved in both. Action is one of the central ideas in the form of therapy I will be describing, both the action of the therapist and the action of the patient. Much of the action that occurs in the office is talking, although not all (for example, with children there is play as well). Action occurs outside the office also, when the parents go home to try something different.

But there is a central mystery at the heart of all this using of words: why should words make such a difference? How is it that they are such decisive forms of action? They are relatively puny when put up against the truly phenomenal forces of nature. Screaming at the ocean to retreat does little good. Yet words are incredibly powerful in most situations that involve people. This book will not approach this question, but here we take for granted that people are language animals, that much of our reality is constituted by and through language.[1]

ACTION

Why do we say action is so important? There are several answers to this question, all of them related, each of them critical. One answer is that compared with feelings or beliefs, action is relatively easy to alter; it is more observable than other aspects of human experience (thoughts, moods, feelings, images), and it can be divided into small segments until eventually there is a segment small enough for a person to work with. An example will illustrate this: if a person is in terrible shape and wants to improve his physical condition, the way to approach this goal is to do a little exercise the first day, a little more the second, and so on, for weeks and weeks. Each small incremental action is relatively easy. For a person who is sitting down to stand up is not so hard. But for a person who is in terrible shape to get into very good shape is not so easy. But one step at a time and the task can be accomplished. All this is possible only because the acts required are relatively easy to describe (lift your leg, bend your knees, etc.), and that is critical to the success of proposing exercise to people. But even such easily observable and external events as exercises are not that easy to describe with words.[2]

---

[1] Two different approaches to this topic from well within the mainstream of psychological commentary are offered in Eugene Gendlin's *Experiencing and the Creation of Meaning* (1962) and Donald Spence's *Narrative Truth and Historical Truth* (1982).

[2] Even simple exercises are not so easy to describe with words; Jane Fonda's exercise records and videos are successful in part because she gives very clear

Another part of the answer is more complex, and perhaps has a moral and philosophical tone. Action seems in some important way to be implicated in the creation of a self. Through taking action, we each discover who we are, what our capacities are, what our limits are. One way to look at this issue is through Piaget's well-known lenses. He emphasized the ways in which development occurs through an interaction between an active organism and an environment. He argued that children adapt through complex sequences of accommodations and assimilations, all of which occur through activity. This general point of view has become pervasive in developmental psychology.

Unless you actually try something, you do not know if you can do it, and there is something productive about actually trying (this may be the moral part of what I am saying). In saying this, I am aware that I am in part echoing an important strain in American philosophy, that referred to as pragmatism. And I am perfectly willing to contemplate the possibility that I am here expressing a typically American bias in the direction of action over reflection or contemplation.[3]

Developmental psychologists show us the underlying patterns behind the surface changes of childhood. Different theorists have postulated variously named stages for this development, but fidelity to any particular one is not so important here as grasping the idea that a child moves through various stages through taking action in a variety of ways. Piaget's descriptions of children are as good an illustration of what I mean as any. He shows us children trying, for example, to reach out and pick up an object. Through trying this, again

---

directions (and shows how the movements should be done). When physicians prescribe exercise for lower back pain, they often hand out brochures with diagrams which give a visual portrayal of what is required. My own HMO has such brochures, which show not only the right way to do something but the wrong way to do it, to help patients see more clearly what is wanted.

[3] That may be true, and if it is, it is not so horrible; I am an American psychologist working with people who are by and large either Americans or are becoming acculturated to American mores. But the fundamental sources of my conviction lie both in my understanding of developmental psychology and in my sense of what works in therapy, how therapy unfolds.

and again, a child gradually gains a sense of the reality of objects in space, of the intricate interconnections between his own activities and the nature of the world surrounding him. Anyone who has tried to teach a child to ride a bicycle has a sense of what the process is like, and I think this example is illustrative of much of the learning children do. The child tries to sit on the bicycle, the parent holds it, the parent exhorts the child to try to push the pedals, although most children have seen others riding bikes so they have an idea that that is necessary. The parent stays next to the child, holding the bike so it will not fall over, providing support and the comfort of his presence. But the fundamental learning, of what it is like to maintain a sense of balance, the child cannot really be taught, but must learn through the doing of the task. Eventually the child learns to ride the bicycle (most children who try do learn, though some more quickly than others), just as children learn how to walk, or skip, or jump, or run. All of these are learned, I would argue, through doing.

Doing, then, is fundamental to certain forms of learning. Does it make sense to generalize from this and argue that most learning involves some form of doing? Proving this is not my intention here, but if you reflect about learning, I think you will see how doing is intimately involved at some point in most learning. One learns to write through writing, to talk through talking, to do most things through doing them and benefitting both from the comments of others on our performance and from our own self-observation.

What role do others play in all this? To start with, they provide enough security and comfort so that we dare try something new (when we are children). A child will try the bicycle only if he has enough confidence, built up through months and years of experience, to believe that he has a chance. He will ordinarily try today only if someone is there to help him. So another is there for support (if not literally, then figuratively). Further, others provide constructive evaluations when we cannot accurately judge our own performance. If you are learning Italian, you try pronouncing something, and ordinarily you cannot hear the mistakes (at least, not at first). So an Italian teacher will tell you when you did it wrong, or may compliment you when you get it right.

How is all this relevant to therapy? In part, because this is what a therapist does. The therapist can help someone else change or do new things through being there for support, and through providing constructive evaluations of what has been done. This is not all a therapist does, but it is one important aspect of therapy which is often neglected or even ignored, and it might be interesting to speculate why. Perhaps it is too prosaic. Certainly this view of the therapist's role understates the complexity of the world of feelings and relationships and human experience. But this may be better than overstating that complexity, and many of those who write about psychotherapy may err in this other direction.[4]

So if we as therapists need to help our patients do something, then I think we need to develop some ideas about how doing is helpful. One such idea I have already articulated: that learning should involve doing, sooner or later. Another idea is that doing leads to self-knowledge, or to the development of a self. This is harder to explain, if only because exactly what a self is remains rather mysterious. Perhaps one approach into this tangled topic is through looking at what people say

---

[4] Perhaps they do so in part because they are selected—through the processes involved in therapist training—to be intellectually inclined people with a talent for academics (who have done well in school) who enjoy thinking and reflecting. Anyone who pays much attention to the mysteries of how people develop and change knows full well that there are many unlicensed and untrained people around who are very very good at helping people change, at listening, at drawing people out about difficult and painful topics. There is scarcely anything therapists do with their patients that some other people cannot do, people who are untrained and do not have the right credentials to do it officially or with reimbursement. To ignore this is to mystify the therapeutic relationship, which after all is usually just two people (or a group of people) sitting in a room and talking. I think we may all mystify this endeavor; certainly there are senses in which we all expect more from therapy than it can deliver, in which we all try to surround this endeavor with more mystery and meaning than it can comfortably absorb. So if I am erring here in the opposite direction, it is partly to redress the balance. For too long the writers who make things seem enormously complex and convoluted have held sway. If you want to know what I mean here, I think the best course would be half an hour with one of Kernberg's books on borderline conditions or with almost any of the psychoanalytic writing on narcissistic disorders. It is all fascinating, but at quite a distance from just having a conversation with someone.

when you ask them who they are. They give various answers, some of which involve assigned characteristics (their name, given them at birth, or in some cases chosen later), others involving acquired characteristics (being a teacher), still others involving biological givens (being a man).

Another set of answers flows from a slightly different question: describe yourself, tell us about yourself. Then you will get some of the same material (I am a man, I am a teacher, my name is————, etc.), but also additional information about what the person can do, or how she sees herself. I am brave, I am sociable, I have no sense of humor (well, almost no one will say that about himself!), I enjoy music. In order to arrive at this kind of self-knowledge, people need to have experience. What does this mean?

It means having tried various things in order to discover what one can do and what one cannot do, in order to discover what gives pleasure and what does not. Until you listen to a variety of music, you have no way of knowing what music you like, or whether you dislike all music. Until you try playing tennis, you don't know whether it is fun, or whether you can become good at it. So through trying things you discover what your characteristics are. This is part of what is meant when we say that you need experience to know yourself.

To profit from experience, one must be able to observe what is happening, and then both to remember it and to integrate it in some fashion in one's evolving sense of self. How exactly this happens is very unclear. We know that children must do this, but the nature of the process is hidden. And matters become very complicated by the fact that one's own experience is so influenced by other people. If you try to play the piano, your sense of what that is like will be in part based on your own ears, but in part based on what your teacher says, and how other significant people react. If every time you sit down to play everyone in the house comes and yells at you to stop because you are giving them a headache, then your own sense of yourself as piano player will be different than if everyone comes in and beams and tells you how happy they are to hear such beautiful music. So our own judgment wn actions is permeated by our sense of how other people are reacting to our actions. The two cannot be separated. This complicates matters enormously.

To return to the therapeutic situation, we all know people who say that they are ending therapy because the therapist says they are better. The therapist's view of the patient becomes integrated into the patient's view of himself, and this of course happens to an infinitely greater degree between parents and children. When Eric Berne wrote (in *Games People Play* [1964]) about the parental voice, he was not just being fanciful. Parents really do inhabit children, and the potential here for malignancy (and for beneficence) is enormous. So there is more to self-knowledge than simply trying something new and then observing to see what happens. There is also a sense in which the reactions of others are integrated into one's own sense of oneself. But although this occurs most powerfully in childhood between parents and child, it can also occur throughout life, and this is one of the avenues for therapeutic influence. There are many patients who will quote their therapists long after therapy has ended, indicating that the therapist's voice is still present, that it has been internalized in some sense. We know that in some cases, this can happen after just one interview; several meetings a week for several years are *not* necessary to have this sort of an impact on someone. Parental impact hinges on many factors, one of which usually is an extensive presence in the child's life, but this is not necessary; there are children who are influenced, to some degree, by parents they have never met (but of whom they have heard), or by parents who died long ago.

So if we evolve a sense of self through action, we also integrate into our self-conception some of the things we have heard others say, or our accumulated sense of how others have reacted to us. Here the therapist has two powerful sources of leverage, one on his own account, through the things he says to the patient, the other through the ways in which he may persuade the parent to alter her way of treating the child. As the parent behaves differently, the child may also, since the child is so extensively influenced by the parent.

How does all this translate into practice? In several ways, all of them very simple—for example, through asking the patient to do things, and helping the patient observe what happens when something new is tried. Or through saying something to the patient that then will enter into the patient's own internal dialogues. Haley's (1973) book on Erickson's methods of treatment *(Uncommon Therapy)* gives many very concise examples of how this might happen, and the model Haley uses is that of the hypnotist, although in general that model has too many negative connotations to seem germane. But there is no question that there is a considerable portion of hypnosis (in some very general sense) in all of what goes on between people, and not just in therapy. However, this is such a general sense that using a word like hypnosis—with its ordinarily restricted context and meaning—does not make much sense. Suggestion is perhaps a better word. We are all infinitely suggestible, although not always predictably so.

AGENCY IN THERAPY

Next let us turn to the intricate question of agency and its role in therapy. As used here *agency* means a sense of being involved in action. One point made already is that a child seldom feels that she has much power in her family. This point, when put in different terms, is that the child seldom feels a sense of agency in the family. This does not mean the child does not do things and initiate action; it means, rather, that the child does not experience herself as the initiating point but instead feels as though she is merely reacting (to her parents, or the situation created by her parents and social institutions like the school). This may be factually inaccurate; children may in fact initiate frequently but usually do not experience themselves in that way. So there is a sense in which one of the aims of our therapy is to help a child attain an increasing sense of agency, although this is possible only with the cooperation of the parents, and sometimes it is impossible because parents object. The parents may want their child to be docile and subservient and reactive, although my experience is that parents are seldom so rigid and bent on complete power that they would assert this unequivocally. Rather, parents may at first have trouble allowing their child to be an initiator, but usually they can be persuaded that this is not a bad idea. In fact, usually we can locate many points at which the parents encourage their child to be an initiator. So the task is to find those points and sometimes to help the parents see in an explicit way that this is what they are doing (since often they have not formulated their behavior in this way).

The more intransigent difficulty is often with the child, or rather with the child as brought up by the parents. To feel in charge of things, the child must be able to tolerate responsibility for what happens. Some children have a hard time with responsibility, and often their parents do not help; they feel that they are responsible for the child's actions, rather than being able to help the child see that she ought to be the responsible one. Here a value issue lies hidden. As therapists we value responsibility and feel that each individual should be taught to act in a responsible way. This may mean taking into account whatever consequences follow from one's actions; it may mean accepting that one's own activities led to certain consequences even when one did not intend the consequences. In our culture we would call this a sense of maturity, and it is regarded as being a good trait. So our own values here are not wildly discrepant from those of the general culture, but it is nonetheless worth drawing attention to the points in therapy—in any therapy—where values intrude into or lie at the basis of some technique or intervention.

So when we use the word *agency*, part of what we mean is the ability to initiate action. Another part refers to taking responsibility for what happens. One aspect of the task in therapy—if you will, of the therapist's own responsibility as agent—is to help parents see that they are trying to train the child to be responsible, and that they need to extend this attempt—an attempt they are already making in certain realms—to the problem behavior which brought the family into the office. This sounds relatively simple, and in some cases it is, although most families who find this truly simple manage to do it on their own and do not come seeking help. If we take the messy room as an archetypal problem between adolescents and their parents, I suspect that nearly all families have difficulty with this issue, but very few families come in to consult a therapist about the matter. So by the time we hear about it, usually there is more going on, or rather, more has been going on for years that gets in the way of the family stumbling onto a solution to their problem. For most people do figure ways out of most of the dilemmas of daily living, and they do so on their own, or rather, with the help of people who are already in their lives, not through consulting professionals. But as we have said, many families come to see us who do not have serious or long-standing problems, because access is so easy and affordable and relatively unthreatening.

Families who are having trouble with children who act irresponsibly usually have trouble giving responsibility to the child. This may be true even when the family values responsibility. In fact, this is sometimes part of the problem: the parents so value responsibility that they feel that they are the main or even only responsible ones. So, paradoxically, some of the most responsible parents have trouble teaching their children to be responsible. Here I am trying to put in a favorable light that which has its unhealthy side, and this is another important principle in working in therapy. For underneath this apparent exaggerated sense of responsibility on the parents' part is usually a sizable component of inability to let go of the child, to tolerate separation. And separation is probably the gist of the complication of training in responsibility. Separation and also caring, in the sense that parents who have trouble separating from their children, or allowing the child to separate, usually care immensely about the child. This in turn can often be traced to their not caring enough about themselves, or about other people and activities, but the positive side is that they do care immensely about the child. So I will always draw attention to this, by saying to the parent something like, it's obvious you care immensely about your daughter. Or something a bit more tangential, such as, it's hard to watch a child growing up, by which I mean— though do not necessarily spell out—that there is pain in being a parent, in watching this being who used to be so helpless and soft and cuddly become larger and harder and separate, no longer such a dependent part of me. Good parents need to enjoy taking care of a child if they are to do well with a baby (some parents do not enjoy this, and that leads to a different set of problems). But the other side of this is that parents who truly enjoy that phase of parenthood may have difficulty with later phases where less caretaking is required, where the job is more one of maintaining standards, watching and praying that things will work out, giving advice, and being available when the earlier kind of complete care is wanted.

So if the child is to have a sense of agency, the parents must be able to help the child in this regard. This means gradually giving the child more responsibility for making decisions, and then living with the consequences. Many parents have trouble doing this at all; most parents have trouble doing this sometimes. I am not talking about helping the child express her feelings, nor am I talking about exploring feelings through play or talking with the child. Instead I am talking about action and responsibility. This may not sound like orthodox therapy talk, but my view is that therapy quite properly focuses on such issues. And in short-term therapy, such issues need to become central.

Why do these issues need to become central? Because they are always germane; because it is possible to work on them and make progress in a few sessions; because they involve concrete behavior, which can be pointed to and looked at in detail; and because looking at them avoids some of the complications of resistance and transference which a more direct focus on feelings leads to (and which can perhaps better be handled in a longer-term setting). This is not to say one ignores feelings, for nearly always there are strong feelings lying underneath, no matter how small the problem is on the surface, when a family makes an appointment to see us. Further, there are times when the most effective direct approach is through feelings. An example can illustrate this vividly.

A pediatrician calls me saying that one of his patients is in the emergency room of a hospital having ingested some as yet unknown quantity of drugs in an apparent suicide attempt. I agree to see the parents and child when the hospital has medically cleared the child. Later in the day the hospital releases the child, having discovered that she probably took a handful of aspirin; whatever she took she vomited quickly (since she told people what she had done and they encouraged her to try to get the drugs out of her as quickly as possible). So the parents appear in my office with their 15-year-old daughter. What is immediately clear is that the girl is miserable, crying, unhappy, but not depressed—rather, feeling hopeless about how her parents treat her; and it is just as clear that the father is furious with her. So on the surface are two strong feelings: the misery of the girl and the fury of the father. These clearly need to be acknowledged, although not explored, in the first session. But if I did not acknowledge them, I would be ignoring an important part of the reality of the situation being presented to me in my office.

It may turn out that these feelings are not central to the suicide gesture, although I suspect they are, and in this case, it turned out that they were. As it turned out, the father was furious with his wife, although he expressed his anger mostly toward the girl, in the form of very strict limits, unceasing demands for compliance with a range of rules, and abundant grounding for infractions of the rules. But when I kept drawing our attention to the anger, which seemed somehow in odd contrast to the situation which had brought him and his family to see me (his daughter, after all, had made a suicide gesture), he became more willing to talk about it, and then suddenly he called me to ask whether I'd be willing to see him and his wife without the girl, since he said they needed couples' counseling. Then I discovered that he was furious with his wife for affairs she had been having, so our work moved forward in the form of couples treatment for marital issues. The girl did not miraculously get better, but some of the heat was off her for a while, and that helped her.

So we are not advocating ignoring feelings, especially when they are clear and powerfully present in the office. But we do not go searching for them when they are hidden until we have tried looking at what is closer to the surface. The danger of probing for the underlying feelings (which as a psychologist I would agree are always present, and in fact always strong in the way that real feelings are) is that one may do more harm than good. One wants to avoid doing harm at all costs, and this is true not just in a medical setting, in which this is the primary ethical rule.

If people's feelings are buried, there is probably a good reason. Unleashing those feelings will not necessarily be productive, in spite of the generally accepted psychological wisdom that being aware of feelings is conducive to healthy living. There are certainly cases in which a buried feeling needs to be revived and brought to the surface as a way of reducing its negative effects on current behavior; this is the original idea elaborated to such effect by Freud. But this is not true in all cases of human misery and unhappiness, as he either explicitly argued or unintentionally persuaded people was the case. And this idea has been taken far too far by the numerous proponents of self-expression in our culture, where the individual self is taken so seriously.

To understand why I emphasize action and responsibility so much, we need to look at the more conventional therapeutic idea that feelings are the essence of human experience—not just the ultimate mover, as it were, of our behavior, but the most effective entry point if one wants to change behavior or experience.

One problem with searching for buried feelings is that the search may absorb so much time that one is not able to look at that which is more directly the problem. If one has vast quantities of time available, this may not matter, but in a short-term setting, the time is not available. The search may take time because the feelings may indeed be deeply buried, and because the forces keeping them out of awareness may be very powerful. Another problem is that the deeply buried feelings seldom pertain to the present situation; they usually pertain to past situations, and discovering that one is sad or furious because of something that happened long ago with one's parents may not be helpful, since there is nothing one can do about it beyond realize it. Sometimes this is precisely what you want, of course: to realize that you are sad that your parents never did those things for you that you wanted them to do. But such a realization is not always liberating (though it may sometimes be). I have met patients who seemed to take pleasure in repeatedly reliving their sadness in their early childhood deprivation. Such reliving is not necessarily a progressive force, for what is needed is to move onward, to stop feeling victimized (even though one was truly victimized, perhaps), and to decide what to do next to make one's life better. This may seem an overly pragmatic or simpleminded approach, but it is unquestionably more effective in changing the tenor of one's feelings than reflecting on the past, which is beyond changing. Doing different things than one is accustomed to doing can change one's feelings. Lying in bed in the morning while feeling depressed is not an unusual state; but reflecting on one's depression may not be the most effective tactic if one wants to reduce or eliminate the depression. Getting up and engaging in physical activity may be infinitely more effective for some people. (Some people are apparently unable to do anything, even get out of bed, but I am not mainly talking of such extreme cases.)

Children do not tend to live in the past, nor do they have such long pasts, and usually their feelings are not in fact very deeply buried. They are more immediately overwhelmed by their feelings, they have fewer well-developed maneuvers for holding feelings in check, and so gaining access to a child's feelings is not always so difficult. A child's play will reveal many feelings and (to an observer who is trained in reading the affectual content of the play) usually in a rather direct way. So with children the problem is not usually gaining access to their feelings, but helping parents and child tolerate the expression of the feelings, and sometimes helping them work toward more appropriate expression of feelings. These then become appropriate foci of short-term therapy: tolerating and containing the expression of feelings, and finding acceptable ways to express the feelings (usually this means choosing verbal expression over physical acting out).

So my statement that looking at feelings is not necessarily the best route to effecting change must be qualified by several other points—for example, that sometimes one needs to stress the importance of acknowledging an obviously present feeling. Other times one needs to stress the importance of appropriate (rather than inappropriate) *expression* of a feeling. Sometimes one needs to focus on helping a patient to live with a feeling: it is real, present, and unavoidable, so one had better learn to live with it. For example, a child who is angry that his parents are divorcing had better learn to live with his anger, since his parents are going to divorce regardless of how he feels. Or a child whose mother is dying of cancer needs to learn to live with the grief, or sadness, or rage, or whatever feelings are being evoked, all of which are perfectly appropriate feelings, none of which need to be avoided, but about which there is little to be done, given the brutal reality of the fact that the mother is dying.

Many people need help containing feelings, not expressing them, and although this is certainly recognized by most therapists, it is not a view with as elaborate a theoretical rationale as that which Freud provided so eloquently for expressing buried feelings. The traditional phrase used for expressing this idea, a phrase with roots in the Freudian theoretical point of view, is to say that the patient needs to build more appropriate and flexible defenses. I would add that action is often an appropriate defense; that is, I would like to broaden the conventional notion of defenses as intrapsychic maneuvers (which go on within a person, as he struggles with the various conflicting impulses he feels) to include a view of defense as intimately bound up with one's way of being in the world.

By being in the world, I mean simply that when one acts, one is acting in the world, and that such action is an invaluable and essential avenue to knowing what the world is like and what one's own capacities are. Further, such knowledge of self and world is one of the best defenses against being overwhelmed by affect, and against outrageous fortune. To take a trivial example: knowing that tomorrow is another day is hard-earned knowledge that babies seldom have, and that children only gradually acquire. A child who is counting on a trip to see the circus next weekend is seldom able to reflect, when he gets measles and has to stay home, that he'll have other opportunities to go to the circus. Instead he may cry and be upset. Knowledge may not be the right word for an orientation that takes the future into account, that tomorrow will come with its own opportunities, but my use of the word includes a grasp of such realities. Similarly, the child who cannot wait until his birthday can be described as lacking several kinds of knowledge: that birthdays are seldom the magnificent events that they are supposed to be, that the birthday will come in due time, that life includes other pleasures besides birthdays which can be enjoyed until the birthday itself arrives.

How does action in the world help one in acquiring that knowledge? Living and having experience are part of what I mean by acting in the world, and through lived experience we gain knowledge, not the sort of knowledge ordinarily taught in school, but a real knowledge nonetheless, a knowledge of what we can expect from life, and a knowledge of what capacities we ourselves have for dealing with life. This is the nugget of truth which educators who promote the importance of real-life activities have grasped. They advocate doing things and argue that a child learns through doing things. And in an important measure, this is indeed true, not because children are eccentric beings who need to act to learn, but because humans learn best through action (although with great effort and the right gifts, a human can learn in other ways: through reading, through watching, through simply reflecting and imagining).

So I am arguing that action can be a defense, and that it has healthy aspects. The phrase *acting out* is used frequently to denote the unhealthy side of action as a defense; the assumption is that the person, through action, avoids truly feeling something painful. But action has another side as well, for through action children and adults can learn, and in short-term therapy this proves to be an invaluable concept. We can ask a child to do something and see what happens; we can ask a parent to try something different at home and then hear later what the consequences were. And all of this can be done from the very first meeting; no long acquaintance with the family is necessary before one suggests particular actions to a family. In this respect, directing a family toward action may be easier than directing their attention toward buried feelings, for the latter may occur most easily only after long acquaintance, and after a substantial relationship has been constructed with the therapist, a relationship which then can help contain whatever feelings may emerge.

Here is another aspect of agency, one that involves the therapist who must be more active than is conventionally the case in longer therapies. Careful listening is only one of many skills a therapist needs; regard for patients is another; understanding of development is vital, but in addition, one needs the nerve and experience to take action, even though this will always seem riskier than just sitting and listening and reflecting back to the patient what has been said. I do not mean drastic action. I simply mean saying things like, maybe you could try this, or have you tried that; or I mean telling patients to stop doing one thing and try another. This may feel authoritarian and dictatorial but it need not be, and how it will be experienced by the patient hinges on the tone, on the relationship which has been established, and on the appropriateness of the suggestion to the presenting problem or on the rationale provided by the therapist for the action.[5]

There is a clear-cut sense in which taking action, for a therapist, means risking doing harm; almost any forceful action will seem potentially more harmful than just sitting and listening, but I think there is no way around this. We need to recognize this fact and act nonetheless. If we therapists do so responsibly, then we are first of all acting as a model for our

---

[5] Here I diverge from the point of view articulated by Milton Erickson in Jay Haley's account of it in *Uncommon Therapy* (1973). Erickson apparently relies on his authority as expert to suggest some rather outrageous things to his patients, and he apparently gets away with this. Erickson is explicitly adopting the stance of the hypnotist who makes powerful suggestions to people, suggestions which they will accept. I do not take such a stance, although I am sure that my own effectiveness in part builds on whatever authority I possess by virtue of my training, my position, my presumed expertise.

patients—for we want them to engage in new actions as well—
and we are also able to accomplish more, since our actions
will propel patients in the directions of positive change. Usually
the worst that can happen in therapy is that the patient will
not get better; the sorts of actions I engage in and recommend
to patients are not likely to make things worse, although
patients may fear that they will, just as patients may fear that
seeking out a therapist's help will make things worse. In short,
the potential benefits considerably outweigh the possible risks.

THE ACTIVE THERAPIST

Any new patient of mine is seen with caretakers in what
we would ordinarily call an evaluation; usually this evaluation
will take more than one session, but given the constant press
of new patients, there is some urgency, in the sense that one
cannot take the stance that time will tell all. We cannot simply
sit back and wait to find out what we need to know; we need,
as clinicians, to be active in seeking out the information that
will help us. We need to be active in several ways, all
simultaneously.

One must be active in the sense of pursuing several goals
simultaneously. One needs initially to become acquainted with
the new family, and building a relationship with each member
of the family is usually important. This means paying attention
to each of them, and making sure each of them has a chance
to be heard, even in the first session. One needs to be active
in reviewing the charts of each family member, if not before
the initial session, then soon afterward, so that information
contained in the charts can be integrated with whatever was
learned during the first session.

Another form of activity involves observation of the child,
of the parents, and of the interactions among them. And this
observation is informed by one's initial understanding of the
presenting complaint, whatever the reason is that leads this
particular family to seek help at this particular time. Who
takes charge of telling the clinician the story of the child?
How do the parents talk to each other? Which of them takes

charge of the child when intervention is needed, or does neither of them? Which toys does the child gravitate toward, and how does the child respond to any interventions made by the therapist? All of this is potentially important information. Usually some history needs to be covered; usually the family constellation needs to be described; but the fact of limited time means that one will not go into much detail about any of this unless one sees that it is important for some specific reason.

The therapist must also be actively considering, even before the first session begins, the question of what will happen next. There will almost always be a second appointment, but will it be alone with the child, or with the parents, or with all of them together? And what needs to be done before then? Ordinarily I will see the child alone at the second appointment, and request permission to talk with the child's teacher (if school seems to be problematical in any way) or with any other involved professional (probation officer, guidance counselor, caretakers who are not able to be at the first meeting), but this is not necessary, and I must always be alert to the possibility that a different approach will make more sense with a particular family.

The therapist's activity is partly cognitive, of course. An assessment is being made of the developmental status of the child, and the whole question of how to understand the problem is always present. This means not so much arriving at a diagnosis, although that may be part of the process, but, rather, coming to some conclusions, however tentative, about what seem to be the main issues. But although one would like to understand what the main issues are, there is always the possibility that one will not understand and have to act anyway. Thus, part of working in our system involves acting assertively and responsibly even without having gathered sufficient information or understanding to know what the main issues are in any given case. This can be anxiety provoking, until one discovers through experience that most interventions that we can make are not terribly powerful. In truth, there is little that we can do directly to change anyone's life drastically;

our influence is small compared with all the other forces for change that are always at work. Life events—new jobs for the parents, divorces, moves, changes of teachers for children, illnesses—all of these have much more powerful effects than we do. All we can do is try to help people change their own lives, and in doing so, make sure we do not make things worse than they already are. So although we may not be very powerful, we are also fairly safe from the danger of making big mistakes.

An example of what is meant here by the therapist's cognitive activity is provided by such family therapists as Selvini Palazzoli when she discusses *hypothesizing*. She insists that the therapy team should imagine many possible scenarios in considering any given family. To start with, they should think about why the family is coming, and use whatever data have already been accumulated to do this. As more data are gathered, once the family is in the office, the hypothesizing changes. But the importance of having hypotheses is not to guess correctly, but, rather, that they give the therapist some idea of which direction to look. Even a well-behaved small family provides vastly more information in ten minutes of a family therapy session than any single therapist (or team of therapists) can possibly assimilate. So the therapist needs ways to sort all this wealth, and hypotheses provide ways to do that. The more aware the therapist is of his hypotheses, the better able he will be to test them against the emerging data of the interview session, or of successive sessions.

One of the crucial differences between therapists who have become accustomed to doing short-term therapy and others is this function. The experienced short-term therapist is making hypotheses even before he meets the patient or the family. Doing this requires energy and time, although to some degree it can occur intuitively and unconsciously; ideally the therapist will make time to hypothesize before each session with each patient. Most settings do not provide the luxury Selvini Palazzoli provides of allowing abundant time for this activity, but allowing some time is crucial. Experience allows the therapist to make and discard hypotheses even while doing the other things that must be done, such as observing the children playing while talking to the parents about what has been happening.

The therapist asks questions, not just to elicit information but to help the patient focus. In short-term work, a focus is much more critical than in long-term work (although it is important in both). So the therapist uses questions or comments to help keep the patient on the track, to make clear when the patient is not being clear, to elicit other relevant information. But the underlying message is just as important: that the therapist has an eye on what matters, and has ideas about what might help; he has seen something like this problem before and has some notions about how to help. Furthermore, he expects some lively give and take between himself and the patient. There will be dialogue, not just narration on one side (that of the patient) and reception or listening on the other.

Dialogue is an important concept basic to most therapy, although Freud seemed to emphasize the talking function of the patient and the listening function of the analyst, and a situation in which one person talks and the other listens does not sound as though it would involve much dialogue. But in most therapy, and certainly in all forms of short-term therapy, there must be much more dialogue, give and take, back and forth between patient and therapist. This is not because the patient cannot be trusted to tell the whole truth eventually, but because the whole project of short-term therapy hinges for its success on there being a focus, and finding and holding to a focus requires effort in which the therapist must necessarily lead the way, at least at first. This whole idea of dialogue is worth exploring further, and we will take it up in a variety of contexts throughout this book, especially when we consider how the therapist and patient together constitute a reality out of their dialogue (see Chapter 9).[6] The dialogue in therapy

---

[6] There is a whole literature on the nature of dialogue. For a lucid introduction to certain facets of this literature, see Elliott Mishler's recent book, *Research Interviewing* (1986).

revolves to some degree around questions and answers, and the questions are very important because they provide a model of activity (the therapist is being active, showing the patient how to be active in his own behalf), and because they help guide the patient in one direction rather than another. A silly question at the wrong moment can be disastrous, and therapists all need to acquire the knowledge of when to ask further and when to wait and listen. But the balance in short-term work is tilted toward being more active; not listening less, but listening with more purpose and intent.

3

Our Work
as Consultation

The word covers a vast portion of what we do, and it refers to a form of help that is ordinarily thought to be very different from what is called *therapy*. Yet in our setting, when people come for therapy they often get consultation; that is, much of what is called short-term, intermittent therapy is in fact consultation when it concerns children and families. As a clinician I am often consulting to a family about a child; occasionally I am consulting to a child about a family, or, more frequently, to a school or other professionals about a child and family. For whatever reasons, the word *consultant* does not seem so imposing as the word *therapist*, perhaps because it sounds more commercial, more like the business world, and less medical, less beneficent, less altruistic, less complicated. Freud, of course, did not call himself a consultant, and the word he used for what he did, *psychoanalysis*, still means something in particular; the word *therapy* covers much more ground.

CONSULTATION TO THE PARENTS

But Freud was quite capable of acting like a consultant in my terms. The best example of this is what he did in his only published case of child analysis, the case of little Hans. Here what Freud did was to talk to Hans's father about Hans. The father would keep track of Hans's dreams and his conversations and behavior, and would report to Freud about them. Freud then would talk to the father about them, about what they might mean, and would give suggestions about what to listen for, and how to respond to Hans.

Freud barely met with Hans at all, and in his own account of this process referred to it as psychoanalysis at a distance. But I think a better way to refer to what he was doing would be to say that he was consulting to the father about Hans. His consultation, like my own, included listening to the parent, asking questions to elicit other relevant information, interpreting the child's behavior, and giving suggestions about what to listen for and how to behave with the child. The consultation also included connecting things that might not have seemed connected. Freud's guiding principles, which helped him see that apparently disconnected bits of behavior and fragments of conversation and dreams were in fact all bound together, were those he was developing, the ones known now as psychoanalytic theory.

My own guiding principles include this theory but a vast array of other ideas as well, some of them from developmental psychology, some from behaviorism, some from the knowledge that researchers in cognitive and perceptual psychology have accumulated. In addition, I draw on the work of family therapists and others who have investigated family systems, and I often rely on what I know about psychological testing to help parents make sense of what schools are telling them about their children's learning difficulties. (In the next chapter, we will turn to a discussion of all these.) I think the best way to make sense of how I use all these ideas is to refer to part of my work as consultation, although in part it is very much like ordinary therapy, and in part it is very much like education (especially when I tell parents what an ordinary two-year-old, for example, can be expected to do; when I try to show them patterns in their relationships with their child which are developmentally normal). Winnicott's writing probably offers the best examples of how therapy can be consultation.

Another reason I like the word *consultation* is that it implies that the main responsibility will remain with the patient. I am there to help, but the main action will have to flow from the other person in my office. Whatever I give must be taken home and used there if anything different is to occur. This I ordinarily refer to as making sure the patient retains the responsibility for what occurs, and responsibility is another key idea in the presentation of this form of therapy which we will turn to later.

So one form of consultation involves my talking with the parents and telling them about childhood development. Many of the parents I see are coming in to discuss their first child; others may have more than one child but have very little explicit knowledge about children, never having studied developmental psychology, nor having learned about children in any formal way. But even those who know quite a bit in a formal sense are often blind when it comes to seeing the relationship between what they have read in books and their own child. So sometimes all I do is point out that relationship; that is, the parents may already have the pertinent knowledge but need someone outside their family system to point it out and to assert that it is relevant. With that help, they turn in that direction and often see rather quickly that what is going on at home with their child is in fact very similar to what they had learned about when they studied children in school.

This consultation, which on the surface is rather pedagogical, works best, however, when it is informed by a deep understanding of and familiarity with psychoanalytic principles, since often what gets in the way of parents using what they have learned is some block which can best be understood in psychoanalytic—or dynamic—terms. To take an overly simple example, a mother who has studied developmental psychology may not be able to see her child's oppositional behavior in the framework she has acquired at school, because she is deeply threatened by her own hostility. She is not comfortable being angry, so resisting her child's oppositional demands is hard for her, even though she knows that children can be expected to test limits (to use the phrase common in books about children). So advice given to this woman about how to handle her child needs to be informed by a familiarity with the difficulties people get into with affect, especially with their own aggressive impulses.

Or it may happen—to continue with this example—that this woman's relationship with her own mother is still so ambivalent and still so unresolved that all her behavior with her own child is permeated with her own unconscious fantasies and wishes about her own mother and her own childhood. She is trying, in some unconscious sense, to redress the wrongs she experienced as a child, and this effort impedes her ability to be resolutely firm with her own child when the child is oppositional. Thus, a purely pedagogical approach will not work; advice given to parents needs to come from someone who is able to see the patterns, both emotional and behavioral, that may get in the way of receiving and using the advice. To use the jargon, one needs to keep an eye on the resistance and one needs to have learned to work with the resistance.

However, I think the word *resistance* is perhaps too parochial (in its embeddedness in the context of psychotherapy) or too general (it is sometimes used to refer to everything that can be construed as interfering with the therapy). A slightly different perspective is to see that there are factors that get in the way of using what one knows. This parent knows something about children, yet she cannot use it with her own child. What gets in the way? A variety of factors, in all probability, some of them unconscious in varying degrees. But raising them to consciousness may not require years or even months of psychoanalysis. For there are many faster ways in which cognition can be improved, in which clearer and more accurate thinking can be promoted.

CONSULTATION AS PROVIDING IDEAS

Cognition or knowledge may be a very complicated affair, but it is not always difficult to improve it. And similarly, behavior—which in humans almost always rises out of a substrate of cognitive understanding—is not always so complicated to change. A trivial example: someone watching me play a difficult passage in a Mozart sonata on the piano may notice, by observing me, that I always do the fingering in such a way as to almost guarantee being tripped up. He suggests I try a different fingering; I try it, and at first it is awkward, but within an hour or less it is easy and from then on the difficult passage is much easier. Or a baseball player can be told to try holding the bat up a little higher, and then marvelously this may turn out to help his batting. In both these cases, there is behavior rooted in some form of thinking, but the crucial aspects of the performance are unconscious (not available to awareness). But they are not heavily repressed (in the analytic terminology). That is, simple advice can go a long way.

This is not always the case, of course. But it is more often the case than anyone trained mainly in psychoanalytic thinking would suspect. Much of what parents do with children is like this. And even when what parents do with children is rooted in their own childhood, in their own ambivalently held parental relationships, it may still be susceptible to alteration without long, arduous psychotherapeutic work.

There will always be some parents who will need a lengthy period of hard work to come to terms with their own unconscious feelings about their own parents. But even this work may occur in contexts other than long-term therapy, although I do not hesitate to recommend long-term intensive therapy to people when I think that treatment, although elective in the sense of not being absolutely necessary, might be helpful. Any recommendation for such work cannot ever be unequivocal, since it is radical treatment, in the sense of requiring a long time and a large expenditure without any sure result. It is, in a word, risky, and therefore cannot ever be honestly recommended with complete certainty. This is an important point, and one worth remembering whenever one hears that someone is recommending therapy, for a global recommendation for therapy is perhaps similar to a global recommendation for surgery. One always needs to ask why therapy might help (just as one would always ask why surgery might help, and how, and with what likelihood of success or failure, and with what attendant risks). Yet this very simple question is one which almost never is asked, and this is very odd. It is as though the goodness of therapy is so much accepted in our culture that inquiring about why it is necessary or going to help is seen as a taboo question (or when asked is chalked up to someone's penuriousness, as though the only reason to inquire is out of a desire to save money). There are other very good reasons to inquire whether therapy is necessary, one of which is the inevitable dependence which accompanies any intense relationship, and the lengthier and more intense the therapy, the greater the potential dependency of patient on therapist. This is not altogether bad, and therapy probably cannot have any beneficial effect without some degree of connectedness between patient and therapist, but we do well to remember there is always latent in such dependency the possibility of harm.

CONSULTATION ABOUT LEARNING

Besides consulting with parents about children, I may consult with parents about their child's education or other aspects of her life. For example, many parents come in to see me with the vexing question of what school their child should attend, or what sort of educational program would be best for their child. There is no simple answer to this question, and often there are not that many different choices anyway, but I proceed by inquiring about the child, about the child's past history and about school history in particular. I examine whatever records the parents have accumulated, or I request current records if the parents do not have them in hand. In some cases, parents who are divorced have different ideas about what is the right school for their child, and they may want me to arbitrate between them, or to meet the child and attempt to determine what is in the child's best interests, or simply to provide a sounding board for them as they wrestle with the complicated question of where to send their child to school.

Even when it is taken for granted that the child will remain in the same school, there may be questions about what sort of class the child should be in the following year, or what sort of educational plan should be put in place. In Massachusetts, there is a state law which allows parents (or schools) to initiate an investigatory process whose aim is the specification of an appropriate school plan for a given child. Parents often need an advocate during this process, since the school has its own procedures and parents may not understand what those procedures are or why they exist as they do. Each of our clinicians is familiar with this process; as a psychologist, I am in addition familiar with the psychological (and educational) tests schools are likely to administer to a child during this process. Thus I can review whatever records are generated in this process. I can if necessary administer further tests (or readminister some of the same tests) in an effort to discover why the child performed as she apparently did during the school administration of the test. Each of us is knowledgeable about learning disabilities, one of the many difficulties which may lead to a 766 CORE (the name given to this process of educational review).

Learning is a complicated arena, vulnerable to interference not only from cognitive deficiencies but from a variety of emotional (and psychological and social) factors. Humans need to learn more than most species; growing up is time consuming and immensely more complicated with us than with other animals; and there is a sense in which it is miraculous that we all learn as much of what we need as we do. Performance in our culture depends on a phenomenal array of knowledge, and almost no one is equally good at acquiring all the varieties of information pertinent to adequate performance in our culture.

Schools are the elaborate social institution (along with families) which have evolved to help each of us learn what is needed. Unfortunately, we have no system for ensuring that each child obtains precisely the kind of family and schooling that will best help him acquire the necessary knowledge; nor have we any way of knowing, when a child is small, what

sorts of information will be necessary when the child grows
up. Thus all education is haphazard with respect to what
may be needed a decade or two later, and with respect
to a particular child's needs. What we call education is
always inevitably a failure in one way or another, and we all
look to the educational system to do much more than it can
possibly do.

Thus I think parents are inevitably disappointed in the education their children receive, no matter how much it costs,
no matter how good the school is supposed to be. Parents
who come in to see us nearly always have some reservations
and complaints about the education their child is receiving,
and connected with those complaints is usually a vague implication that perhaps part of the problem is in their child.
The child may not be able to learn what is needed because
he lacks some vital capacity. So learning disabilities become
a gigantic topic, one that interests most parents (and sometimes not just on their child's account but on their own account
as well).

Taking a strictly educational view of this problem is a mistake. Nearly always, there are other important factors wound
into the situation. For example, most parents have memories
of their own learning experiences; many have some wish that
their children have better experiences than they had. Most
parents have a perhaps exaggerated sense of the importance
of formal education, and nearly always parents are bothered
when the reports from the teachers are less than glowing.
Part of this reflects normal parental narcissism: that is, as
parents, we each want our children to do well and thus
indirectly to give credit to our good parenting. We want our
children to be perfect. Another part reflects our sense that
what is done in school now will affect the future in some
crucial way. This is almost always exaggerated, although telling
parents that is hard. It is especially hard when they are sac-
rificing to enable their children to go to school, but even
when they are not paying directly, they are paying indirectly,
and most parents are inclined to see school as much more
serious than most children do. Thus the seeds of conflict are

there, deeply rooted in the situation: the parent sees formal schooling as vital to the child's future; the child sees it as an imposed and often unenjoyable task. Thus consultation to parents about school involves, necessarily, some mediation between the child and the parents. They look at the dilemma from different vantage points, and this must always be taken into account.

Part of the difference rests in the social roles of adult and child as defined in our culture. Adults take care of children; children are taken care of. To some degree this is always (necessarily) true in all cultures, but we extend this process more than is necessary. Infants truly cannot take care of themselves, but we infantilize our young more than we have to, and this whole process is attended by a variety of complicated emotional and sociological factors. For example, many Americans have a hard-boiled, grown-up sense that life is tough, and that children should be protected from the rawness and pain of life. We may think that worries about life are an adult province, and that children should be protected from them. And we associate an intense concern about money with adulthood, thinking that children should not have to worry about money unless there is real poverty. All of these tendencies work together to complicate any analysis of what parents do with children, and all of them need to be taken into account by any psychologist who works with children and families.

CONSULTATION TO THE FAMILY

One role I play with families is that of advocate for taking children more into the adult world. For example, I like to see the child with the parents in the first session, in order to discover what the child understands of the reasons for his visit to me; and I want to see how the parents handle the task of talking in front of the child about their view of the child's problems. The more laborious and complicated and tangled this process is, the more the difficulty can be traced to these parents' tendency to see their child as somehow special, different, needing protection, fragile.

Many parents object to having their child present at the first meeting, but most accede to my wish even when they find it peculiar. There are some parents who refuse, or who throw up so many objections that I give in, hoping that if I go along with their idea of how things should be done, I will accumulate some leverage in their family system that I can then use productively. As soon as they come into the office, after I introduce myself and find out who they are, I ask the child what she understands about her presence in my office that day. Most children mumble and do not give any clear reply, although the older the child, the greater the chance of some acknowledgment on her part that she knows why she is here (even if she does not wish to say anything about it). But my interest is not so much in hearing the child talk, as in seeing the process which unfolds as the parents hear my question and listen to their child's answer. The basic question I want to answer for myself is how these parents are connected to their child, how they see the child, how the child sees them, how they talk to one another, how they understand one another. For no matter what the presenting problem, this other realm is of vital importance, for a child's problems are almost never encapsulated and separate from the parents. This is not to say that the parents are responsible for the child's problems, but rather that the problem does not exist autonomously.

Talking about this without sounding vague and mysterious is difficult, but the truth is that any symptom (or problem) exists in and through the eyes of whoever is looking at it. This is less true with certain symptoms (a mortal heart attack kills someone and this fact is insistent and pressing) than others, but nearly all the problems I am told about in my office depend for their comprehension on a complicated web of social construction. Parents and child and often the school must all cooperate in the construction of a problem, and different people do this in different ways, depending in part on social factors.

This may sound excessively sociological and subjective. I do not mean it to be. Certainly there are sociological factors which enter into the construction of problems. What is a problem in one context is a joy in another; there is almost

no human predicament which does not have both bad and
good sides to it; what bothers one couple in their child may
strike another couple as trivial. But to say this is not to argue
that therefore the problem is not a real one, merely subjective.
For I believe that all problems are constructed through a
process with subjective aspects which can be seen from a
sociological point of view.

Reality is socially constructed, but saying this is not tanta-
mount to saying that reality is imaginary or fantastical. Rather,
the fact that reality is socially constructed—or my insistence
on the importance of this view of things—means that in all
of my contacts with my patients, I need to find out who sees
the problem, and why they see it as a problem. I always need
to know who is defining the behavior as a problem, not because
I am interested in ascertaining who has the power to make
these definitional statements (*This* is a problem, says the powerful one), but because I believe that when one is working
with children and families, all of these issues are germane.[1]

In our culture, parents always have more power in this
regard than children; I have never had a child come to me
and say, look, I have a problem with my parents, they are
too rigid, too constricted (or whatever). Children may say to
me, after they have come to know me, *"He's* the one who
should be seeing a shrink," but children never call on their
own to make this kind of complaint. This fact reflects a clear-
cut reality of our culture: parents exercise more power and
responsibility than children.

Is this always bad? Of course, it has its bad aspects.[2] But
that it is always bad I would contest, and my view of this
matter is central to my stance with my patients. For although
I am always on the child's side in some fundamental way, I
also always regard the parents as having the prerogative to
make the crucial decisions. Much of what I do is to reinforce

---

[1] The importance of ascertaining who defines the behavior as problematical is
especially emphasized by most family therapists.

[2] Alice Miller has written several interesting books which address this topic. Hers
is a psychoanalytically informed perspective which I will discuss at more length near
the end of this chapter and then again in Chapter 5.

the parents' right to make decisions, to exercise power, not because I think children should be dominated by parents, but because I think it is realistic to see parents as needing to have more power, because they have more responsibility and therefore more rights. Furthermore, children benefit enormously by being taken care of, although when the time comes to break free of the parents, the process is made more difficult the more closely held the child has been by affective bonds with the parents. I often say this explicitly to parents: you people have taken such good care of your child and you and she are so attached to one another that for her to break away is a major developmental task for her, so the whole separation process is more laden with intense affects. I also mean that the parents are so attached to the child that for them to let her break away is a major developmental task for them as well.

When parents come to see me with their child, I ask the child what she understands of the reasons for her visit to my office. Then I usually listen to what the parents tell me of their concerns. During this interview I attempt to engage the child, partly to see how the child responds, partly because I am in truth there for the child and need to establish some relationship with the child, and partly so the parents know that I am interested in the child. And my ear is attuned to the family dynamics: how do these people handle one another? how do these parents see their child and one another? how does the child cope with their concern for her? Additionally, my orientation has a sociological side: into what larger context can their view of this problem be placed? Here we have two parents who are worried about their child's grades. What is the best way to understand this?

The possibilities are endless. There is no one way to see this parental complaint. Thus our whole enterprise is one that does not lend itself to recipe formulations. In no way are we able to say that when this problem walks in, you do one thing, and when that problem walks in, you do another. And this sheer fact is problematical, since in part we aspire to the status of a science, and—in my workplace especially—we are connected with the medical model, and medicine in turn is usually seen as part of science, and that in turn is usually glorified in our culture. Thus therapy with a child and family is assimilated to medicine and science in a way that is not always accurate, although sometimes it is helpful (in the sense of helping the parents to be predisposed to listen to us when we tell them what we think the problem is).

So the parents have entered my office with their child and told me about what appears to them to be a problem. If the child is old enough, I inquire about the child's view of the problem; nearly always, the child has an opposing view, or a different way of construing the problem. In part this springs from the child's different position in the social order (the family, and the larger society): the child is not only smaller and younger, but dependent and powerless relative to the adults around him. Children nearly always feel powerless with respect to important decisions: where they will live, with whom, how much money they have, where they go to school, how they manage their time. Nearly always, most of those decisions are made for them by their caretakers, although less and less so as they grow older. But children do usually have a very real sociological powerlessness, a lack of organizations to help them, and a general dependency, which colors their views of almost everything.

In part, however, the child's different view of the problem springs as well from the boundaries of the problems we are presented with. The problems we encounter in our office cannot be picked up and examined by several people from a variety of points of view; rather, their very existence is contingent on a social construction; and the problems always emerge out of a social context.

The problems of the children I see often emerge out of the social context of their relations with their families, or out of their relations with their schools. There are a few patients who seem to do all right in school and whose families have no complaints about them, but who have done something that gets them into serious legal trouble outside the family. Courts often send such children for a psychiatric evaluation, or for counseling, on the assumption that whatever is wrong is psychological, and on the assumption that counseling or therapy will help. Such cases are almost always problematical for us, if only because the child is coming with his parents but not with the injured party, as it were. Whomever he offended is not in the room, and thus the social context of the troublesome act cannot be constituted in my office, and I am left with only a child. Unless the child is bothered by what he did, and eager to discover why he did it and to talk about that in order to stop himself from doing it again (and this is rarely the case), I really have no idea how to be helpful, beyond satisfying the demand of the court that an intervention occur.

But most of my cases involve troubles at home or at school. Nearly always there is more going on than the specific presenting complaint, and I always inquire about this. With older children, I ask them not just for their point of view about the worries the parents have, but whether they have any additional concerns, about themselves or about the way things go in the family. I invite them to make a complaint, as it were, against their parents or siblings. The point of this is to try to reduce the degree to which the child is being made to feel—by the whole process of a family consultation with our service—that he is at fault, that he is the problem. I never believe the child is the whole problem, if only because, as I have already argued, I see all problems as existing within a social context. A crying baby is a problem only when the parents are distressed by it, or perhaps we should say that crying does not emerge as a problem from the complicated web of life until it bothers someone (usually the parents). This is true with all the problems I encounter in my office, and so I never see the problem as residing solely in the child. But beyond that, I want the child to see that the process of my being consulted gives him rights too, rights to ask for changes (if he is old enough to conceive of things he would like different at home).

And when children are unable to articulate changes they would like, I often help them, once I have gotten some sense of their view of things. For example, sometimes I get a sense during the first session that the child feels picked on. In such a situation, I might suggest that perhaps the child would like to feel less picked on, less criticized. Saying this is not very adventurous, since most children would like never to be blamed for anything, and since most parents would argue that they only blame the child for things the child has done wrong. If the child stopped doing things wrong, he would never be blamed; this is the conventional parental position. But many of the families I see come in to complain about behavior in their child that is not very outrageous, and parents often respond very well to some guidance with regard to discrimination: which behavior needs a firm disciplinary response, and which could simply be allowed to occur, and which should be commented on as bothersome without being met with punitive measures. Most families try to make these sorts of discriminations on their own, but many families have trouble doing so, and a substantial part of my practice consists of such families.

SCHOOL PROBLEMS

Often the problem mentioned by the parents centers on school behavior. The child is not doing very well academically (this can mean anything from being bored, to failing all his courses). Parents are often upset when their child fails to work hard, regardless of what the grades are; I never hear parents complaining that their child works too hard (except in those cases where the parents are concerned about some nonschool problem, e.g., depression). Thus hard work is taken as a sacred value by most of the parents I see. They usually assume a number of things: that hard work today pays off tomorrow (hard work in childhood pays off in adult life), that hard work occurs when someone is motivated, and that a lack of hard work reflects a lack of motivation. They often go further and assume that a child's life is mostly play, and therefore the child ought to work hard at school, since he does not have to work hard at anything else. Behind this may lie a parent's resentment about having to work hard to support a family, and in some cases there lurks as well a very narcissistic sense of injury, that one's child is getting lots of goodies in life although the parent is not and never did, even as a child. But most often, a parent simply worries about the future. Parents know that a given grade in one course in a particular year is not crucial, but they do worry that a failure in application and studiousness now reflects a character defect that will affect the child's future. And they nearly always feel responsible (to a mistaken extent) for the child's future character.

Here is one of the central interventions I try to make, the more forcibly the older the child: trying to help the parents see that their responsibilities, although real and weighty, do not include the child's eventual character, in spite of what they may understand from reading psychological and psychoanalytic works. Freud was certainly effective in persuading all of us that character has roots in early childhood, but to say this is not to say that we are created by our parents, nor is it to deny that change occurs constantly through the life cycle. There is a certain grandiosity connected with being a parent in our culture, in part because so much weight is attached to having children.

What do I mean by this? I mean that parents overestimate their influence, and certainly exaggerate their responsibility for what their children do. And I would argue further that this is inevitable given our way of raising children, our family structure, our American ethic of individualism, and our attitude toward possessions. A sustained argument on this issue belongs elsewhere, but in essence I think that the pathology of parenting which I have been describing is a normal pathology, normal in our culture because of all the factors I have mentioned. We raise children in individual families in which one or two people, called parents, defined in certain sociologically limited ways, are given the primary responsibility; this increases our sense of the importance of the role of parent and neglects the immense importance of all the other people who come into contact with the child. Our families are ordinarily more or less nuclear families, existing in separate dwellings, with few other adults mingling on an equal basis in the family, and this likewise helps create an exaggerated sense of responsibility in the parents for the children in their charge.

The ethic of individualism in a paradoxical way contributes to this situation, since children become overvalued in a culture where each person feels so much on her own. This occurs because the parent-child relation seems as though it ought to be one of the closest and most intimate relations we ever have. For a woman, this view may be especially compelling, since she carried the child within her for nine months; but for both men and women, there is a tendency to seize on having a child as a support in what can feel like a lonely culture.

It is as though we reflect: this child looks like me; this child has the same last name; this child acts like me (often). This child is an extension of me, we then feel, and this view is necessary perhaps because we have such a paucity of stable and meaningful supports for our fragile selves. This in turn makes the parent-child bond much more intricate, since not only is the child dependent on the parent for nurturance and protection during the early years, and dependent on the parent for guidance and support in later years, but in addition there is a closeness in the relationship that often has a hothouse quality. The passions become very intense in a way that is not universal, not necessary in all cultures, but very much part of the very fabric of our culture. And this needs to be taken into account in working with families. This topic is not ordinarily considered in the curricula of our child-therapy training centers, but it ought to be. Bettelheim (1969) touches on this theme in his consideration of the effects on character development of being raised in a kibbutz (in his *The Children of the Dream*) and provides a thoughtful analysis of some of the issues involved.

The very large question lying behind all this analysis is that of how we in our culture bring an individual into being. Sociological and anthropological and historical perspectives are very helpful in understanding the contemporary families we clinicians encounter. Perhaps intensive study of all these approaches to the family is more than most clinicians would have time for, but having some feel for the dimensions of the problem is important, and one way to acquire that grasp is through studying the approaches of these other disciplines. What is this entity we call a family, and how are children raised by our families? Many specific aspects of this question are worth examining, and clinicians would benefit from doing so. For example, as Bettelheim argues, it may be that our very American brand of individualism, with its very complicated mixture of opposing values (creativity and initiative on the one hand, and conformity on the other), is supported by our family structures.

To some degree, children are seen as possessions of parents, and there is a general reluctance in the culture to interfere in this relationship, although there are many forces working in opposite directions as well. Schooling, for example, is an interference with the private relationship between parents and children, and some parents have fought mandatory state schooling on that ground, and argued that they should be allowed to educate their children in the bosom of the family, or in schools of their own choosing, whether or not they are state-approved schools.

Regardless of the individual contributions of each of these factors to the texture of the parent-child relationship in our culture, there can be little question that a substantial proportion of the affect behind many of the problems I encounter in my office arises out of the peculiar intensity of that parent-child connection. So when the parent comes in saying that her child is not getting good grades, there is a sense in which she might be asking me for advice about how she could help the child do better, but this is almost never the sense in which she makes the complaint. There is much more freight being carried in her complaint, and much of it arises from her identification with her child and her projection onto the child of all her hopes for the future, hopes for herself and for her child. And this is not a simple materialistic issue of her needing the child, for example, to help her on the farm, or to support her in her old age. Rather, it is an intricate interpenetration of parental feeling and thought on the one hand, and child on the other, or image of the child as held by the parent.

One of my ways of trying to defuse the intensity of this connection involves trying to help the parent focus on simple practical things which can be done by the parent. The child's future life is too far off to be immediately available for inspection; so instead, when faced by a question of grades, we look at how the parent can help the child study. Quite often the parent cannot help the child study, since once a child is over eight or 10 the child will ordinarily need to study on her own and will resent the parent trying to take over the studying function. So all a parent can do is try to enforce rules for studying, rules which, for example, prohibit television watching or interdict phone time until homework is done.

Nearly always any attempt of mine to focus on such practical matters runs very quickly into a wall of resistance, from child and parents, resistance which can only be understood in terms of the complicated nexus of factors I have been discussing. For if such practical intervention is to be successful, the parent and child must come to some understanding of their different positions. And often such understanding is impeded by the intense affect surrounding the whole parent-child relationship.

In order to state a rule about studying, for example, a parent must be able to step back from an overidentified relationship with the child, step back from feeling as though a huge life drama hangs in the balance, to see that all she can do is set a rule and try to enforce it. In order to feel that she can lead the horse to water but not make him drink, she must feel that she and the horse are separate beings, and many parents have difficulty with this with regard to their children. They may have no difficulty at all with regard to other people's children, which is why therapy groups for parents of adolescents, for example, often work very well; one couple can see another couple's problem in a way they cannot see their own, even when their own may be very similar.

For younger children, there are other ways a parent can help a child study; for example, through better communication with the teacher about homework. If the parent knows when there is homework, and in what subjects, and roughly how long it is supposed to take, then he is in a better position to be effective at home in creating the conditions for the child to do the homework. But that technique will not work so well with adolescents, although many parents try to set up an intricate system of check-ins with the teacher around homework assignments. Such a system can always be defeated by an older student if the child is uncooperative; and if the child is cooperative, that system is not necessary.

However, poor grades are not just a matter of not doing homework, and when a family comes in complaining of poor grades, I always investigate further in order to ascertain what is happening. Some students seem to study hard and yet still do badly; in such a case, the parents may need to be encouraged to approach the school and initiate a review of the child's educational program. Perhaps the courses are too hard, or perhaps the instructors are not using the most effective teaching method for this child. Sometimes what is called poor grades is in fact one poor grade, in a subject the student hates. In this case, even when the parents are convinced the subject is crucial to the future happiness of the child, I often try to work with the child to persuade the parents that one bad grade is not so critical. Sometimes the parents can accompany the child to the school to see about changing from that course to another, or from that teacher to another (if this has not already been tried). Sometimes the parents admit they hated that subject too when they were in school. Admitting that helps them sympathize more with the child (in situations where the child appears to be interested in school and is generally cooperative except for the one course in which he performs badly).

There are many situations where the poor grades occur because the student does not know what is interesting, and is engaged in a struggle to define for himself what is worth doing. When I worked at a counseling bureau at Harvard College, I encountered many students whose poor grades were a function of their existential quest for meaning. Such a phrase may sound pretentious, but it reflects some of the reality of what was happening. The student was searching and did not know what was truly important. Typically, with the Harvard students I met, the student had formerly taken the position that all that mattered was good grades; now suddenly good grades no longer seemed the most important thing on earth, and part of that discovery surely hinged on the fact that the student had left the family home and was no longer enmeshed in the family network, so whatever the parental contribution was to the child's sense that all that mattered was good grades is now attenuated (by distance and psychological separation).

But not all young people wait until college to make this search, and I see a significant number of high school students who are very much caught up in what Erikson would have called identity issues. Parents of such adolescents often have some sympathy for their child's struggles, and many of these cases involve children who come on their own, without their parents, or with minimal involvement from their parents— that is, for an adolescent to be involved in an identity issue, there must be some separation between the child and the parents to start with, or else the issue of individual identity would never arise. Parents who have children who are caught up in these struggles are usually able to allow their child to go see a therapist on her own. And then the work I do with these children is similar to that I did with the Harvard College students, although the children I see now are still living with their parents.

Thus a presenting complaint of poor grades may have varied meanings, and exploring these is important before deciding on any particular mode of treatment. Exploration must include specific details about the poor grades (how many, what courses, for how long); information about how the child feels about the situation; and some glance into the educational histories of the parents and their aspirations for their child in order to better grasp why they are upset about the poor grades. I also want to know whether there are other areas of conflict between parents and child, whether the parents are united in their attitude toward the poor grades, and how they have handled conflicts with their child in the past. What forms of discipline have they used over the years? Which have been effective, and which not? In particular, I want to know what they have already tried with regard to the presenting problem, since I do not want to waste time recommending avenues to them they have already explored.

There are always some cases where students do poorly because they are depressed or anxious, but these are not the majority of the cases I see. Instead many of the adolescent cases I encounter involve children who are in conflict with their parents about the meaning of life (ultimately), about how life should be lived, and about who is in charge of their life. And therapeutic responses to these varied situations need to range from individual work with a child, to family work around conflict and how it is handled, to consultation with the school about the curriculum of the student and how it might better be handled.

Occasionally the child's problems may be connected with his identification with one or another parent; if the child's parents have varying educational attainments, the child may identify with the parent who did less well educationally and thus the child may, to some degree, be caught up in a struggle between the parents (about who is better, who has lived a fuller, more meaningful life). And if divorce has complicated this picture, then often the parent who brings the child in can be helped to see that what is being played out, in the child's school drama, is a script whose beginnings go back quite far, and whose end lies in the child's eventual choice of a life. If the child chooses a life in which educational attainment is not significant, then there is little the parent can do no matter how wasteful she may consider that.

HELPING THE PARENT GIVE UP

Often parents need help giving up—not giving up their aspirations for their child, not giving up all responsibility, but giving up their unrelenting effort to force the child to be what they want the child to be. They need to see that there is only so much they can do and from then on it is up to the child, and the child's chosen path may make them sad, but that does not mean that they can change it just by wishing the child would do differently. There is a substantial sadness connected with raising children, and acknowledging it does no harm; in fact, since acknowledging it is foreign to the dominant ideology of family life, often simply pointing out the sadness is beneficial.

Sadness arises, for example, in watching a child grow older and more independent. Insofar as a parent enjoys having a helpless being on his hands, he will enjoy taking care of the baby; eventually most babies become more self-sufficient, and a parent who is very identified with the role of nurturer will find it hard to give up this role.

Sadness arises in observing the decline of the spontaneity and wild energy of the child, although most of this sadness is accompanied as well by some degree of relief, since coping with a young child's energy for more than a few years would exhaust most of us. Kids say the damnedest things because their view of the world is so discrepant from that of adults. As kids become socialized and learn how others in their culture see things, their perceptions become less fresh and new, more prosaic and conventional. This is not to say that we adults want the child to stay childish forever, but simply that there are many parts of childhood that are wonderful and exciting, and seeing some of them fade is sad. There are accompanying rewards, of course, which for most parents suffice. And sadness overwhelms very few parents, although I am convinced that it affects many.

Another form of sadness has to do with the vantage point of the parent who has experienced more than the child and who knows more, in some sense, although the knowledge is not transferable, and lectures about that knowledge do not do much good. Children need—as did we all—to discover things for themselves. Thus from the parents' point of view, the child's chosen path may be mistaken or even dangerous. Nearly always the parent sees difficulties in the child's path which the child is oblivious to, and sitting with that perception is difficult, but necessary, since hectoring the child about the pitfalls lying ahead is not very constructive. And for the most part, the pitfalls are not so dangerous as the parent conceives, but even when they are, there are few constructive alternatives to giving advice and then standing back and observing. The sadness here is of knowing what is best but being unable to make it happen.

So sadness accompanies this role, since it is such a limited role compared with our importance to our children when they were very young, when we could do everything for them, when they were helpless and incapable of doing much beyond crying. Parents suffer an enormous loss of control as children grow older, and since age in our culture is not a valued attribute to start with, the loss of control which comes with age is almost never greeted gladly by any of us. Children are unfortunately able to make us vividly aware of our waning powers.

Children start off almost entirely helpless and then, day by day, gradually grow in power and control until, by the time they are adolescents, they have substantial powers (and even more substantial interest in exercising whatever power they can lay their hands on). So having an adolescent in the house is a daily lesson in humility, one which stands in stark contrast to all our vivid memories of taking care of that same child when he was a baby. And this whole process is accompanied by significant sadness, a major part of which resides in our growing awareness of how helpless we are with our children. We want to make their lives wonderful, but we must sit back and watch them make mistakes. We remember the toddler running to us for a kiss after a nasty fall and we want to kiss away the tears forever but we cannot. In fact, we can seldom kiss our children at all during adolescence; they do not seem to like it. And sitting and watching our own child suffer is very difficult, more than most of us can comfortably manage.

Many of the parents I see are struggling with this issue, although they will not frame it in these words. Instead they come in talking about poor grades, but underneath what is fermenting is their own sense of themselves aging, their own regret that they cannot protect their child from harm, their own sadness that they are so helpless with what seems of such critical importance. Thus giving up is necessary but almost impossible, and much of what I do with many of the families I see is try to help the parents give up, in all the senses I have been discussing.

The parents need to give up their wish to be omnipotent, their wish to be the perfect caretakers and the all-providing nurturers, even though they usually have vivid memories of playing just such a role and quite successfully, too, when the child was younger. All of this becomes acutely exacerbated when children are adolescents, since it is during that period that they are most rejecting of parental involvement; even saying good-morning seems to be felt as an intrusion by the child. All boundary issues become highly defended, as the child is attempting to protect an identity which is still barely established and quite tenuous.

A typical adolescent issue discussed in my office is that of the room: parents typically think it is too messy, and children typically think that it is their own space and should be in their own control. So the battle occurs over the issue of how neat the room needs to be. The underlying issues are those of control, boundaries, and identity, and the parents in addition need to come to terms with their own helplessness: if they are going to give the child a room of her own, they need to relinquish some control, and there really are no two ways about it, although coming to terms with this often requires years of struggling between parents and child.

Unfortunately the phrase *giving up* does not have very favorable connotations in our culture. We have all sorts of clichés which emphasize the importance of never giving up, of struggling onward no matter what the odds, of triumphing over all adversity through sheer doggedness, and parents who have successfully managed to work out a life-involving job and children are often unaccustomed to giving up on anything important, and they typically define their children as of immense importance. So I can never tell the parents in my office that they need to give up; instead I need to use phrases with more positive connotations, or I need to deflect their attention to the issue of how much they are living through their children.

What do you do for yourselves, I may ask, as a way of getting them to look at the fact that there is more to life than struggling with an adolescent about a messy room.

To some degree the issues I have been discussing—the need for the parent to learn to give up some part of the control and sense of total responsibility which were so familiar when the child was a baby; the way in which giving up the need for complete control is complicated by changes in the parent's own development, since aging involves a loss of other forms of control as well—these not only are pertinent to battles with an adolescent over poor grades or a messy room, but reside at the heart of some physical child abuse. Here is where Alice Miller makes her most telling points: she collapses any distinctions between clear-cut child abuse (involving violence) and all forms of control exercised by parents over children, which she insists are, as well, permeated by violence or the threat of violence. And she makes much of the rather ordinary parental tendency to hope that one's children will reflect one's own high ideals and aspirations and, ultimately, one's self.

Doubtless there are dangers inherent in all this; that is, parents do ordinarily become too invested in their children's performance and character, parents are narcissistic to some degree in hoping that their children will reflect their own ideals and aspirations. But the alternatives are difficult to perceive, since all of this pathology—if that is what it is— flows from a sort of parent-child attachment with very deep roots in our culture. So parents who do not have this over-investment in their children are often not very good parents in our culture's terms. They may neglect their child, and this may have consequences just as injurious as the consequences Alice Miller portrays so vividly. Thus I think Miller's arguments suffer from the same difficulties as other by now familiar arguments that take some indubitable fact and then argue that it is the one central fact that characterizes our culture in general. For example, you can take the fact of rape and argue that it is the crux of male-female relations in our culture.[3] Or you can take the fact of schizophrenia and argue that it is the

---

[3] Susan Brownmiller did this to some degree in her book *Against Our Will* (1975).

crux of family relations in our culture.[4] But I think all these attempts go beyond their germ of truth and err in the direction of exaggeration, and similarly I think Alice Miller has strayed too far from her central germ of truth in her books. (We will return to Miller's ideas in Chapter 5; they deserve a more extensive discussion.)

A more sensible approach is to retain the category of physical child abuse at one end of a complex spectrum, and to ac- knowledge that all parents feel some desire, occasionally, to control their children, and to see this desire as not so much pathological as flowing from the overidentification with the child which most parents experience. This latter cannot be done away with, either; it is a natural consequence of our socially and culturally accepted ways of arranging our families. In this view, problems arise because parents look to children for more than can be obtained; parents feel frustration; they are accustomed to some measure of control; they feel a waning sense of control; and in an effort to reassert their own powers, they sometimes go too far and move into the realm we would call child abuse. Abuse, then, is seen less as sadism (the desire to inflict pain) than as a desire to reassert control over a recalcitrant reality, namely, the other person, who was for- merly a baby and is now a growing child. (Sexual abuse is most likely another story, at least in part, although how great a part is difficult to specify.)

So this form of therapy necessitates talking with parents about their children; exploring their view of the children; exploring the parents' own histories; taking into account the sociological perspective all of the involved parties bring to bear on what is happening. One way to refer to the entire process is to call it consultation instead of therapy, since a major portion of what happens involves my talking to the parents about what they see and giving them various different perspectives from which to view it. Whether this helps them depends on what happens when they go home and try to put these different ideas to use.

---

[4] Ronald Laing apparently tried this in several of his books.

4

Guiding Points
of View

One way to obtain an overview of our short-term and intermittent therapy would be to describe it as flowing from a set of guiding points of view. They are not guides that tell us specifically what to do; rather, they are points of view that in any given case may or may not have some pertinence. In discussing these fundamental vantage points, I will try to indicate why they are particularly helpful for anyone doing the form of brief therapy I am describing.

Fundamental points of view for anyone working in our field include those of developmental psychology and psychoanalysis, the former because it refers to all that has been learned (and continues to be learned) about how people evolve and change over their lives (not just in infancy and childhood), the latter because in a general sense it continues to provide the basic concepts which guide most of what is called dynamic psychiatry. I will explain more clearly what I mean in a moment, but first let me continue with a list of fundamental points of view.

Another is provided by family therapists, all of whom see families as systems of one sort or another, and all of whom tend to think that each of us is influenced by his family in

79

important ways, but even more important, that one effective way to modify what is happening in any given person is to work with his family. Some of the work we do in the Child Unit is family work, although not all of it, since we have no doctrinaire belief that only family therapy is effective; but even when we are not seeing an entire family, our work is informed by what can best be called family perspectives.

Behaviorism contributes a great deal in the sense that looking at behavior is basic to much of what one does in brief therapy. The behaviorists who have become interested in therapy have developed various forms of behavior therapy, none of which we espouse enthusiastically but all of which contribute a way of looking at what is going on in a person or group of people. What I mean here by behaviorism is perhaps somewhat idiosyncratic, and I will explain this in more detail.

Three more points of view I find particularly valuable because of my own background and training derive from sociology, from psychological testing, and from cognitive psychology. I have long been interested in social psychology; I am inclined to see individual behavior as in part a function of the larger systems in which each person exists. Thus I think it makes sense for any psychologist to be aware of larger social trends, such as those that currently affect the position of women in the family (the high divorce rate; the continuing trend toward women being employed outside the home full time, in careers which are taken seriously), or the growing number of children in day-care or other partly or completely institutional settings during their early years. Any investigation into anyone's life needs to take into account the larger social realities that govern that person's life. So, for example, if a teenager is having many fights with his parents about use of a car, it helps to know where the family lives and how vital the car is to transportation. Living in the city means there is more public transportation; in some suburbs, a car is almost the only way to get around if one is going farther than one can easily with a bicycle or on foot. Perhaps this should not be called a sociological factor, but whatever it is, it needs to be looked at, and one needs to consider similar factors in designing any treatment plan. In another example, if I think a father should spend more time with his son, I need to know what the father's work life is like, and what the constraints are within which he lives. Finally, any clinician needs to be aware of the ways in which his location in a particular system influences the care he provides. Someone in private practice may think he is not part of any system, although that is never true; but many clinicians work in systems whose character-istics are rather clear to everyone, and the point of view I have developed about short-term work with children and fam-ilies is very much a product of the particular health-care system in which I work and through which I provide my services.

Psychological testing is a skill I acquired during my training. I do not do very much testing in my present setting, but I do some, and there is a general sense in which knowing about testing is helpful. First, it helps in conversations with parents about their child's school performance; often the school has done testing, and my knowledge of the tests helps me under-stand what the school is seeing as a problem, and helps me talk with the parents about it. Second, there is a process basic to testing which I think has general applicability.

Cognitive psychology provides me with useful ways of think-ing about the dilemmas I face in my office. The gist of this is my belief that in short-term work, some of what gets done could be called cognitive therapy; that is, we are working with how people think about things. Further, there are many chil-dren I see for whom the presenting problem is connected with school, and often in these cases it makes sense to be explicitly concerned with how the child thinks or, more broadly, how she uses her mind. Let me consider each of these seven points of view in more detail.

DEVELOPMENTAL PSYCHOLOGY

Since I am primarily a child psychologist whose referrals nearly always include a child, it makes sense that I should be interested in development, for children are developing in ways so vivid and obvious that no one could miss them. Any examination of any child needs to take into account how old the child is, and almost any behavior or event will have varying meanings depending on the age of the child involved. All therapists surely take this into account, so the fact that we do so is not unusual. What we do in addition is: (1) to see entering therapy as a stage in the development of a family; (2) to see therapy as occurring in stages, and as never really ending, just as all true development does not ever end but unfolds until life itself ends; and (3) to see families and parents as well as children as in a stage of development.

Entering therapy is a stage in the sense that it marks a significant point in the family's life, the point at which the family turns to an outside expert for help in its own internal affairs. This is not commonplace, although there are admittedly some families in our practice for whom it is perfectly ordinary and done repetitively over the life of the family whenever there seems any need. But many of our families are embarking on therapy for the first time when they come to see us; or even if this is not the very first contact with a therapist for all of the members of the family, it is nonetheless a significant event. The family is looking for outside help, or at least one member is, who has persuaded the others to come along. So when we apply the term *stage* to therapy with families we mean in part that the family is at a certain stage in its development.

We also mean that they are in a process of change, one piece of which is our contact with them. Our view—perhaps overly optimistic—is that change is occurring whether we like it or not; the only question is which direction it is going. So the therapist's participation in this process influences the direction the change will take, but it is not the only force active in the process. Grasping this is essential if the therapist is to engage in short-term work, since the therapist's occupational hazard is feeling overly responsible for and involved with the patient. The patient's fate comes to seem the natural result of and entirely due to the therapist's presence in the patient's life, even though this view is patently ludicrous. In a very real sense, the problem here is not one of comprehension but one of experience. The therapist needs—as does the parent, for that matter—to experience herself as *of* importance, but *not the only* important ingredient of what is unfolding; and the therapist needs to feel that a process is unfolding whether she likes it or not.

So one meaning of the term *stage* is an explicit identification of what is happening as a developmental process, and the development is partly of the patient, partly of the family of the patient, and partly of the therapy with the patient and the family. There is a critical sense in which these processes must be respected. For example, the developmental process of the family must be respected, although one must not be so respectful that all intervention seems heavy-handed and meddlesome. This is a complicated point, but it is not dissimilar from what some family therapists explicitly declare.

For example, Karl Tomm's (1984) version of the Selvini Palazzoli (Milan) school of family therapy argues that an essential constituent of their approach is to respect the family's present functioning as a sensible way of coping with whatever they see as their dilemmas of living. They may not be entirely satisfied with their solution, and they may be asking for help in changing, but one of the keys to helping people change in this regard is to feel a substantial respect for their present way of doing things, even when it does not make sense to you as therapist. There is a sense in which this is conventional therapeutic wisdom, but another sense in which it is an extraordinarily difficult task to accomplish; most therapists do not really feel this in their bones, although they may acknowledge it intellectually. Acknowledging that the patient's or family's way of doing things has its merits and has evolved for good reasons—if one can manage to gain access to their way of seeing things, can develop empathy for their experiential position—is easier in a system like ours, and when one is engaged in short-term therapy, than when people are either in private practice or doing longer therapy.

Understanding this point hinges on seeing clearly the ways in which doing short-term work within a health care system like ours is made possible because of the variety of ways in which the health care system supports each individual clinician, and supports each patient. The clinician is supported, for example, by an elaborate on-call emergency system which all of us take turns participating in; by colleagues who are ready to consult about difficult cases, and ready if necessary to take referrals of patients with whom we may be stuck; by access to abundant information about patients through the charting system. The patients are supported by having several providers, not just the one in mental health; and by feeling (when the system is working) that he is being taken care of in general, even when there are specific aggravations and disappointments (e.g., with the mental health care, or with some other specialty).

How does all this make it easier for a clinician to respect a patient's ways of doing things? First, the clinician in our system is less likely to feel solely responsible for the patient, and thus less likely to be grandiose in his expectations of himself and his hopes for the patient; second, the clinician has an easier time refraining from holding on to the patient. Holding on in what sense? In the sense that some clinicians try to keep patients returning to their office when they are convinced that there is a "need" for therapy. The clinician is likely, in other systems, to want to keep the patient returning because he fears that if the patient stops coming, he will drop out of sight (this is harder for patients to do in our system, although not impossible). In addition, the clinician may have other less noble motives for wanting to keep the patient returning (because he needs his time filled and there is no one waiting to fill it, because if the patient does not come no one gets paid, because it is more comfortable to deal with the same familiar patients than with new ones, etc.).

All of this occurs because the clinician sincerely sees the patient as needing therapy. The patient is doubtless in distress, or is symptomatic, or is exhibiting some sign which can be taken without any distortion as implying a need for improvement (that is, a need for therapy, as the clinician would put it). But in our system it is easier for a clinician to say that the time is not right for therapy (for example).

This patient could, perhaps, from our point of view, be living his life in a better, happier, more fulfilling way, but he is not ready to commit himself to making the change. Saying this is for us not difficult, given the system within which we work, and I am arguing that saying this is possible for two sets of reasons. One set is systemic: because we work in a system which permits us (encourages us) to say this, and because we are inclined, by our own systemic pressures, to insist that people who are not ready for therapy will not get therapy. The second set of reasons has to do with our readiness to look at patients in a way which permits us to say that they are determined, at this particular moment, to go on doing what they have been doing already. We can see that they are attached to their own ways of doing things and are determined to continue with them. This is what I have been calling respect for the patient's point of view.

There is a fine line here between abandoning the patient (well, if that's the way you are going to behave, then too bad for you; I certainly am not going to waste my time trying to help you), and respecting his right to live his life as he wishes even if to us it appears destructive or miserable. But I think this is an especially important point for any therapist who works with children and families, because this is, after all, the crux of one of the major dilemmas of parenting. All children will at times do things that parents are convinced are stupid or self-destructive, and allowing children to do this without abandoning them is one of the most severe strains on any parent. Similarly, the therapist will be stressed by the constantly evolving task of deciding for each patient whether what is needed is more pressure (for example, to keep appointments, to make changes), or more distance and freedom (for the patient to make his own choices).

All of this is related to the developmental point of view because it arises out of a conviction that therapy itself is characterized by developmental aspects. Psychotherapy is peculiar in that it cannot be applied without the patient's consent and, even more, his participation. Thus the patient needs to be ready for change, and no amount of pressure from outside agencies or people is going to create that right moment. I do not mean to imply that I can always tell when someone is ready for therapy and when he is not. It is all a complicated process of assessment and reassessment (a patient who is not ready one month may be ready the following month). Furthermore, any patient's readiness for change is a complicated process in itself which the therapist can influence by what he says and does with the patient—that is, the therapist may persuade the patient that the time is ripe. But allowing people to say no, they are not ready, is important, and doing this is easier for us, and easier when the clinician sees therapy as something for which a given patient may not be developmentally ripe.

Another aspect of our use of the idea of development is our sense that all interventions—anything we therapists do during our encounters with the patients, and any effects this may have after our patients leave our offices—are bound by or contained in the developmental stage of the patient or family. Thus, an intervention that is effective with one patient at one time may not be effective with the same patient at an earlier or later time, or with a different patient at the same time. The clear analogy is to children: what works with one child at one age will not work with the same child at a different age, or with a different child at the same age. Seeing this clearly, and holding this in front of one as one works, is a tremendous aid to short-term work, for it gives one the courage to try something more than once—the fact that something did not work last month does not mean it won't work today— and it gives one the patience to wait and see what happens (it may work next week, or next month).

Thus the view of the patient being offered here is not of a person with fixed character and fixed conflicts whose repressed feeling is amenable to change through the process of insightful interpretation by the analyst, for such a view assumes (among other things) that an interpretation is either valid or not valid. The view being offered here is that perhaps an interpretation that was valid a year ago is not valid today. Or that today's interpretation may be valid but the same interpretation next month may no longer be valid. What if that which is being interpreted is constantly changing? This seems to us in fact to be the case. In his interesting book, Donald Spence argues this among other things (in an analysis I will consider at greater length later).[1]

The point of view being offered here has other implications also. What if the psychoanalyst's interpretation is akin to what the hypnotists call a suggestion? Perhaps Freud never moved as far away from hypnosis as he thought! This would imply that the therapist is not so much an objective scientist observing the "truth" of a person as an *active agent* who *does* something by talking to the patient, and part of what he does is to change things by talking. Here I am not trying to imply that the therapist is putting alien ideas into the patient's head, but I am positing an active therapist as someone who intervenes by making observations, and I would suggest that his observations have not so much the status of verifiable truth, but rather constitute an intervention which has some shaping power of its own. The therapist is making a difference by his observations.[2]

Grasping this idea requires a more complicated view of what people are with one another and what they mean to one another than most social scientists can readily accept. Discussing this without drifting off into a rather ethereal realm is hard. I find that philosophers have more of pertinence to say on this topic than most psychologists, and I especially recommend the work of Macmurray (*The Self as Agent* [1957]). But the one crucial idea, which pertains to both what the therapist is to and does for the patient, and what the parent is to and does for the child, is that each of us, although apparently separate and autonomous, is in fact bound up with others.

In this country we have an elaborate ideology of independence, some of which I will be apparently supporting when

---

[1] See his book *Narrative Truth and Historical Truth: Meaning and Interpretation in Psychoanalysis* (1982).

[2] For a cogent and detailed analysis of this way of looking at therapy, see, for example, Haley's account of Milton Erickson's work, *Uncommon Therapy* (1973).

I talk later of the need of the adolescent to separate from the family, but we are simply mistaken when we extend this value—our belief that it is important to treat people as autonomous, independent beings—and act as though it describes reality. For no matter how much we value independence, we have to recognize—if the mysteries of raising children and of doing therapy are to make sense—that we are not indeed so independent. We exist through and in relation to others; we come into existence in that way (from physical gestation through psychological gestation), and we live that way.

Developmental psychology and psychoanalysis have in common their acknowledgment of such ideas, although I am bringing these ideas more to center stage than most psychologists or therapists would. For the developmental psychologists have gone to the trouble of painstakingly documenting the amazing psychological importance people have to growing babies; and the psychoanalysts invented a vocabulary for talking about the ways in which people are multiply constituted, and constituted through relations with others (via internalizations and identifications and projections, etc.).

One of the values of the developmental model is that it clarifies how we can do a piece of work with a person or family during a few sessions and then do another piece of work perhaps six months or a year later; by that time either things in the patient's life will have changed, or the patient's understanding of his life will have altered under the pressure of unfolding events. And it makes explicit our sense that therapy is never finished; it is truly interminable, but not in a bad sense, just in the sense that life goes on and on much longer than seems possible. Since change is ongoing, there is no arriving at perfection of development, so there is no point in searching for the ideal therapist, or the ideal therapy. No matter what criteria we use for assessing therapeutic progress, we must always recognize that what seems to be substantial progress today or tomorrow may contain within it the seeds of substantial difficulty a year from now. Recognizing this explicitly is a tremendous relief for a therapist. It removes the burden of trying to be perfect, of trying to finish something and get it right once and for all.[3]

Thus part of what I mean when I refer to a developmental view is a thoroughgoing belief in the inevitability of change, in the dynamic tendencies inherent in human existence. Therapy is never the only route to change, nor is it the sine qua non of change, for change is occurring continuously. So the therapist is not the person who is responsible for creating change, not because the patient has to change himself, but in the more complex sense in which development is always occurring and is always multiply determined. What the therapist says and does matters, and being responsible means acknowledging that; but it is not the only thing that matters, and it is grandiosity to lose sight of that.

PSYCHOANALYTIC THINKING

Another major underpinning of our point of view is provided by certain aspects of psychoanalytic thinking. The analytic view needs to be discussed because so much of what is called therapy is based in this view, and the psychoanalysts have been very influential in creating a climate of opinion within which most writing about therapy occurs.

Psychoanalysis is conventionally described as having three aspects: it is a method of doing therapy, a body of thinking about people, and a way of collecting data about people. Of these three, it is the body of thinking which is of most interest to us. Some psychoanalytic ideas are critically important for us: that behavior is multidetermined; that some of what we are experiencing is unconscious (or out of awareness); that we each fend off unpleasant ideas and feelings by using defense mechanisms (which can be interpersonal as well as intrapersonal); that we each are more primitive and childish than we

---

[3] If one wants to feel certain about what has been accomplished, this point of view can also be very depressing. But then, this is not a field for people who want certainty. Most of what we do is permeated with uncertainty and lack of clarity.

like to think (that is, we develop through stages and never leave the early stages entirely behind).

The point about much of human experience being unconscious is of critical importance because it leads to the conclusion that the patient does not know how to tell the therapist what is of critical importance, and this in turn leads to a lengthy therapy; if the therapist believes that crucial aspects of a person's experience are difficult to obtain access to, he will be predisposed to believe that the important knowledge and understanding of a person's character will take a long time to obtain. There is some truth in this. People *are* hard to get to know, and many important aspects of each person's character are hidden. Therapists who do short-term work have not discovered any magic way around these problems. But the important question is whether there are other ways to help people change, whether understanding a person thoroughly is the best and most effective or only way to generate change. There is abundant evidence that understanding is not crucial for change, neither self-understanding nor the understanding of the therapist obtained through psychoanalysis (and conveyed, presumably, via interpretations given to the patient).[4]

Furthermore, there are many situations in which people are unaware of what they are doing, and have no great investment in continuing the behavior. The fact of lack of awareness does not in itself imply resistance to change. If someone is whispering and is not aware of it, simply asking him to speak up may lead to the desired result. (A separate issue would arise if you were to ask him why he was talking in a whisper. But to change the behavior, it is quite possible he does not need to know why. And it may be that the why is not so terribly complicated anyway. He might say, oh, I thought the baby was sleeping, so I was afraid of waking her up; and you could tell him that the baby is not sleeping, and even if she were,

---

[4] This is a complicated topic; I touch on it at various points in this book, but there is no way to summarize easily all the kinds of evidence which may be brought to bear here.

the noise of people talking in ordinary tones does not wake her.)

Analysts have devotedly observed that although we are each constantly changing, we each also resist change, sometimes rather strenuously. The factors that impede change they call resistance, and one important aspect of therapy in their view is the necessity of working with the resistance, or getting around the resistance. In the analytic view, resistance is best handled within the context of a relationship which has been built up over time with the analyst; this cannot occur quickly and requires in itself many meetings over a long period. Part of the analyst's art, which requires years of learning, involves working through the resistance.

Each of these is a familiar and important idea in the psychoanalytic framework. Although we have discussed them only briefly, they are crucial, and we all owe the psychoanalysts a tremendous debt for developing these ideas and for gathering the evidence to support them (through their psychoanalytic work).

Certain other important psychoanalytic ideas seem less useful in our setting, or are useful in new ways. An example is the decreased usefulness of the idea of termination, since in our setting, therapy often has no clear-cut end point, and it may be restarted again at any time. Thus we seldom say goodbye to a patient in the final, absolute way that the original idea of termination presupposes. We sometimes do schedule meetings to say goodbye to a patient whom we have seen regularly, but this is not the norm; and even when we stop seeing a patient, the patient so often returns to the Center for other health care that we may see him in the halls or waiting rooms and say hello; patients seldom have a clear sense of having finished with a therapist, even when they are not currently in active treatment.

The idea of transference is useful but in a new way; in addition to the ordinary forms of transference (and countertransference) between a patient and a therapist, we also observe a form of institutional transference. Many patients develop a strong attachment (which can be ambivalent) to our Center. Whether it is the building, or the various individual providers the patient is accustomed to seeing, we do not know. But there are many patients who develop a strong attachment to our setting, and usually this works in our favor even when we have not seen the patient before, or do not see the patient very often. Patients expect help, and this predisposes them to receive it.

Another aspect of psychoanalysis, which is no longer specific to analysis but which characterizes most therapy, is that it inculcates a way of listening to people, and this is useful for us. We listen to the unspoken messages; we attend to the varieties of communication that may be occurring simultaneously; we listen to a patient's associations as a way of getting at what is going on beneath the surface. However, we do this in a way which is very different from what a psychoanalyst does, in that we do it in a context of wanting to effect a change fairly rapidly. So our primary focus is not on the unconscious, not on what is happening beneath the surface. But we must pay attention to that realm in order to work with what is closer to the surface.

Another aspect of psychoanalytic thinking involves its method of doing therapy, which makes the analyst's listening and the patient's talking the fundamental activities. Here we part company with the analysts, since a posture of careful listening whose context (in Freudian terms) is a period of months or even years is not possible for us. So we must be more active, must talk more and listen less, or rather—since we do want to listen to whatever the patient has to say that is important— we must take a more active stance in our therapy. And our model for such a more active stance has had to come from areas other than the psychoanalytic, so we turn to the behaviorists and to the family therapists for such models. In saying this, I am not ignoring the numerous analysts who have attempted to develop a more active form of psychoanalysis (such as Ferenczi). Nor am I ignoring the early history of Freud's own psychoanalytic work, since it is clear now that Freud himself was capable of being very active. He gave advice to patients, probably interrupted them, smoked cigars, and sometimes even did very brief treatment (his treatment of Bruno Walter was exceedingly brief, as the account by Richard Sterba [1951] makes clear). I am merely reflecting the general sense of contemporary psychoanalysis as a form of treatment which takes years, and in which a patient is encouraged to talk freely and uninterruptedly about whatever comes to his mind (following what Freud called the fundamental rule).

So when we needed to develop ways of being more active, ways that would not abandon the important psychoanalytic insights contained in some of the ideas I have mentioned already as being of crucial importance, we have of necessity turned in other directions, toward behaviorism and toward family therapy.

BEHAVIORISM

Even though we may not identify ourselves as behaviorists, we still borrow many ideas from them, chief among which is a more active stance in the therapy. Behaviorists were among the first to take an unabashedly active role in therapy, and although their theoretical base may seem rather thin in comparison with the richness of the psychoanalytic perspective, there is no question that they have given the rest of us the courage to make suggestions to the patient, to answer questions directly, to tell the patient what to try in a way that is, after all, perfectly ordinary for a doctor, but which over the years since Freud developed his theory has become very unordinary for a psychiatrist (in spite of various attempts by Ferenczi and others to develop a form of more active analysis).

Another important ingredient of a behavioristic perspective is its focus on behavior. One of their typical questions is, What is happening? and concrete and specific detail is required. Although almost any therapist of any persuasion might ask this question, the behaviorist's focus on the details of the behavior is very important. So when a man comes in saying he wants to lose weight, we would want to know details of when he eats, and we would want to consider at least the that there is a way to get him to modify his eating ... is would not be addressing any underlying issues of ... steem or unmet basic needs or counterdependency or masochism, partly because addressing them in a short-term setting does not make sense, and partly because a different way may be more effective in producing change, change that endures (and is not just a transitory reflection of the brief on-going therapy relationship).

Behaviorists often tell patients to try something at home, and this is a technique which often is of immense use to us. The "something" may be a new way of responding to a child's temper tantrums; it may be a planned time together for a couple who seem not ever to have time for one another; it may be almost any specific behavioral response to a particular act or situation. And many of the guiding ideas behind the particular suggestion may derive from more general behavioral tenets.

To take a simple example: responding to a baby crying may stop the baby from crying, or it may not. When a situation evolves in which the baby cries until it is picked up and then resumes crying when it is put down, the crying may represent something other than physical need. In this situation, respond-ing to the crying may prolong the crying. So parents sometimes need to be told that they should limit their responses. The baby won't die of crying too much (the neighbors might, but that's another story). The general point of view here is that a piece of behavior of one person is influenced by the responses to that behavior by another person. This is certainly not always the best way to look at a given problem, but sometimes it is a very powerful way, and this is partly what I am referring to when I talk of a behavioral approach.

This approach may be most easily applied when the therapist has more than one person in the room; that is, if we want to look at how one person's behavior is responded to by another, we need both people there. So this approach may be used most easily when a clinician is working with a parent and child, or with a couple or family. But there are other behavioral ideas easily applied to working with individuals (for example, to help people stop smoking, or lose weight).

But the most general debt we owe to the behaviorists is the idea that behavior counts as much as feelings do. So the time-honored and typical therapist question *how do you feel* about this is not the only important question to ask. Another very important question is *what do you do* when this happens. Some people need help looking at feelings, and therapists may find this an important focus with certain patients. But there are many other people who have all too many feelings, and all too few ways to modulate them. Such people may benefit most from being encouraged to look at their behavior. Behavior is also important. There is a point at which talking more about feeling bad does not help; more effective would be doing something to feel better. And insofar as feeling better is incompatible with feeling bad, things will improve.

I am not advocating this as the only approach to take; there are clearly some people who need help discovering their feelings, who need to act less and feel more consciously what is being experienced, although even here a behavioral approach may be pertinent. Gendlin's work (1981) on focusing provides a very relevant example of how this might occur, insofar as it breaks down the rather vague and general question "Tell me about your feelings" into more specific perceptual and cognitive acts of paying attention one can carry out in order to learn more about feelings. In his approach, the therapist suggests ways for the patient to become more aware, instead of just sitting back and waiting for the therapy to do its job, hoping that the power of the interpretations will cut through the resistance. In other words, much of what may appear as the patient's unwillingness to share his experiences may be lack of ability to be aware, and it is possible that people can be trained to be more aware. The behaviorists who have done biofeedback research have surely taught all of us that greater awareness is possible with practice, even of aspects of our functioning that we traditionally think of as biological and inaccessible to awareness (body temperature, blood pressure).

Training in awareness can be done in a short-term context, as can training in relaxation, and both of these can be invaluable tools in any therapeutic endeavor. Both seem related to the contributions behaviorists have made to our field. They may refer to the surface of things, and anyone who thinks only the depths matter may be contemptuous of such efforts. But although there are depths, and there surely is a place for a Zen approach to everything and a psychoanalytic approach for everything, short-term therapy is probably not that place. So we need to broaden our definitions of therapy so that short-term attempts also count. There is surely a sense in which a lifelong attempt may be necessary to attain nirvana, or perfect enlightenment, or complete psychoanalysis. But our rejection of that sense is not due simply to our desire to save money; it is also due to our respect for the importance of other life tasks. There is more to life than understanding oneself perfectly, and if the other tasks are to be gotten on with, we need to develop respect for less than lifelong attempts to change our ways of being. These attempts are surely superficial compared with the lifelong discipline of a Buddhist monk or a man pursuing the perfect psychoanalysis, but they are not therefore worthless.

As is apparent, I am in part arguing here for the importance of respect for short-term therapy. We need to develop a theoretical framework within which short-term work appears valuable not just because it is cheaper, not just because it is quick, not just because it is responsive to an environment of limited resources, but because it is useful and it works and it makes sense. In our area, we have arrived at the point of being able to say to people that "we do short-term work" and they nod and seem to grasp the idea, but their response is mainly contained within an understanding that this is all we can offer because we have limited resources. They have no grasp of how valuable this approach is, and how it may in fact be the treatment of choice for many people even when capabilities for longer treatment are available.

So our phrase about short-term work is heard as a statement of our limitations, not of our strengths. The assumption of those who listen to our description is nearly always that we would do more if we could, that we would agree to see people weekly if we had sufficient staff and time. But in fact, I think this is a fundamental mistake, for I think our approach has more to justify it than sheer economic necessity, and one of the goals of this book is to present arguments from different points of view that support this position.

FAMILY THERAPY

There are many ways of doing family therapy, but our interest in family therapy is less in any specific theory than in certain general characteristics most family therapists have in common.

First, we think it makes sense in many cases to see a child's problems as connected with his family, not that the family causes them, but that the problem and the way it is greeted within the family are inextricably bound up with one another. Often an effective intervention needs to be directed not just at the problem but at the whole context, which means that one needs to work both with the problem and with the way it is responded to in the family. For that, one needs ideally to have the child and the parents present in the room, or at least accessible to the therapist.

Second, family therapists are accustomed to being active, and being active is an important part of short-term therapy. Activity means governing the process (when there is more than one other person in the room, the conversation may need a traffic manager, someone to allow one or another family member to talk, someone to draw out a silent family member). It may mean rearranging how people sit, or suggesting tasks for the family to carry out either in the room or later, on their own, at home. It always means doing something other than or more than just listening to the flow of free associations (as one might with an individual patient in long-term therapy).

Family meetings are also an invaluable way to collect information, about the role that each member plays in the family, about how each of them feels about the others, about how the process in the family unfolds. All this information can be essential in generating a wider sphere of understanding within which the presenting symptom, whatever it might be, can be grasped. And these meetings offer an unprecedented opening for seeing what happens when one makes a suggestion to an individual. To take a simple example, if a daughter fights frequently with her mother, then having the family in the room may allow one to observe a fight. One will also see how the other family members handle the fight. And then the therapist can suggest to the fighters that they do it a different way and can observe what then happens. Can they take advantage of a suggestion about a different way of doing a fight? If one has met with one individual only, and then sends her home with instructions about something to try at home, it is much more difficult to be sure what was actually tried. One has only the individual's report of what transpired. But in a family session, one can either see it unfolding in front of one's eyes, or minimally will have other readings—from other family members—about what happened in an event that occurred at home.

Some of us are more dedicated family therapists than others, but all of us share a strong belief in the importance of the family for the identified patient and his symptoms. There is usually no value in forcing this point of view on people, but even when we see patients individually, the family point of view often guides our thinking about the patient.

SOCIOLOGY

I see the family therapy approach as a movement away from individual psychology toward a broader, systems-based understanding of people's behavior and experience, although family therapists usually are not trained sociologically and see their intellectual debts as being more to clinical fields. But a sociological perspective informs my work in two ways. First, I look for social roots or aspects of whatever problematic behavior is being brought to my attention. Second, I think of my intervention as occurring from my position within a system of care that is having an ongoing impact even when I am not explicitly drawing on it or trying to get it involved in a case. Let me discuss each of these points separately.

What might be the social roots of a presenting problem? The most general answer is that all human behavior has social roots, although in any particular case they may be more or less relevant. For example, if a patient comes to talk with me about a writing block, I need to know why writing is important. If he is in a Ph.D. program, he needs to write papers for his courses, and a dissertation eventually for his degree. Unless he abandons his ambition to get a Ph.D., he must write. But the need to write has a social structure to it; he needs to do a certain kind of writing, a kind that will be acceptable to his teachers. And the ambition to get a Ph.D. only has meaning within a particular social structure. Or to take another example, dyslexia can arise as a problem only in a society which takes literacy for granted as a plausible ambition for nearly everyone. Or we could see school phobia as in part generated by a social system which insists on school attendance for all children. Our field is dominated by social complaints. This is true in all mental health to some degree, but it is especially obvious in work with children, since they almost never come on their own. They are brought by someone who sees a problem, and if it is not the parents who feel the problem, it may be the school or some other concerned agency or person.

Why does it matter to see that there is a social context for most behavior? Part of the answer hinges on the way in which a clear view of this aspect of the problem takes some of the responsibility off the shoulders of the deviant person. If I cannot read, it may help me cope with my shame if I can see that this is a peculiar society which insists that everyone must read. A high school student who is made fun of because he studies will have many fewer problems if he eventually arrives at a college where studying is more the norm. A woman who likes taking care of children may need to find a social network for support, since in our local parochial social world most women work outside the home and there are not large numbers of women insisting that they really love taking care of children.

Thus, seeing that one's problem has a sociological aspect may lead one to take the important step of trying to gather social support for oneself. Looking for a supportive network is one important avenue for improving (though not curing) many human predicaments. Admittedly a therapist may not be needed to point this out, but for some people, the most useful thing the therapist does is to help them see this. The disposition or plan may be a referral to a group, or it may simply be helping the patient to see that finding a group would be an important step. (It need not be an official group with regular meetings; it might instead be a circle of supportive friends.)

Most clinicians know that only a small fraction of people with a given problem come to see us. Why does one person come and another not? Part of the answer surely has to do with social context. A boy who likes to stay at home to avoid school will not be brought in to see one of us if his father likes to have him home for company. The school may find the boy and his father a problem, but it is not usually a problem that will make its way into our offices. Here there are two kinds of relevant social contexts, the family and the school. Occasionally we consult to a school about such a problem, but ordinarily our avenue is through the family; the parents bring the child, if we are going to see the child. But there are certainly therapists working in school settings where the client would often be the school or the teachers, who would bring their own perspective to bear on whatever the problem might be.

We too consult to our own social world, namely the pediatricians and various primary care providers and also the adult mental health providers (who may have patients with children). This consultation is part of our therapeutic process, since it brings other professionals into consideration of a particular case, and, in a way not simple to grasp, this process often helps the patient. For when the patient sees or infers that several professionals are in touch with one another about his situation, that can be reassuring; it can help the patient feel heard and taken seriously. (It can also scare the patient if the patient feels the problem is trivial and he does not want to consult a specialist about it, but in most of those cases, we would never meet the patient; he would simply refuse to come in for an appointment.)

PSYCHOLOGICAL TESTING

As a psychologist, I draw on my knowledge of psychological tests and the process of administering them in much of my work. One part of this is very straightforward; since I work with children, and since some of the children who are referred to me are having problems in school, I find that there are often test results already available for the children. If the parents are willing to bring copies in to me, or to authorize the school to release copies, then I can examine the test results. Knowing how to read them helps me talk with parents. Sometimes this simply means I can explain to the parents what the test scores mean and do not mean. This sort of conversation is most critical with regard to intelligence testing, since there is substantial anxiety and misapprehension about IQ tests. But it is also valuable with regard to tests for dyslexia and for learning disabilities in general, and with tests of personality functioning, which some schools give (the Rorschach, the Thematic Apperception Test, or other forms of such projective tests).

Schools usually give these tests when they are puzzled; their hope is that the test results will guide them toward more effective teaching. Unfortunately this is seldom the case, and most often the tests are given as part of a bureaucratically required package. In Massachusetts, for example, if a public school is to offer special services, they must be justified; the justification process is called a CORE (a comprehensive review of the education of a child), and the CORE process mandates various procedures. There are different kinds of COREs (partial and full), and each has its own requirements. But educational and psychological tests are often part of the mandated requirements for a full CORE, so their administration is simply part of this whole process. Seldom is there a clear-cut, focused question which needs answering, and tests function best when that is the case; usually when there is a question it is large and unfocused—What's wrong with this child; he behaves so differently from other children?—and tests can almost never answer the question by themselves. Of course, tests may be able to help answer the large question of what this child is like, and that answer may in turn help teachers design an educational program for the child.

But in part I help parents interpret the test results. When the test report says this child has emotional problems, or this child has difficulty with sequential processing, I try to explain what is meant, and I point to the kinds of evidence the tester has used to arrive at the conclusion. If I cannot figure this out from the test results, I can always call the person who did the tests and discuss what occurred.

Another part of what I do is talk with the parents about their questions and about whether the tests already given, or others which might be given, could help answer their questions. Occasionally there is another test or part of a test which might yield results pertinent to something which puzzles the parents and in that case, I might do that test myself. Usually, however, what is more to the point is a discussion with parents about what tests can help with, which is actually a more limited range of problems than most parents realize. Psychological tests can sometimes indicate problem areas in personality functioning. Educational and cognitive tests can usually pinpoint areas in which what a person knows is limited, or ways in which a person could improve his way of acquiring knowledge. But tests can seldom answer all the questions that people have about a child (or an adult, for that matter), and for many parents this comes as an unpleasant surprise; often they are asking for "testing" as though it would yield specific conclusions about exactly what is wrong with their child.

Another more complicated way in which my knowledge of psychological tests is useful to me is that it offers a paradigm for discovering useful information. The gist of the paradigm is that one develops a routine way of putting certain questions or posing certain dilemmas or tasks, and then can observe what happens. Most clinicians do this automatically, without thinking of this as a technique that owes anything to psychological tests. But when one thinks about a patient's responses in the ways that professional test interpreters find useful, a broader, more interesting vista opens, because those who interpret tests need to take into account the amazing variation in response which occurs both within and between people. The same person may respond differently to the same question in two successive testing sessions, and, of course, two different people are likely to respond differently to the same question given the same day. Variability of human behavior is a crucial concept which I think those who do not do research and do not think in statistical terms are not accustomed to appreciating.

Let me talk about each of these in turn: first, the sense in which tests offer a paradigmatic way of discovering pertinent information about a person; and second, the way in which a grasp of the statistical basis of test interpretation is relevant to all understanding of human behavior.

The simplest way to indicate how tests offer a way of discovering information is to talk about a test as a miniature situation which, to some degree, is comparable to a real-life situation. My discussion here draws on the very interesting use by Sebastiano Santostefano of what he calls the Miniature Situations Technique (MST), which, in brief, is a test that offers a child (or a child and a parent) a choice of actions, each of which must be undertaken by the child, although the child can choose which to do first. For example, Santostefano asks a child to choose among the following three tasks: breaking a lightbulb with a hammer, cutting a piece of paper along a line with a scissors, and hammering a nail into a board. Each of these is a situation that might arise in ordinary life. The point of asking the child to do the tasks is to see which one he does first, and just as important, what his associations are (thoughts, memories, and feelings). This particular test is aimed at discovering something about how the child handles aggressive activity, and, if possible, elucidating the internal structures that accompany his way of handling aggressive action. By internal structures I mean feelings, thoughts, associated memories, all of which cannot be seen directly but which are revealed through behavior and talk. So we ask the child who is doing these tasks what his associations are, what his feelings are. Does he think of his father, or does he feel scared, or does he start laughing?

My point here is that one can see almost anything one asks of a child in an office during an interview as constituting a miniature situation, comparable to the situations that arise in ordinary life. So in the office, one is observing a sample of the child's behavior—not a random sample (more about this in a moment), but a sample in the sense that one does not see all of a child's behavior but only a small portion of it, the part that can be displayed in an hour's visit in the psychologist's office.

My point is further that when a child is in the office with a parent, the actions the two of them engage in together, or the ways in which they engage with one another, are miniature situations representative to some degree of ordinary life situations. And Santostefano has used the MST to ask a child and a parent to do something in the office, to engage in a task together, as a way of observing how the child and the parent get along. If the tasks you ask the parent and child to engage in involve important themes—autonomy, nurturance, dependence, aggression—then you may learn something about how those themes are played out between this child and this parent. And this sort of observation is often more powerful than simply asking a parent to describe how she handles requests for nurturance—for example—from her child. Family therapists who ask families to take different seats, for example, or who give other tasks to families who are in the office, are using this technique, although they would not label it in the same way. They are asking for a form of action and then waiting to see what happens. This emphasis on action is crucial, as is the related insistence on close observation of what behavior, both internal (feelings, thoughts, memories) and external (observable and clearly displayed), accompanies the action.

In practice, all clinicians who work with children and families are observing what goes on in front of them in this way, through this sort of lens. They may not think in terms of giving psychological tests, but they definitely think in terms of comparing the family in the office at the moment with other families who have been in the office before. Through this sort of comparison, the issue of who takes the child's seat—though this is not posed as a test—becomes important to the clinician. Or the question of how the parent will either intervene or not when the child tries to clamber on the bookcase becomes important, because this issue arises whenever a family is in the office. Who holds the baby, who interrupts whom, who diverts the conversation when a difficult topic is broached: all these are phenomena which any clinician would observe and take note of. But being trained in administering psychological tests gives me a context within which to think about these questions. The context is one of comparing individuals and families in their responses to certain situations; and the context is further in knowing that there is variability in how people respond, but being able to assimilate that variability within a point of view enriched by the usual psychological point of view, that associations matter, that sequences are important, that feelings often accompany actions.

Another aspect of the training in giving psychological tests is that it is a training in being active, in posing dilemmas to the patient and being ready to reframe one's question if it is not understood the first time, and having a reservoir of other alternative questions if the first one does not lead anywhere fruitful. When Huck Finn is dressed up like a girl and stops in a woman's cabin for dinner, the woman is suspicious and throws a ball of yarn at him. How will Huck react? is her question, and from his reaction she draws a conclusion (as it happens, the correct conclusion, though we can never be guaranteed of that). He moves his legs together, forgetting that he has a skirt on, which if he spread his legs apart would catch the ball of yarn. The woman here has constructed a miniature situation, as it were. If one is accustomed to giving tests, then even an ordinary interview with no formal testing component can partake of some of the qualities of a testing situation.

To take another example: most family therapists use the arrangement of chairs as just such a miniature situation, although they do not ordinarily frame what they are doing in the way I have done. The therapist watches to see who sits next to whom. Later the therapist may ask one person to move and sit next to someone else; this is essentially the same kind of device which those who administer psychological tests are accustomed to using. You set up a fixed situation; then you vary it, and watch to see what happens; and you may even explore behind what you see by asking people how they feel in this new situation, what thoughts occur to them, what it reminds them of, in the same way that a miniature situations test might require.

The statistical point of view is the other important aspect of training in administering tests, and by this I mean simply that one learns to think of what one is seeing in the office as a sample of behavior. The fact that it is called a sample emphasizes the probability, which one should never lose sight of, that a different clinician on a different day might elicit a different sample of behavior from this same patient. So one is never looking straight into a personality or character; rather, one is seeing through the sample which reflects not just the character of the patient but also the situation and the dynamic relation between the tester and the patient (which would alter with a different tester). Roy Schafer's discussion of psychological tests is most lucid on this issue; the gist of the matter is that giving psychological tests is much more complicated than taking a person's temperature with a thermometer or taking an x-ray.

This is part of what I meant before when I talked of a general misunderstanding about IQ tests, for part of the misunderstanding is that many people think of them as like x-rays, which peer into a person's mind and give an accurate picture. In fact, IQ tests are constructed by taking samples of a person's behavior, and the conclusions one draws from them vary depending on the degree to which the sample resembles the target behavior, the behavior one wants to predict. As it happens, school work is a target behavior that IQ tests often do predict, although far from perfectly, and parents often benefit from some discussion of why the prediction is less than perfect. But another associated issue is whether IQ scores predict any other behavior with any greater exactitude.

This way of thinking is invaluable, since it helps us shift from thinking of IQ tests as measuring a trait called intelligence, a mode of thought which leads us into such puzzlement. For example, how can a person be so smart and yet act so dumb? Why does this smart kid do such stupid things? The thinking which assumes that because a child scores low on such tests, his life chances are limited is especially pernicious, and schools do not help; in fact, they exacerbate the problem, since they themselves are prone to believing that success on tests—intelligence tests and school tests—is an important index of what will later become success in life. This is probably erroneous for many, and certainly erroneous for some, although the details of the relevant arguments are too complex to be entered into here. Other things probably matter much more in life, such as the ability to apply oneself, and to express oneself verbally, and to take the other person's point of view. Parents think that grades are important not just in themselves, but because they are an index of the student's ability to apply herself, and often they talk about how it is application they want—hard work—not just grades. Here I am inclined to agree that the trait matters—being able to work hard—but I am not convinced that being unable or unwilling to work hard in school necessarily means one lacks the trait in life. So I always inquire when I hear about a child not working at school whether the child works at anything persistently. And here we are back to the question of whether a sample of behavior reflects character or predicts the future.

If we take school as a situation that collects samples of behavior, then the question is whether those samples are reliable and valid. A reliable sample is one that can be obtained again at a future time. So if a student does well on a test in

October, and is still doing well in March, then the test-taking behavior being collected can be said to be more reliable than the samples taken from a child whose test scores zoom up and down from week to week or month to month. The next question is whether the tests are valid, and here everything becomes more murky, since to answer the question one needs a grasp of what one is hoping to measure with the sample. The easiest sort of validity to postulate for test-taking behavior is that it is a true indicator of how well the student takes tests. But seldom does a teacher or parent—or student, for that matter—want to know just that she's good at tests. So other forms of validity which test givers and takers hope for include those of accurate measurement of knowledge (a history test collects a sample of behavior which the teacher hopes is valid in the sense of accurately measuring the entire domain of the student's knowledge of history), and future ability to learn additional material (her college admission directors hope that high school test scores are a valid index of this ability, and—and this is much more tenuous—intelligence or ability in life).

So when I talk to parents about psychological tests and about school performance, I have as background a knowledge of the statistical language which is used for interpreting psychological tests and which, I would argue, ought to be used in interpreting all school tests as well. The language involves words like *sample* and *domain, reliability* and *validity*. Parents almost never know this language; even when they know some of the words already, they are not accustomed to thinking in this way. Being able to think in this way is a tremendous help, since it has the potential to clarify what is otherwise an anxiety-arousing situation.

When parents come in to discuss school performance, they almost always are coming in not because they are worried about one grade on a test or in a course, or even the grades of a school quarter or semester. Rather, they are worried about the future. What does the fact that my child is not doing well now mean about his future—that is their anxiety.

So we explore what ideas and hopes they have for their child's future, and part of this discussion is psychological in a psychodynamic way, which may lead us to explore their own childhoods, or their varying images of success in life, or the affect-laden aspect of their relationship with their child or with their own parents. But part of the discussion can involve issues such as those I have been addressing, and engaging in that sort of discussion always leads me to explore the parents' view of the child's other strengths and weaknesses, since to predict the future (always a perilous task and one almost guaranteed to be a failure), one needs as complete a knowledge as possible of a person's character and attainments, of which school performance is only one part, and perhaps a subsidiary part.

Here we enter into a social problem in the sense that because the society places so much weight on school performance, a child may have self-esteem problems as a result of not doing well in school. Fending off the negative judgments of important adults is hard for a child, so a child who persistently does poorly in school may have problems which flow not from doing badly per se, but from the negative evaluations which attend that performance. But many of the children I see are not doing so badly in school; rather, there is a parent-child conflict in which the child's school performance plays a role. The parent thinks the child could do better, or often, that the child should work harder.

The child sees things differently. He may be using school as a way of playing out separation issues with the parents, although that is almost never clear to the child, so the child will say many other things in his own defense. He will say, for example, that he's not doing so badly in everything; he did well last year; he's doing better in one course now than he did last quarter. The child points to the variability in his behavior as a way of saying that he can do better sometimes, he's not all bad. Part of my role in such cases, besides trying to support both the child and the parents at the same time, is making clear that this sort of behavioral variability is an important matter.

Thus part of training in interpreting tests involves learning to take this into account. One assumes some variability of behavior and tries to draw conclusions on this basis. This is a much more accurate and sensible way of thinking about school performance than the usual way, and parents and children often benefit from learning to think in this way. (Of course, there are some children who do badly in school for numerous other reasons: depression, learning disabilities, or even greater character pathology, and I am not talking about all children here.) Further, parents benefit from hearing about an alternate view of test performance, thinking about tests as samples of behavior, and thinking even further about school as a large sample of behavior which may or may not be representative of the behavior needed to survive or excel in life.

Another way of using the statistical ideas of sampling is in considering what happens when a patient comes in the office. Traditionally, the therapist assumes that he is gaining an unbiased and whole picture of the patient. Much more sensible is the assumption that one is getting a sample of the person's behavior, for making that assumption will encourage one to think about factors that might make that sample less than perfectly representative of the patient's entire repertoire. For example, the patient may be nervous, and this will make today's sample different from what would be obtained if the patient were more at home in the office or with the therapist. Most therapists naturally take such factors into consideration, but they may not do so unless they are forced to (when a patient's anxiety is blatant). It is always wise to think in terms of such contaminating factors when one is trying to make sense of whatever has transpired during a patient's visit. Contamination is perhaps too strong a word; in this context, it means simply that some factor other than those one is counting on being present is influencing the sample of behavior one is obtaining.

My own bias in assessing this issue is to ask what the patient is trying to do, rather than asking what the patient is feeling. Feelings matter, of course, but feelings are bound up with action, and are integrated—except in extreme cases—with action. Thus I often ask myself and sometimes even ask the patient what she is trying to do. I see an angry father berating his daughter and although I might just comment on his anger (to find out if he's aware that he is expressing it so openly, to see how he makes sense of it, to draw the attention of the daughter to the fact that I see the anger so that she does not feel she's imagining it), I might also inquire what he's trying to accomplish.

This is a major theme, which was discussed in Chapter 1 and which will be returned to throughout this book: that of action in therapy—not just the necessary activity of the therapist, which I have already discussed, but the action being carried out by the patient as well. Focusing on action is one of my main techniques, not as an alternative to focusing on feelings, but as a necessary complement to the traditional single-minded focus on feelings, which is not always so useful as therapists like to believe.

COGNITIVE PSYCHOLOGY

Here I do not mean to discuss the academic research on cognition which is considerable and interesting but not directly pertinent. Rather, I want to talk about attention, concentration, memory, and thinking. These topics permeate my work, not just when I am seeing someone who is explicitly presenting with a cognitive problem, but when I am seeing most patients. For cognition enters into most problems, just as affect enters into most problems; therapists have overemphasized affect to the neglect of other important issues, and cognition is one of them.

Cognition seems directly pertinent to school and learning situations, and part of my interest is in patients who are having trouble learning. Many of the children I see come in with school problems as part of the presenting complaint. Sometimes, as I have said, we quickly discover that the parent is unhappy with the school performance of the child, and the issue is not so much one of the child's cognition as one of conflict between parent and child. Furthermore, there are many other possible sources of school problems. But when the problem is more clearly cognitive, then I draw on my background and training in problems of cognition.

Learning is a very complicated endeavor, with many component parts. Studying cognition can help one learn to discriminate a problem in one area from problems in other areas. Some people have difficulty registering information—learning new information, especially when it does not fit into any available context—but have no trouble remembering it later once they really know it. Registration here refers to looking or listening in a certain direction, and seeing or hearing what is happening. One is taking in something. If a person cannot register information, then he will not need to worry about memory problems because there will be nothing to remember. Paying attention is a more complicated task, since it requires that one look (or listen or bend one's senses) in one particular direction over a sustained period. Memory enters in when we consider what happens to that which one has registered or attended to, and there are clearly differences between short-term and long-term memory.

But attention can be deployed in a variety of ways. To take one simple contrast, we can go into a room and scan the room with a once-over-lightly look, as we might if we're looking for our glasses, for example. Children are notoriously bad at this when they are young, although they improve in this ability with age, and it is possible to devise tests of this scanning ability.[5] Another form of attention involves close scrutiny of some limited area. Ordinarily we do both constantly. For example, in driving we need to pay close attention to what is happening directly in front of us on the road, but we also need to scan constantly, both behind us for overtaking cars, and to both sides for pedestrians or cyclists who may veer into our path. But some people are much better at one than the other, although whatever abilities we each have can be improved by practice and learning. For example, if one goes to an airport and scans the field looking for a particular plane among the rows of parked planes, the task will be hopelessly difficult until one has spent a long time learning how planes vary. Once one learns what planes look like,

---

[5] Some of my discussion here draws on the work of Santostefano.

through study or experience, the scanning task becomes markedly easier. Similarly, most cognitive tasks can become easier when one masters the requisite information.

People vary immensely not just in their attention-paying capacities, but in the extent to which they know what helps them to pay better attention, or what decreases their ability to pay attention. Until one encounters a situation in life where one wants to learn something new and is having trouble, one will not really make the effort to figure out what will make the task easier. Children typically learn what they truly need (speech, walking, etc.) almost effortlessly (barring some grave pathology), but school learning does not come under that heading, except when it involves learning that they do in fact need immediately. So a child will learn where her seat is, or what the name of her friend is, but have trouble learning the names of the Iroquois tribes, or the main imports of Egypt.[6]

I have often seen college-age students or adults who want to learn how to learn more effectively; I occasionally see high school students who have the same question, and very rarely grade school children who have this question. But I am interested in working with such people, and I think there is a lot to be done with people who want to learn how to learn more effectively. So one way in which I use my interest in cognitive abilities is with such patients. But most of the children I see who are brought in because of what may be a learning problem do not want to think about their learning style, about what makes learning easier or harder. So I cannot discuss such issues with them, although I may discuss them with the parents or the teachers (if the child will allow these adults to be helpful).

But another way I use my knowledge of cognition is in helping parents see how complicated the learning tasks are, and how seldom it is that we can take a child with poor school performance and say that he truly has trouble learning.

---

[6] George Dennison has a wonderful book (1969) about children and learning in which Egypt becomes the symbol of all that which schools force us to learn that is not directly pertinent to our American lives. This is certainly unfair to Egypt, but very pertinent to the school experience for all too many people.

Much more often it is the case that the child has trouble learning certain things in a certain way in a certain place, even though the capacity to learn is still there. Quite often learning abilities become enmeshed in other battles which are not especially cognitive, which have more to do with the development of autonomy, with relations to authority, or with identity struggles.

My interest in cognition also leads me to be interested in using metaphors having to do with attention and concentration and memory in discussing other more affect-laden issues with parents. So if parents are telling me about their daughter's messy room, I will talk about how they pay attention to that rather than to her well-developed social skills, which later in life will probably turn out to be more important for her self-esteem and success and happiness than her room-cleaning abilities. And if they talk about how she owes them and the family a certain amount of cooperation and gratitude, which should lead her to do her share of the work of the house, I will draw their attention to how cooperative she is in other respects. Thus, I wonder with the parents what they are attending to, and hope to get them to reflect why it is that when they scan their daughter's life, all they see is a messy room. They screen out so much other information that is also pertinent.

This almost certainly will sound like a peculiar idea, since it seems to veer so far from the surface of the presenting problem, which is most likely a conflict between parent and child. But often such a veering away is the most sensible procedure in helping the parents get some distance on their preoccupation, and it may be helpful to them to think in cognitive terms about what they are doing. Here they are, paying such close attention to such a small detail; have they ever wondered why? Calling this an aspect of their cognitive style almost surely neglects the substantial emotional content of the conflict, but such neglect is useful with some families. Not all affect needs to be explored in depth.

The phrase *cognitive style* refers to the ways in which people obtain and process and rework information or experience.

People have varying cognitive styles, which are just as important as their varying personality styles (see the work by Gardner and his colleagues [1959]). Personality styles are referred to by words such as obsessive and hysterical; cognitive styles by words such as sharpening and leveling.

Sharpeners look for small differences in whatever array of objects or events they are examining; levelers tend to collapse small differences and smooth things out cognitively. Furthermore most of us vary in this regard, and become—for example—inclined to level more when we are anxious. Even here there are personality differences; for some people anxiety serves as a trigger to increased cognitive sharpening, for others a trigger to increased leveling (see Santostefano's interesting studies on this topic).

For some parents, this way of thinking about what they are doing is pertinent, since they often are using one cognitive style with regard to their daughter and other cognitive styles in other areas of their lives. So the question is: what triggers their use of a particular cognitive style with their daughter? Either extreme—too much sharpening or leveling—can be a problem in raising a child, but the parents I see usually err in the direction of sharpening too much. They pay too much attention to details that would be better ignored, or at least pushed aside for a while. So the color of the blouse the girl is wearing, the tone of her voice when she says good morning, the hour she arrives home from school, her choice of courses, all these become the subject of intense scrutiny. Of course, there are affective roots of this scrutiny, and the overinvolved parent is no stranger to any of us when we think dynamically about families. But there is something to be gained from thinking about this in another way: if we can think about it cognitively, then the door is open to ask a question like, Don't you have anything better to do? Wouldn't you rather be reading a good book or going to a good movie than worrying about what color blouse your daughter is wearing?

"Put your attention elsewhere for a while" may be the important message. We are not saying ignore your child, although for many parents, not paying attention to the color of the blouse is possible only by complete withdrawal of attention, and then this must in turn be dealt with. But if we can ask parents to put their attention somewhere else, on each other, or on some other absorbing interest, then we have a chance to see what happens. Some parents find this impossible, and then we can discuss what got in the way. This is often a much faster avenue to the affect-laden side of the parent-child relationship than the route of careful history taking or lengthy periods of free association, which aims toward an improved dynamic understanding of the child and the parent.

Thus, one starts from the presenting problem—the child does not study—moves to other areas of conflict—she wears the wrong clothes—and suggests that the parent look somewhere else for a while, and then discovers that the parent cannot look somewhere else. Then we can discuss that difficulty, which is probably just as important as the difficulty which brought this family into the office, and has the advantage of involving someone who wants to make a change, that is, the parent. For the child seldom wants to make a change, or, rather, seldom has any sense of leverage with the parent and so would never dream of dragging the parent to a therapist's office to improve things at home. When asked whether she wants life at home to be different, a child may answer with a heartfelt yes, but children will seldom initiate contact with a therapist, nor will a child typically see a therapist as a possibly ally in helping to create a new home situation. But the crucial point is that the child does not feel in control of the home situation, and so does not imagine that she has the leverage to create a change. So bringing the parent who more explicitly wants a change and is seeking a change into the center of the picture has a huge tactical advantage, and in fact in many cases unless one can involve the parents little or no progress will be made.

5

Practical Applications

I have outlined several constituents of our theory of therapy. We see action as central; we think of much of what we do as consultation informed by therapeutic thinking; I have outlined several points of view which provide a background to our approach. How is all this applied in practice? In order to discuss this, we need first a general discussion of the enterprise of therapy.

Let us begin with the fact that we are working with children (and their families). One fact that is clear about children is that they change constantly. Change for children is not, then, a rare or complicated occurrence which requires the ministrations of highly trained professionals. It occurs willy-nilly. Anyone who lives with children knows that what is happening today will probably not be happening in a month, or will be happening in a different way. This is a boon to parents when the behavior of the moment is painful. If Johnny is waking up at three in the morning, chances are that in a month he will not be doing so, unless—and this is an important point for those of us who work with families—something is happening, currently that maintains that behavior. It does happen of course that children wake up in the middle of the night and then continue doing that for months. But when this is presented as "the problem," chances are that something is occurring to maintain this situation. The child may be sick, or may be having nightmares, but in addition the parents may be fostering this situation in ways they do not see clearly.

There is a sense in which all psychotherapy is self-therapy, which makes doing therapy very complicated: what is necessary is for the client to be active, yet the context in which most of us do our work as therapists is one where people come to us for help. They look to us to help them and we cannot very well say straight out and unabashedly: look, you really must help yourself. Yet that is certainly an important though tacit part of whatever we do say to them. The sociological structure of the situation is, at the outset, one in which a person comes for help. The seeker's role is relatively passive; the helper's role is relatively active, since he is the one who is expected to make things better. The challenge is to transform this situation into a different one, in which two active beings work together. The therapist's power to be active, which is created by the situation (it is his office, he decides at what hour to meet, how long the meeting will be, who will be included, etc.), must be conveyed to or absorbed by the client. Conventional ways of discussing this process are to say that the therapist must instill hope in the client; that confidence in the future must be fostered. However it is done, the therapist must keep an eye out from the very beginning for opportunities to give the patient power. This can mean asking the patient for advice about who should be included in the first meeting; it certainly means listening to whatever suggestions the patient may make about such matters, even if the therapist eventually decides to handle things somewhat differently.

This whole project is complicated when we work with children by the fact that the people who come in saying "We want therapy" are usually the parents of the person to whom the therapy is supposed to be given. So we must find a way of saying to them that what is important here cannot be given by me to your child unless the child engages in this process. And that usually means that the parents have to see the child

in a different way, as an important participant in the therapeutic process. That is, they must relinquish their view of the
child as someone who can be treated whether he likes it or
not, and they must adopt a different view of the child as an
autonomous actor whose wishes and feelings and thoughts
must be consulted in a respectful way. For some parents, this
becomes the main part of the work; once they have been able
to change their way of looking at their child in this regard,
often the problem melts away, or rather, the parents come to
see that the problem is the child's problem and it is up to
the child to deal with it, not up to the parents to solve the
problem. Thus therapy in these cases consists mainly of a
change in point of view, a change on the part of the parents
often, and secondarily on the part of the child.

There are a few cases in which a parent comes in with a
child—we ask the parent to come with the child in most cases
at least for the first visit, although we listen when they want
to discuss this plan or to suggest alternatives—and says, "My
child is asking for therapy." Sometimes the child actually
confirms this assessment of the situation, and in these cases,
we may meet individually with the child much as we would
with an individual adult who came in with the same statement
about himself. But these are not common cases. And even in
these cases, it is very rare in my experience that the problem,
whatever it might be, is truly only the child's problem. There
is nearly always a reactive portion of the child's predicament;
that is, the child is nearly always reacting to something in his
larger environment, and this usually means his family, and
this usually is most effectively addressed by working with the
family in one way or another (if not through explicit family
therapy sessions, then perhaps through contact with the parents and suggestions made to them about how to improve the
situation).

But much more common are the situations where the parent
accompanies the child and says: "We have a problem; Sam
is too difficult, at home and at school." The parent continues
by saying, not overtly but in words to this effect, that he wants
the child to change, and expects that we can be of help. My

child smokes pot and I don't like it; this is a problem; he would not be smoking pot if he did not have psychological problems, so fix them. Or: if he did not smoke, we would not have conflict; the conflict is a problem, so get him to stop smoking and then we will have peace in the family. Or: he smokes because he hangs around with the wrong people; find out why he insists on these inappropriate friends, persuade him to drop them, and then he will stop smoking. Or: he smokes because he is depressed, so help him with his depression and then he will naturally stop smoking.

In some of these situations, individual meetings with the child may be helpful. In my own practice, I nearly always meet individually with the child at least once or twice, so as to hear the child's side of the situation and to become familiar with the child. Talking with parents about their child is easiest when one knows the child, and individual meetings with a child are a very direct way to gain important knowledge. But beyond these evaluation sessions, I may find that individual meetings with the child are important even when I think that the main problem is in the way the parents are construing the situation. I may wish that the parents could change the way they view the situation but there are cases where the parents appear rather inaccessible, either literally, because they will not come together because they are separated and at war with each other, or psychologically, because they are rigid or so encased in their own view of things that they are in my judgment unlikely to budge, especially given the time constraints within which I operate.

In these situations, I may conclude that individual meetings with the child will, first of all, help the parents see that someone else is trying to help (I am helping by agreeing to take on their child as a client). Second, I may see that this child is very responsive to the support I can give him. I will be another adult who knows his parents; I may be able to reflect, in my conversations with the child, my knowledge of the parents as difficult and rigid and yet do so in such a way that I make clear that they must be lived with, they cannot be discarded, and in spite of their peculiarities, they are the parents. The child must, in short, come to terms with their presence in his life. Some children are extraordinarily responsive to the power of meeting with another sympathetic human being who sees the reality of their life, who knows that it cannot be easily changed, who does not take sides and condemn his parents as horrible people (as the child's friends may do), and who does not feel constrained (as his adult acquaintances from his own social world may) to offer the parents unqualified support. Some children can find such helpful adults on their own. But the fact that a child cannot find what will help him on his own does not mean that he will not respond to the help if it is offered to him. And this is a central fulcrum of some portion of the work I do as a therapist.

ACCEPTANCE OF DIFFICULT REALITIES

There is a strand of thought about therapy which runs counter to the dominant American ideology of self-determination and control (an ideology which may be masculine in some sense but which is embraced by men and women in this country). I call this the acceptance of difficult realities. I want to discuss this in a variety of different contexts. To start with, we can say that most therapists have addressed this issue—for decades—when discussing the subject of one's parents. Ever since Freud's investigations of the experience of his individual patients led him to see the importance of childhood experiences, most patients in therapy have discussed their parents. However, how we were treated by our parents as a child is out of our control. Whatever they did is done; we can change the way we look at it, we can change the way we make sense of it, but we cannot go back and relive the experience, whatever it may have been. Trying to understand what the experience was is a reasonable goal, though full understanding may forever elude us. But a second chance is impossible. Thus therapists have tried for years to help patients "come to terms with" their parents. This is the therapeutic phrase for admitting that one cannot change the way they treated one. It may even extend to admitting that one cannot change them in the present, if one's parents are still alive and are still not giving us what we want. My father does not respect me, a patient says; the therapist may try to help the patient see that he will not be able directly to alter that fact. It is a brutal fact of life. You had better accept it. What choice is there? ("I accept the universe," Emerson reportedly said; "By God, he'd better," replied Carlyle.)

Thus one arena within which therapists have conventionally tried to help patients accept life has to do with one's parents. Another arena has to do with limitations. Many people have grand aims for themselves. Often these aims turn out to be grandiose, or unrealizable. A child dreams of being a great baseball player; he later discovers he does not have the talent or the drive. That child might become an adult who feels dissatisfied with himself; a therapist then might help the patient see to what degree the sense of dissatisfaction is rooted in childhood (childish) dreams.

In many fields of medicine, doctors try to help patients come to terms with their illnesses. Doctors try to respond to symptoms so that the patient will feel better, but there are many medical situations in which the symptoms cannot be eliminated. They are going to be present, the doctor must say, for as long as the patient lives. Thus the diabetic adolescent must eventually come to terms with his diabetes. He cannot get rid of it. The Parkinsonian patient must accept his condition; medication may alter the symptoms, but it will not eliminate them. Life can be seen as a process of coming to terms with a series of problems. Within this context, the idea of cure begins to seem rather utopian, or better, like a mirage. It sits there on the horizon holding out great promise, but one never really gets close to it.[1] This is a medical fact, which most doctors and nurses have no trouble accepting; however, they encounter resistance in patients to this idea, since for many patients the idea of medicine and symptoms are com-

---

[1] A very interesting discussion of this general issue is contained in Rene Dubos's *The Mirage of Health* (1961).

bined to create the idea of a cure. The patients go to the doctor to be cured and they are often not happy with anything other than that. Perhaps this is the fault of doctors; they have perhaps oversold themselves. I am more inclined to see this as a product of a general ideological situation, which insists that all problems are susceptible to solutions; in this view, doctors are just part of this. But whatever the sources of this belief, it is powerful, as anyone who sees patients can testify.

I work in a medical setting. The medical doctors see many patients with back pain; they have prepared several handouts about back pain, and the gist of most of these is that the patient must learn to live with having a bad back. This means, usually, taking sensible precautions so that the back will not be aggravated, and doing exercises to keep various relevant muscles strong and supple.

I would like to argue that this approach is pertinent to most human predicaments. People sometimes need to become accustomed to thinking about how to live with something, rather than thinking in terms of how to get rid of it. A patient comes in complaining of insomnia. The "let's get rid of it" approach says here, take these pills, then you can sleep, and the assumption is that then the insomnia is gone. A different approach would be to ask the patient what he does with his insomnia, how he endures it, what tactics he has evolved for handling it. This is the approach which I often take with my patients, not that it is pertinent in every case, but just that it is one of the principal directions in which I may move after assessing the situation.

Let me give a simple example. Mr. Green comes in with his 15-year-old son Jamie. It seems the problem is that Jamie never does what he is supposed to do. I ask for examples. Mr. Green says, well, he never cleans his room. Of course, there are other examples, and each example needs to be taken and considered seriously. Most parents who complain about their adolescent children will admit that not everything is bad; this is one topic I try to discuss before addressing the presenting complaint. Usually there is, however, a list of problems as presented from the parents' point of view. I try to find out the boy's point of view. He usually is not entirely opposed to doing what his parents want but—often—feels that some of the demands are unjust. Typically we will end up discussing the parental demands one by one (not all in one session). With regard to the messy room problem, the solution is often some middle ground between insisting that it is clean to the parents' standards, and letting the child do what he wishes. But one important ingredient in the solution (by which I mean a way out of the tangle in which the parent and child find themselves) is the parents' coming to accept the fact that the child has a different way of seeing the world. The parents may need, that is, to accept the fact that the child is messy in ways which distress them, and will perhaps also need to look into the possibility that one reason this is so upsetting is that the parents are worried about the future.

The parents, that is, seem to think that the child will never amount to a hill of beans in life because he does not make his bed. When stated in this form, most parents will admit rather quickly that this is nearly always unrealistic. My point here, though, is not what I would say specifically in this situation, but simply that one thrust of my intervention would be to explore the possibility of the parents accepting the mess to some degree. Acceptance of a child's characteristics nearly always means living with them only for the time being, since, as I have pointed out, children change often, and the fact that a child's room is messy this year does not mean that it was always messy, nor does it mean that it will always be messy. Even if it is always going to be messy by parental standards, the parents need to explore the possibility that the mess is in the service of some important aspect of the child's growth toward autonomy (which means, inevitably, some degree of pushing away from parental standards).

Nearly always there are forces, accompanied by varying degrees of emotion, which impede the easy acceptance of the child; otherwise the parents would not be coming in with the child, since most families survive these kinds of parent-child struggles without consulting a professional. However, as I have said already, the fact that a parent comes in with a child in our setting does not necessarily mean that the problem is severe, since access is rather easy and uncomplicated. But even so, most parents who need to consult a professional about such a matter—such an ordinary matter, we must make clear, the sort of issue that arises in every family between parents and adolescents—probably have "more going on," as we say. Exploring what this might be is important. In fact, in some situations, the issues that the parents bring to the conflict may impede any resolution of the conflict.

There are life predicaments in which learning to live with the problem makes no sense whatsoever; for example, a woman who is being beaten by her husband should not improve her coping skills with regard to beating, but with regard to independent living if her husband will not stop. Part of being a therapist means learning to recognize when the problem situation is one crying out for remedial action and when it is one that must be survived, and to some degree this discrimination hinges on judgments that are not simply a matter of clinical wisdom but, rather, have to do with choices about life, with fundamental values. Therapists are guided by their own values, and these will sometimes not benefit particular patients.

OUR IDENTITY AS THERAPISTS

In returning to the question of how often we meet with our patients, I would like to discuss our identity as therapists, since that is one important component of our way of doing business. Our own need to be helpful and to believe that what we do matters leads us to feel as though it is a significant fact in a child or family's life if we can offer to see him or them one hour a week regularly, or two hours weekly. This ignores the other 167 hours of the week, and grossly exaggerates the helpfulness of such brief meetings. There are certainly forms of therapy, in the field of medicine and elsewhere perhaps, which have very obvious effects closely correlated with the dose of the treatment—pharmacologists are very interested in the dose/effect relationship and study it closely—but in the field of psychotherapy, we are deluding ourselves if we look for large effects solely as a result of the frequency or quantity of the interventions we make. In therapy, this relationship is of marginal importance, according to present evidence. More hours of therapy are not more effective, and even the psychoanalysts who believe change is slow and arduous will acknowledge this. But there is still substantial disagreement about what the minimum dose of therapy is which will have an effect, and using the word *dose* implies more precision about what is being given to the patient than is realistic. For therapy is not like a pill whose potency can be calculated independently of who is giving it and to whom. Furthermore, there is substantial disagreement about how to treat different people, how much and what kind of treatment is desirable for this particular patient.

But our aim is interventions that make a difference in the child's life, such as those which in addition to engaging the child directly are able to recruit the other resources of a child's environment (not excluding those the child possesses). Thus in work with a child, care must be taken to ensure that these other forces are working with one, not against one. And this becomes one of the principal goals of the therapy or the intervention: to marshall the available forces so that they are all dynamically tending toward the state which is assumed to represent greater health or adaptation or happiness.

In practice, this means that a substantial proportion of what one does in treating a child involves talking with the others who are important in the child's life: the parents, whether together or separated; the teacher; and other professionals who may be involved. This in turn raises many problems of professional identity, and of the arrangement of our work situations.

Our identity as therapists is predicated on our doing therapy, and we all learn that therapy means sitting with a patient or client in a room during a scheduled time. This is the psychotherapy we all learn in our training programs. But if therapy with children means talking with parents and teachers, then it is possible that there is a set of skills that need to be learned that are not exactly the same as those we learn when we learn individual psychotherapy. To take only the most obvious example, family therapy may need to be learned as an adjunct to any child work, not that one will always do family therapy, but because the family needs to be considered in all work with children.

So far as work schedules go, many work environments in which psychotherapists are employed assume, for convenience, that a therapist's day is divided into discrete components, each of which can be accounted for, preferably in advance by scheduling. The most conventional way of doing this is to divide the working day into hours or half hours and to label each segment with either a client's name or the name of whatever administrative meeting is occurring during that time. This makes it possible to assess what is often called productivity: how many patients a therapist sees in a day or a week. But what if there are crucial components of the therapist's work which cannot be so labeled? What if doing work with a family means being available to talk by phone? A rigid schedule in which each slot is filled with a patient leaves little room for phone conversations. Phone time is almost never regarded as "billable," although lawyers and other professionals have discovered that phone time is important and therefore have figured out ways to make this time count; one way to make clear that it counts is to evolve an algorithm for translating phone time into money. But even when it is not billable, it may still be important. One difficulty here is persuading the administrators who run the clinics or settings within which we therapists work that the phone time is crucial. There are other, related difficulties.

For example, another aspect of work with children can involve visits to the school. The same sort of difficulties arise here: time is needed for such visits, the time usually is not available in the conventionally structured schedule, and the time required is usually substantial, involving travel time as well as the actual meeting. The solution is probably not billing for this time (in our setting, of course, we therapists rarely bill for time as such) but, rather, seeing this time as a necessary part of the treatment and assuming that each clinician will need some time for such trips. There are many administrative ways to handle this once the chief administrator is convinced that it is necessary.

Thus there are several issues that arise when one considers the therapy we do as involving more than individual meetings face to face with a client in our office. One set of issues involves our own identity as professionals: we need to escape that view which sees the individual therapy session face to face with a client as central, the view which regards issues of transference and resistance and insight and working through as the crucial aspects of therapy and sees all those as occurring in the context of an individual session (or series of sessions with an individual client). The other issues are more administrative and require the support of the chief administrator to make room for phone and travel time in each child clinician's schedule.

Earlier I referred to issues of professional identity as intertwined with the primacy of individual face-to-face psychotherapy. There is a sense in which doing therapy is regarded by each of us as legitimate; we have learned how to do therapy; we think we know what therapy is; and we are comfortable saying, when asked, that we are therapists. People ask me what I do; I say I work with children. They ask if I do play therapy, since that is one label people are familiar with, and the easiest recourse is to say yes, that is what I do. Another answer I often give is that I talk with parents about children (in fact, I do that much more than I do play therapy). Knowing what to answer when asked what you do is in some ways a small matter, but the issues that arise in such ordinary situations point to larger, more significant questions of professional identity. The question of what counts as therapy is wide open; certain acts are clearly unethical or immoral, but with those few exceptions, almost anything can happen. However, therapists as much as others need some confidence that what they are doing is legitimate, and so they tend to do the kinds of things they were taught to do, chief among which is staying put in an office and working with an individual or a couple or sometimes a family. Different settings usually have to retrain clinicians to broaden their horizons; in our setting clinicians quickly learn that phoning is very important, and the child therapists learn as well that visits to the school are often crucial.

Another force militating toward doing the familiar emanates from the fact that the situation of the people we see is distressing, not just to them but to us as well. One way for us as therapists to cope with the anxiety that such distress generates is to retreat to doing something comfortable. A phrase which is often used in this regard is *providing services*. Are you willing to provide services? I am asked, and the answer is most easily understood if it is couched in terms of frequency of individual (or family) meetings. So there is an external press to provide the conventional service (i.e., therapy). But there is an internal press as well: for us to feel competent we need to do something familiar, and therapy qualifies. We cope with our own anxiety by doing something—offering services—and we become rather proficient at ignoring the degree to which the services we offer are paltry compared with the problem. We cannot rescue the child: often that is the bottom line. We need to help the child and the family cope, or to admit that they cannot cope (in which case they may need outside help). In the latter case, we may help the family obtain outside help: a short-term crisis placement for an adolescent child, a foster family, a residential school, or, in extreme emergencies, a hospital.

This is all done in the name of doing therapy, but a better way to describe what we are doing might be that we are working with the family to help them regain a measure of control, of power over a situation which has gotten out of hand. And usually it does not make sense to go along with a view of the sick child as the one who needs help. Rather, it makes sense to inquire how this situation, of parents who cannot cope with a child, came to exist; and how can we help the family either reconstitute their ordinary ways of coping, or help them recognize that they cannot (because the mother is dying of cancer, or for whatever reason).

PARENTAL POWER

Alice Miller's books on children offer a perspective that is perhaps extreme but nonetheless must be taken into account. In essence, she argues that parents use their superior power to force their child into modes of being which are distorted and warped, which lead the child away from her true essence. Parents do this not because they are evil, but because they have children partly for their own self-interested reasons, and the way parents raise children reflects their own preoccupations and desires more than it reflects their desire to do what would be best for the child.

Assessing Miller's argument judiciously is not easy. When she points out that parents have more power, there is little reason to dispute her. But it does not follow that this situation is bad; in fact, in America (Miller lives in Germany, and her experience perhaps reflects a problem which, however universal, is more common in Europe) there are as many problems arising out of parental discomfort with superior power as there are the opposite problem: I see many families in which the children would benefit from their parents exercising more power. Often as a therapist I ally with the parents and say: You people should be in control here, but you are not, so what are you going to do about it? I try to help them reassert their legitimate power. Miller does not ordinarily address this side of the problem (although she is an experienced clinician and I am sure she recognizes it; she is simply talking about the other side of the coin almost exclusively).

When Miller argues that parents misuse their power, it is hard to disagree; that is, most parents do sometimes, and some parents do frequently. But it is hard to see what the alternative is, short of abolishing power differentials, and I do not think that is possible when children are involved. Certainly in the United States the idea of equality is a powerful one, but it is far from being perfectly realized, and I do not think that children would benefit from increased equality with parents.

So for me the question is whether there is a way for parents to exercise responsible power without abusing it and without using it to force the child into an alienated existence (or whatever phrase should be used for the situation that obtains when a child is forced to abandon her true wants in favor of parental wants without realizing what is happening). I myself encourage parents to exercise their power, but I try to discourage them from mystifying the process. My approach encourages parents to feel that the exercise of power is legitimate in certain situations but to recognize that their responsibility is to make perfectly clear to the child that that is what is happening. When my child is ill I tell him he must go to the doctor and I use my power (arbitrarily, in the child's view) to force him to go, but I do not try to persuade him that this is good for him, or that it is for his own good, or that he should want for himself what I want for him. Rather, I try to assert responsibility (my own, as parent, to make certain the child is well cared for) and assume that eventually the child will come to agree with me. But I must be willing, as parent, to run the risk that he will not agree with me and when he is old enough to make his own decisions he may choose a different path. Thus I think the warping which Miller is concerned about occurs when parents try to cloak their superior power in the mantle of love or concern for the child's own welfare. I think the whole process works better (for the child's welfare) if the parents simply admit that power is being asserted and do this after having persuaded themselves that this is a reasonable course of action.

Let us take another example: I think my child should go to bed, because I have noticed that if he is allowed to stay up as late as he wants, he is hard to rout from bed the next morning for school, whereas if I force him into bed earlier than his own inclinations dictate, he finds getting up in the morning easier. I am convinced of this, after talking with my wife or other adults who have had the opportunity of observing the whole process. I then force my child into bed at some outrageously early hour, let us say 8:30 for a nine-year-old. I am convinced that this is for the child's own benefit, but I do not try to persuade him of that. I just say, You're going to bed, period. Much later I may notice that my boy, who is now 18 and old enough to decide for himself when he will go to bed, stays up very late and sleeps very late and has trouble getting up for school. But by that time, I am finished; by that time, I must hope that my son has figured out that there is some connection (real but not invariant, different at different times for various people) between sleeping and having energy in the morning.

I think that there is a way for a therapist to use Miller's ideas in working with children and families. The gist of this approach would be to say that parents and children are not equal (in terms of knowledge or experience), that parents must be responsible when the child is very young, and that responsibility means deciding what must occur with regard to certain critical issues of food, sleep, cleanliness, health, and the like. Further, I try to persuade parents that they have rights that they can justifiably assert against their children's opposing assertions. The 12-year-old child wants to play the radio very loudly so that no one else in the house can read; the parent can say, Turn it off or Turn it down or Don't play it when I'm trying to read, and this is not necessarily an evil imposition of arbitrary parental power. The "evil" enters in when the parent tries to sugarcoat this assertion by pretending that it is not an assertion of power, by trying to get the child spontaneously to turn the radio down out of love and consideration for the parent. When that occurs, the child can become entangled in a fog of conflicting impulses and loyalties. The child can lose track of what he really wants, and become confused about where self regard ends and love for parents begins. Internal conflicts may be inevitable (this is another topic), but they do not need to be inextricably rooted in these situations. If parents were willing simply to assert their power more nakedly, children would be less likely to be mystified and confused about what they really want in life. The child would know that he wants the radio loud but that he can't have it. Later he may turn it up loud, when he is alone in the house, or much later when he has his own place. But he is unlikely to be confused about what he wants.

Another part of the lesson I derive from Miller's writings is that parents need to come to terms with their own imperfections. To start with, they can never be completely correct about everything. In addition, they have children for some selfish reasons as well as unselfish ones. Admitting that there are selfish (self-interested) strands to one's attachments to children is helpful, since it makes it easier to perceive situations when what the parent wants is for his own benefit. Then there is less likelihood of the parent pretending that this is what the child wants. The parent is going to the grandparents for a special occasion and wants the child to dress up; the child resists. The parent can insist that the child dress up, not for the child's benefit, but because the parent wants the child to reflect favorably on the parents.

Finally, parents need to recognize that their children are never going to give them everything they want. The children are—in short—defective when weighed against the grandiose desires for perfection which most parents have. Recognizing that the child is not going to be perfect in action, in love, in thought, word, and deed, makes acceptance of the child easier, and in turn this recognition undercuts much of most parents' relentless push for perfection. And this in turn might take a lot of the heat out of many child–parent conflicts.

6

Containing Feelings

Earlier I referred to the possibility that some patients are more in need of help containing feelings than help experiencing them or expressing them. This is an especially important point in working with children and families, since many very caring parents err in the direction of respecting their child's feelings far more than they ought to, though their motives for doing so are nearly always good ones. When a small child gets angry with his mother, he does not ordinarily need help expressing his anger; he can do that without any particular difficulty. So the parent's role is not to draw the child out, to hear more about the anger, but rather to place a boundary around its expression, to make clear where the expression of anger is hurting the mother, or damaging something or someone. The parent needs to say, in essence, It's OK to feel angry, but not to hit me, or not to kick the dog. Similarly, although this is harder for many parents, a child who expresses sadness about something does not ordinarily need to be drawn out on the topic; rather, he may need to be heard briefly and then diverted. The message would be that it is all right to feel sad and to show that you are sad, but not if you are doing this to get me to hold you or pay attention to you or feel sorry for you; instead let's do something else. This situation arises most frequently when a parent feels that a child has had a rough time in life. For example, because the parents were divorced when he was five, the parents may feel that he has suffered from the lack of an intact loving family. Or a parent may feel the child has suffered from lack of sufficient parental attention, since the parents both work full time and the child therefore has gone to a combination of school and after-school program for a full day for several years. So some degree of parental guilt may lay the foundation for a form of parental overresponsiveness to a child's expression of feelings.

In this situation, a parent may overreact to a child's expression of feeling, and may even serve in effect as an amplification device, making more vivid and substantial what would otherwise have been rather muted and transitory. This in turn may lead the child to express this feeling more frequently than he might otherwise have, and an interaction is established wherein the child and parent together work on the development and articulation of what was originally perhaps a vague wisp of a feeling, but which over time becomes an important component of the relationship between the child and the parent. For feelings serve this function: they connect people together, and arise in part out of the interconnections between them.

Saying that parents may need, at times, to help children contain feelings is the opposite of the usual psychological advice to encourage the expression of affect, advice which has an important place in relations with people. The latter is usually less important in raising children than the opposing emphasis on putting a boundary around the expression of feelings, of making the child feel safe in spite of an unpleasant feeling. Most parents do this containment instinctively at certain times, for example, when a toddler falls and scrapes her knee; the parent picks up the child, hugs her, perhaps inspects the injury, or perhaps just kisses the child. Usually the child is ready to continue playing in a moment, and the parent typically can return to whatever was going on previously. Here all that is needed is transitory attention. If the attention paid is less than adequate, the child may continue crying until he gets his parent's full attention, and most parents learn with toddlers that it is most effective to pay attention immediately. Then the injury seems to heal most quickly—that is, the injury to the child's sense of himself.

FLEXIBLE ATTENTION

This is one of the complicated arts of parenting: learning to pay full attention on immediate demand when the child needs this. But once this skill is developed, there may be problems consequent to demonstrating it too often and beyond the point where the child will benefit from it. Some parents have trouble turning this sort of attention on and off; they have trouble shifting gears from whatever they were doing already, to the child, and then back to whatever they were doing. But with toddlers who are becoming mobile, this is important, and most parents seem to manage it most of the time. Certainly this necessity is part of what parents are talking about when they say that they never have time which is truly their own. A parent is in a sense constantly on call, and escaping this necessity is difficult unless one has the cooperation of other adults who will fill in so that the primary caretaker can have some time away.

Some parents seem to feel that this need for attention is inappropriate, and that children should learn to wait until the parent is free and ready for them. Even very young children can be taught this, and with older children, parents should insist on having their own time, and should feel free to try to teach the child to wait until the parent is ready. This is the point at which the earlier skill of providing full attention needs to be put aside, and once it is developed, putting it aside is hard. But with young children, I think there is a different situation, and one of my approaches with parents is to point out how children of different ages make varying demands. The developmental age of the child, then, is always an important consideration in deciding how to handle any particular problem. So with young children, parents need to be able to devote full attention to a child on short notice. Even though young children can be taught that sometimes they must wait for the attention they crave, their ability to wait is never substantial, and a parent who relies on it too much will discover that the child is not thriving emotionally. Knowing when to insist that the child wait and when to give in to the child's pleas for immediate attention is a delicate art, and some mistakes are inevitable. And the chief necessity for the parent of the very young child is this flexibility to put aside other tasks for the most important one of attending to the child.

But this skill needs to be tempered later by an ability to stop paying such concentrated attention when it no longer seems calming, and this is another part of what I mean by containment. When a child is young, simple attention and affectionate warmth—the parent hugging the child with the scraped knee—is very effective. The child pulls himself together and returns to active play. When a child is older and more verbal, the parent will do more to help the child by realizing that there are times when more attention is not going to be an effective calming device. So the parent needs to be very flexible, able to pay attention when the child seems to demand it, and then able to realize that sometimes even though the child is saying, in effect, pay attention to me, more attention will not help. For some parents, this is very difficult.

Actually, all parents find this sometimes difficult. But some parents become more stuck here than others. They function like a device which seeks a signal *I need you* and then locks onto this signal, unable to let go. But this metaphor is not very accurate, for although people are somewhat like machines they are infinitely more malleable. So the child gives a signal, the parent responds, and the child may then give the signal again, even more strongly; the parent responds more strongly, and soon the two of them are locked together with only one main mode of connection, that constituted by the particular signal, whatever it may be, and its response.

In the example we were using, the signal is "help me" and the response is "I am here to help you, for I love you infinitely, you are so precious to me that I cannot bear to see you suffer." This process occurs frequently, although there are always elaborations and complications, since no parent–child relationship is monotonal.

For many parents the early stage of a child's life, when the child seems so infinitely needy and helpless, is very appealing, so the process of the child's growing out of that stage is painful for the parent to watch. Most parents feel the sadness of watching the small helpless infant become a larger active being, but the sadness is not so much that the child is growing but rather that the parent is becoming dispensable. An infant needs a parent more of the time and in more ways than a toddler, and vastly more than an adolescent, although children always need their parents in some sense (eventually, perhaps, just on stand-by, as it were). So insofar as the joy of parenthood inheres in being needed, there is pain in being needed less, and part of parenting is living through these stages and adapting to them. And it is probable that for each stage of childhood development, there is a stage of parent development; and just as child development can, as it were, derail at any stage, so can parent development. But neither occurs in isolation; the child and the parent are developing additionally in relation to one another, and that relationship has its stages as well. All of this becomes very complicated very quickly.

Another kind of emotional message is constituted by a child's becoming angry with the parent, and this likewise can be either soothed or amplified by the parental response (and a host of other factors, since a child's anger is rarely simply at a parent, but more often at a life circumstance for which the parent is perhaps blamed). So this is another affect which needs containment, and perhaps these are the two main affects which parents need to contain: sadness and hurt on the one hand, and anger and frustration on the other. And just as couples can become locked in marital combat and appear to find something about the combat sustaining, a parent and child can become locked in combat, for at the start, a child surely possesses no skills of diversion, has no power to calm the troubled waters. So at first it all rests on the parent's shoulders; if the anger is to be absorbed into some larger structure, the parent has all the responsibility for doing that. Later the child can acquire techniques and capacities to re-direct anger, or integrate it into some larger structure where it serves a more useful purpose.

CONTAINMENT THROUGH A RELATIONSHIP

The larger structure in which anger inevitably becomes integrated is that created by the relationship between two people. Affects help pull people together; they help connect one person not just with other people, but with projects in the world around them. When affects wither, the person with-ers to some degree, so the parent has a very delicate task: aiding and abetting the emotional experience of the child, without prolonging or intensifying the emotion beyond what the child can tolerate at his particular stage.

A good example of how this works is provided by the child who is fatigued. Most parents gradually develop a sense of their child's rhythms. So a parent may be able to say with some conviction that the child is tired and needs to sleep, even when the child is claiming that he does not need to sleep. Most children go through stages when they resist bed mightily; some children, if allowed to stay up as long as they want, will fall asleep when their bodies need the sleep, but most children's bodies are not so imperious and other factors become increasingly more important, psychological factors. Although a two-week-old infant will almost surely fall asleep when it needs to, a two-year-old's bodily need for sleep is not so dominant over other motives that have by that time been established—motives, for example, to maintain contact with the parent. So the two- or three-year-old will often want to stay up later, to be with the parents, or to avoid the separation from the parents which comes with bedtime.

So we have, let us say, a three-year-old and it is early evening, after the child has eaten. The parents think it is the child's bedtime; the child resists and wants to play some more. The parents may think, he is getting older, perhaps he does not need to get quite so much sleep, and besides we just got home from work and it is fun to play with him, or Aunt Molly is coming over in half an hour so it would nice if she could see her nephew. So the child stays up an extra hour or perhaps two hours. Some children bounce out of bed the next morning none the worse for wear, and then perhaps take a longer nap that afternoon, or collapse in fatigue somewhat earlier the following evening. But other children have trouble getting up the next morning, or will not take a longer nap and just become more whiny and cranky. With such children, the parents will eventually conclude that the child needs more sleep than he is getting, and they force the child to go to bed earlier the next night.

But what if the parents have difficulty forcing their child to go to bed, or what if they find it hard to resist his pleadings to stay up later another night? Nothing terrible happens in one or two nights. But eventually the child may be in a cycle where it is hard to get up in the morning, where he is cranky much of the late afternoon and early evening, when he catches up on sleep while riding in the car or at odd moments through the day. In this situation, the parents can be most helpful by ignoring the child's pleadings to stay up later. They should force the child into his bed at an earlier hour than the child would choose, and they will do this if they are secure in their knowledge that they have interpreted the situation correctly (the child is indeed tired), but, more important, they will do it if they are united (if the caretakers, whoever they are, agree) and if they can tolerate the child's anger over this treatment. So they need to be able to acknowledge that the child has a right to be angry (he does wish he could stay up; he is being pushed around by his know-it-all parents!), but they are in charge and he will do as they say. This means both that they must be comfortable in the role of ultimate authority (a problem for some parents, especially those who had problematic relations with their own parental authority figures), and that they must be able to absorb the child's anger without being dissuaded by it. So *absorbing* an affect is one way of containing it. The parent essentially says: Go ahead, be angry at me, I can take it, and calmly picks up the screaming child and marches him up to his bed.

This sounds simpler than it is; what complicates it is the very intense emotional connection between parent and child, a connection with an intricate social and historical context. This child is not just any child, being picked up. This is the child as embodiment of hopes and fears which have a long history, some of whose roots are in the parents' own childhoods, some in the conversations the parents had when they were talking about eventually getting married and then about having children, some in the thoughts they each have about this child's future.

Thus is happens that some people can be very good at putting someone else's child to bed because the action has a rather meager context: a crying child is just a crying child who needs to be put in bed. But when they turn to their own child, they hear not just the noise of the crying but something with resonance which extends in many directions simultaneously. So parents can lose touch with their own common sense and can often, very readily, benefit from someone else articulating what their own common sense is telling them.

The therapist, then, can ally with the common sense side of the parents when discussing many problems. The child will not go to bed; well, why don't you just put him in bed? A revolutionary and completely ordinary idea. Often I find when I describe to friends some of the situations I encounter in my office, they will say something perfectly sensible. I am fairly certain that most of the parents I see in my office have the same reservoir of common sense, and that if I met them somewhere else and told them about some of my cases, they would be very capable of thinking of good ways to handle the problem. But with their own child, no. There is a often a short-circuiting of common sense, and this is why a brief series of meetings with a therapist may be helpful, or why participation in a parent group is often helpful; the process is one of a parent being called back to her own common sense parenting abilities.

Notice that this rationale for brief therapy says little about insight or understanding. The parents do not really need to understand why they are having trouble handling the problem of their child's messy room or the homework tangles. They may become curious and want to explore that in depth, in which case they may elect a longer-term investigation. But for the moment, their need is focused: they need—in their original view when they walk into the office—to get their child to clean up his room or to do his homework, or they need to get their child in bed. This may sound prosaic, and in a sense it is.

But the other side is that this approach is immensely helpful, and parents feel grateful when it works. And with it, one can help more people more quickly. Through the brief therapy the parents shift from saying, for example, that their child must clean his room, to seeing that the problem has two sides. The other side is that the parents are upset by the child not cleaning his room, and further that they have no techniques for persuading him to do so. So first their understanding of the problem is broadened; then they learn various ways to ameliorate the problem.

I have been discussing the role of feelings, the ways in which a child's feelings can be responded to by the parent, and how the parental response can help the child contain the feelings. What happens when feelings are not contained? At the extreme, they take over and dominate a person's experience and behavior. A person who is immensely fearful may not move; a person who is immensely angry may rage so much that almost any constructive action or relationship with another person is impossible; a person who is immensely sad may cry so much that any positive steps requiring initiative simply do not occur. Infants who are in these states can be helped rather easily; adolescents who are still this way, or adults who are this way, are much harder to help. Such people often are treated on an inpatient basis; in this book I am mainly discussing outpatient treatment. But it is important to point out that often what is being done for such people in an inpatient setting—the main treatment—is a containing of the impulses. Someone who is out of control will benefit from being controlled, since it is scary to be out of control, and hospitals and other restrictive settings (such as residential schools for some adolescents and children) have this capacity to provide control. The title of a well-known book about children is *Controls from Within* (Redl & Wineman, 1952); the implication is that treatment is aimed at helping the child gain control of himself, so he does not need the restrictive setting. This is what most hospitals and residential schools promote quite actively. So the idea of containment is not just pertinent to outpatient therapy, although the tasks involved become immeasurably more complicated when the child is older, and when there is a longer previous history of failure in this regard.

AFFECTS AS CONNECTIONS

Affects play a crucial role in connecting a person with other people and projects, and the parent plays an important role in nourishing the experience and expression of affect. All the books that give advice to parents stress this topic, so I am not going to devote much time to it, but it is an important one. The books—for example, those by Haim Ginott—tell parents to avoid phrases like "Don't say you hate me" or "Oh, you don't really hate me, you love me." The simple message is that the parent should not contradict a child's statement of feeling. If the child feels something and says so, then the parent must accept that that is the child's sense at the moment. Feelings are almost never permanent, so that fact that the child is raging now does not mean he will be raging this afternoon; and if he wishes me dead right now, that does not mean he will forever wish me dead. But the parent accepts the child's statement of the feeling not just because he knows it's not permanent, but because he has some sense that the child needs to have feelings authenticated in order to feel whole.

This is a complicated issue, and in discussing it, we inevitably use complicated language. First of all, there is authenticity: feeling like a real person. People have feelings; if parents support a child's right to have feelings, they are helping foster authenticity. Parents also foster authenticity by making clear that they are listening to the child: simple statements (I can tell you are angry; you seem very upset; I guess this is really bothering you) will go a long way toward letting the child know that the parent hears him. Certainly the parent does not intend to succumb to the feeling, whatever it is, but recognizing it and succumbing to it are two different things. This is a very powerful idea, and one which many parents have particular difficulties in using with their own children (although they may be able to use it with other people who are less important to them).

Arguing with the child about his feeling is a response at the opposite end of the spectrum. The child says, I'm scared, and the parent says, Don't be, there is no reason to be scared, or even, Oh, don't be silly, big girls don't get scared of the dark" (or whatever). These statements do not authenticate the feeling. They are directed at getting rid of the feeling, and this is unfortunate because they never really work, and because they imply to the child that the feeling is dangerous or bad or harmful, which is not true. Feelings can be uncomfortable, but not bad.

Furthermore, the child needs feelings. Why? To feel alive in some fundamental sense; to feel like a person, or, as we said earlier, to feel whole. There is no way to prove this; the relevant evidence consists of our accumulated psychiatric knowledge of people who have found having feelings too dangerous to tolerate and who have gotten into various forms of psychological trouble as a result. But even if this idea is not provable, there is another fact which is easier to demonstrate: feelings do not go away just because they are inconvenient. So parents never succeed in talking a child out of all feelings, though the parent may succeed in driving the feelings underground far enough so the parent cannot see them (and in truly unfortunate cases, so the child himself loses track of them). Since the feelings cannot be gotten rid of, perhaps accepting them makes more sense. The psychological point of view, further, is that a parent needs to help a child learn to tolerate the feelings when they come, and learn to work out a very intricate combination of internal adaptations and external expression to make living with the feelings tolerable.

So when a child of four picks up a toy gun or a stick and points it at someone and says, Bang bang, you're dead, the psychological assumption—which accepts such fantasy play as healthy and which regards such hostile impulses as are being expressed here as inevitable parts of being human—is that this is a contained expression of a feeling. The child is not out of control, no one is being hurt, so nothing need be done by the parent. However, if the child picks up a stick and looks as though he is going to bang his baby brother on the head, the parent needs to intervene, because someone is going to get hurt. Or if the child points the stick and says, Bang bang, and then collapses in tears, the parent may need first to comfort the child and then try to see what happened. Was the child scared by his own hostility?

This is a rather peculiar example, since a young child is very unlikely to be so uncomfortable with his own aggressive impulses that he collapses in tears after pretending to shoot someone, but comparable things do in fact occur, especially as children grow older. And it is quite common for children of four to awaken at night with a very scary nightmare. What is the nightmare about? Monsters, often, which in the psychological view spring from the child's mind, or which have been read about in a fairy tale or seen in a movie and which become very real for some part of the child's mind. So the monster springs to apparent life in the dream and scares the child. Here exorcism may be called for: Go away, Monster, says the parent, you leave my child alone, you are going to be locked up in the basement if you can't behave better.

A parent might object that this behavior is treating the monster as real and that this might scare the child even more. This is a plausible theory but one which underestimates the power of the mind. Bettelheim's book *The Uses of Enchantment* (1976) presents a very useful discussion of this topic; he makes the sort of psychological argument I am presenting very compelling, and I will often recommend this book to parents if they are inclined toward reading, and if their discomfort with angry feelings in themselves and others is not too extreme.

So the parent's goal is to help the child contain the feelings, whatever they may be, and there are numerous pathways to this goal. Crucial ingredients of all the approaches include being comfortable with the feelings the child is displaying, and parents need to have at their disposal at least two different tactics, one designed to draw out the feeling (in talk or play or appropriate action), the other designed to calm the feeling, through affectionate holding, through talk, through sharing presence (e.g., sitting with the frightened child in the middle of the night for a while, until the child is less scared or falls asleep again).

There is a parallel way in which the therapist's job is to help the family contain its feelings, and similarly there are these two different tactics needed in the therapist's repertoire. One set involves skill in drawing out feelings, helping patients talk about them, helping them find appropriate expressions. The other set involves skill in dampening the expression of feeling, or being careful not to amplify distressing feelings. Oddly, it often happens that a therapist's calm comfort with a display of feeling has the effect of helping the display diminish; a parent's calm acceptance of a child's upset feeling has a similar effect. In both cases, there is a violent feeling, a display of this feeling, and then observation that the violence does not scare the other person, and this in turn helps the person having the feeling be less scared by the intensity of whatever is occurring.

THE COMPLEXITY OF FEELINGS

Let me turn to the orthodox therapeutic tactic of urging a person to search for and express her true feelings. I have a variety of reservations about this tactic, one of which I have already made explicit—namely, that a therapist needs to have an opposing skill as well (that is, drawing out feelings is never all of what needs to occur in therapy). My other reservations are rooted in what may appear a slightly unusual view of the phenomenology of feelings.

This unusual view centers on the possibility that feelings are not just lying there waiting to be observed. If you walk into my kitchen, I can say that I just bought a new stove, and you and I can look at it together. But feelings cannot be observed in the same fashion. Even worse, it may be that the feelings are not only hard to see because they not accessible to direct consensual perception, but also that they are not there in any concrete, simple sense the way, for example, a bone buried in the back yard is there. They may be, first of all, more of a flowing process than a discrete thing. Second, they may be an active creation which owes much of its energy to what goes on between people, or between a person and a project in the world (by project I mean an activity which we have undertaken, a goal). So when I ask someone how he feels about me, the reply I get may be in part an attempt on the part of the person to search within himself for the hidden strand of feeling I am asking for, but in part it is going to arise out of internal events and out of what has happened between us.

I am not referring to the ways in which people choose their words carefully, keeping in mind not just what they want to say (assuming they know) but who their audience is, the listener's feelings, and the like. Instead I mean something more complex. What we call feelings are more transitory, less concrete and specific, more vague and less certain than we often suspect or hope. We would like to think that the realm of feelings is not entirely murky and formless, and of course it is not. But it is possibly much more vague than we often suspect. Our access to our own feelings (those we call our own, although as I have made clear I think feelings arise out of and contribute to an interpersonal nexus) is not ever perfect. We never know the whole story, even about those events we like to refer to as our own experiences. The conventional psychiatric way of formulating this idea is in terms of what Freud called the unconscious. But there are other ways to think about this.

Let me draw on the work of two writers in explaining this further. Eugene Gendlin (1981) has written a book *(Focusing)* about the ways in which we pay attention to our feelings and experiences. He argues that it is possible to bring feelings into focus by using a variety of skills which involve relaxation, association, reflection, and self-observation. He shows how awareness of experience emerges gradually, piecemeal, out of a background that includes a vast array of feelings and sensations and memories and thoughts. For our discussion, his most important point is that awareness of experience is not immediate, is not easy, is not automatic. It takes hard work, and there is a way to learn to do it better. I think he is right, because experience is not simply there waiting to be looked at. Whatever its ontological state—whatever form of being it takes—it is not easy to pay attention to or see. Thus we cannot realistically expect people to say in a simple, direct, unequivocal way what they feel, because in most cases people do not know what they feel. To become aware, they need to work at it. Awareness is not inevitable, and not just because of the forces of repression, as Freud would have it. People are too complicated to start with, are constantly changing, and awareness is not nearly so complex as experience. And awareness to be expressed needs words, which have their own limits and grammar and syntactical requirements, which surely are not completely isomorphic with those of experience.

Another relevant strand of thought is contributed by Donald Spence (1982) in his book *Narrative Truth and Historical Truth*, in which he analyzes the process through which therapists, in particular psychoanalysts, arrive at an understanding of a patient's character. The process is usually referred to as interpretation. In essence, Spence uses certain forms of contemporary literary criticism to shed light on the process of interpretation in therapy. There are two important parts to his argument. The first is his insistence that interpretation (of a patient's story, or of a literary work, or of a historical era, for that matter) involves finding a structure, and that this finding is as much a creating as it is a finding. The second point is that the creativity, if you will—the use of active imagination and intelligence—is expressed through selectivity. There is always more going on than one can record or attend to, so one selects. The patient selects certain parts of the story for presentation to the therapist; a novelist selects certain things to include in the novel and the critic selects certain parts of the novel as representative of the whole; the historian has access only to those pieces of the historical process that were recorded, and even then he makes, necessarily, a selection of the ones he conceives of as crucial.

All this selectivity is with a purpose: to tell a coherent story. The big question is whether more than coherence is at issue. We cannot help wondering if truth is also in question. The historian tries to tell the truth, and his aims are clearly higher than just telling a plausible and interesting story. But most fiction writers aim to tell the truth also, although it is perhaps a different form of truth. Or is it? Spence's title divides historical truth from narrative truth, though there may be real questions whether this division makes sense. But in any case, he thinks that therapists and patients are searching for narrative truth, which has more to do with coherence (the story has to make sense, to fit together) than with some other form of truth (validity according to some external criterion).

Admittedly nowhere in life in this distinction a hard and fast one. If you study validity in statistics, you find that there are different forms of validity, or, rather, different ways to assess it. One way has to do with what is called internal validity, another with external validity. According to this distinction, coherence would be a form of internal validity. So it is an open question whether these two forms of truth—the two referred to in Spence's title—are truly separate, or distinct. But there is no question that in looking for narrative truth, as therapists do, there is enormous selectivity, and as professionals, we should always keep this in mind.

So when we ask a patient to tell us what he is feeling or thinking, we should remember that we get a selection of what is occurring in his experience, a selection limited not just by the possibility that he is not fully aware of everything he feels (as the Freudians have made clear, although their explanation of this phenomenon may not be correct), and not just by the limitations of language as an expressive device, and not just by his hesitation at telling us even the part that he is aware of (for fear we will think badly of him), but limited as well by the probability that the process of answering the question in part creates a kind of experiential reality. By selecting one part to talk about, and searching for words with which to describe it, the patient is possibly making something more real than it was before. One way to refer to this process is to call it *discourse:* the therapist and the patient engage in a form of creativity called discourse, and understanding that process is vital if we are to comprehend what occurs in therapy and how we might improve the therapeutic process. So it is not just talking, but something complicated and even creative.[1]

An additional selectivity occurs on the therapist's part; from the vast array of information we accumulate from a patient or a family even in just one session, we in turn select a few key items to focus on, and by focusing on them we make them central. The culmination of this process may be advice; try this, or your problem may be here. But in order to arrive at this conclusion, a gigantic reduction has to have occurred, first of all on the part of the patient—who reduces his experience to that which can be talked about, for which words exist, and who selects even from among that portion the parts that seem more important—and second on the part of the therapist, who takes a few items from that vast array and arranges them, as it were, like beads on a string. Once placed on the string, they and the string seem bound together in what may appear an inevitably sensible and illuminating whole. But we should always remember that we may have picked the wrong beads or strung them in the wrong order on the wrong string.

Is this view too corrosive of the sort of informed initiative that therapists need to exercise in the office? I think not, though it is possible, both in life and in the therapist's office, to feel overwhelmed by the intensity and range of what is occurring, or to feel that it does not fit together, and then taking action is hard. It is also true that if the therapist always takes the stance that piecing things together is too hard and

---

[1] There is a literature on this way of formulating conversation; one useful book (among many) which contains very helpful suggestions for further reading in this field is Elliott Mishler's *Research Interviewing* (1986).

too likely to be mistaken, then the therapist may be paralyzed. But for the most part I think therapists can simultaneously work on making sense of what is happening as a patient or family talks, and on taking initiative in deciding what to try next, all the while keeping in mind that he does not know the whole story. And this is where I started a while ago, by saying that we never know the whole story.

If we never know the whole story, then maybe other things matter more than the story. This is my fundamental point, the one which informs my work in short-term therapy. For the essential struggle is not, in my work, to arrive at the truth, but rather to make a difference, to try something new and see what happens, to persuade the patient that there are other ways to live and other possibilities for him and his family. He need not go on doing the same things over and over again unless that is ultimately what he chooses to do. These are the placcs I placc my principal effort, rather than on the grandiose desire to know the truth, to make the correct interpretation, to hear the whole story. I think that is a doomed enterprise, and I do not see it as essential for the process of change.

THE AMBIGUITY OF EXPERIENCE

There is another important point here: that experience is both ambiguous and continually being reshaped through personal relations. To take an example: a child has certain experiences with his parents as he grows up with them. Later in life, he may try to describe those experiences to someone else (for example, to a therapist). But there is an important sense in which those experiences are never set and finished and stable. Rather, they are a shifting and changing array of complicated events that will appear different in different lights. Furthermore, they are, in some way we do not understand, accessible to change, both through the process of an ongoing relationship with the parents (if they are alive) and through the process of reliving the events in imagination (while the parents are alive, and after they die).

Moreover, the process of talking with the therapist (or with anyone else) about the parents affects the experiences. This may sound mystical, and proving it is hard. But there is some important way in which an experience does not exist, psychologically, in a pure form, hard and forever like a diamond. Rather, experience is somehow constantly occurring and being rewoven through an intricate developmental process which includes what we call real conversation and discourse with real other people, but also includes our imaginative reworkings of those events. Thus we have the commonplace phenomenon in which several people experience the same event in some sense and yet seem to have experienced different events.

A different way of talking about this draws on the literature of what is called *hermeneutics*.[2] All texts require interpretation according to hermeneutics; words are texts, and gestures too perhaps. So the way a person (a patient) uses words requires interpretation (by the therapist), but in a more complicated sense, therapy offers some people the chance to discover which words are going to be most useful, which words make sense for them. In this view, therapy offers a chance to explore the meaning-making power of words, a chance to talk and be taken seriously (in the prosaic, widely acknowledged sense), but out of that a more complicated meaning-making opportunity may emerge.

When we are seeing a family, this situation becomes very complex, since what is at issue is a shared meaning-making enterprise (the creation and sustaining of what are often referred to as family myths). Inevitably each family member has slightly different views of the family, so it is usually impossible to find only one interpretation of a given event. The legal system often tries to get at the truth behind these various and sometimes conflicting versions of what is presumed to be one event. But psychotherapists need not do this. Searching for the truth of who said what to whom is unnecessary, even though we may sometimes feel that some security would be

---

[2] A useful introductory guide to this field is contained in Richard Palmer's book *Hermeneutics* (1969).

gained if we could only grasp firmly some one event, without feeling buffeted by the conflicting versions we may hear from child and parent, or from mother and father. Much more to the point is the fact that different people hear things differently, and the task of helping people take this into account in their conversations with one another. This is a form of psychological sophistication that many people do not possess but can easily acquire, once their attention is drawn to it. When parents tell a child she needs to stay in every evening to study, the child may feel this is a punishment and react accordingly; the parents may mean it as a helpful aid to getting the necessary studying done. Each party—child and parents—will do well to realize that there is another point of view. If the child can see that the parents are trying to be helpful, then she may see and hear what they tell her differently. If the parents can see that the child is feeling punished, then they may be able to design a different approach to the problem. This process, then, would be an end run around the complicated question of what exactly happened when the parents told the child she needed to stay in and the child became angry and they had a fight.

Anyone who works with couples knows that it is often futile to try to get to the bottom of what really happened during a conflict. Much better simply to accept that there was a conflict, and to look for other themes, one of which is almost always that one person will hear something as insulting or demeaning (for example) even when the other person does not intend it to be so. Admittedly, not all fights between couples arise out of miscommunication and misinterpretation—there are, after all, real conflicts in life which lead to fights—but a substantial proportion do.

To review briefly, we have been talking about what may be the essential ambiguity of experience, and about how this phenomenon, taken together with the imprecision of words (which are obligatory to convey the experience to another), the necessary selectivity of all speech, and the changing nature of experience (which is always contingent on relationships with other people and projects), all can lead us as therapists toward a particular stance. We can decide to downplay the search for feelings, for what really happened, for the truth of the experience, in favor of taking action *to change what happens next time*. And since experience is so intimately dependent on relationships and projects, changing relationships through action is one fairly direct way to have an impact on the nature of the experience.

I have already talked about working toward a change in a relationship—between couples, or between parents and child— as one way to have an impact on the nature of a person's experience. But I have not said much about projects, and I would like to do so now. By projects I mean activities—goals, aims, or plans—that are connected with initiative and action in the world. Engagement with reality is perhaps the element that relationships and projects have in common: for a person to be in connection with people, or to have projects, he must be engaged with reality. And this is a powerful meliorative factor; people get better when they engage productively with reality. This is a fundamental belief that underlies my form of short-term therapy. It is especially crucial in working with children and adolescents, but it is important with everyone. Thus with everyone we see we should inquire: which parts of reality is this person engaged with, where does he find meaning, in what are his life projects centered. And we need to keep in mind that even apparently self-destructive forms of behavior may have a basic life-enhancing meaning, insofar as they help keep the person engaged with reality. So to change such patterns of behavior, we need to think about what will take their place. What will you do if you stop smoking, or stop using drugs, or leave the marriage; all these questions make sense when we are talking to someone who is considering a drastic change in a life pattern. For always something else must be substituted for any meaningful activity, at least if we take seriously the importance of all repetitive activities in sustaining a sense of being truly alive.

So we have a vocabulary and set of ideas for considering much of what happens in therapy in a new light, one that is fundamentally different from the traditional explorative psychotherapy, which essentially provided one person with an opportunity to talk freely for a long time to a careful, intelligent, sympathetic listener. The fundamental question changes. The old question was: tell me what you feel, tell me what it is like. The new question is: let's figure out what you are going to do, or sometimes let us figure out why, when you try to do this new project, something gets in the way. Thus action becomes as central as feelings.

7

Family Dynamics

One does not need to subscribe to the view that a child's problems always reflect familial dynamics in order to see that the child may be brought in to the therapist for what may turn out to be mainly a couple's conflict or a marital problem. In my practice, children provide an entry point for health care; many parents seem to talk to their pediatricians more readily than to their own doctors, and even healthy children are brought to a pediatrician for regular checkups at more frequent intervals than adult patients usually consult their own doctors. Thus parents usually have abundant opportunities for talking with the pediatricians, and the pediatricians often serve as a crucial link in the provision of mental health services to our population. So it often happens that a pediatrician may be the referring source for a family, even when the child is not symptomatic. And even in cases where the child is symptomatic, the parents often may need treatment themselves, either individually or as a couple.

There really is no rule of thumb that can be used to identify those cases in which a child's problems mainly reflect a parental predicament. Almost *any* presenting problem may, when seen more fully, reflect parental tensions which ought to be

156

more directly addressed. My experience has been that there are a few cases in which the pediatrician will say, at the very beginning as the referral is being made, that the child appears basically to be all right but the parents need to see someone. But there are many other cases where the pediatrician and the parents see the child as symptomatic but where we later find, on closer examination, that the symptoms—although real and important—are better seen as reactive to stress and more sensibly treated through the parents or family.

The parental stress can be as simple as disagreement between two partners about ordinary household rules (bedtime, chores, diet); or it can be such an ordinary problem complicated by the fact of separation and divorce and possible animosity between the partners following their divorce. Or the stress may inhere in any of a myriad other possible situations. For example, a woman may come in with her children, complaining of various behaviors, and a picture may gradually emerge of a household in which the children can derive support for their behavior from a grandmother who lives with them or in an easily accessible apartment. Usually the mother in such cases knows perfectly well that the grandmother is part of the problem, although this is not usually presented right at the beginning. But once the therapist points out that there seems to be a problem with the relative who lives with them and who influences the children, often the parent will agree and sometimes it seems that simply supporting that perception is enough to help the parent take action which will be effective in reducing the severity of the problem. The possibilities for other permutations of this fundamental situation are considerable.

For example, a 12-year-old girl was brought to me with what was described in the referring note as a sleep problem. The girl arrived with two adults (one of whom was her mother) and it was quickly made clear to me that these two adults, both women, considered themselves the parents of this child. The women were lovers and had been for years; the household was a stable one in which these two women had been living with this girl for over 10 years. They wanted me to know of this situation, although they did not consider that it was pertinent to the presenting problem.

After we talked generally about this girl's life, her situation in school, her interests, her friends, her earlier history, I began to inquire more closely about the nature of the sleep problem. My experience is that the more detail one can gather about such presenting problems, the better. Sleep problems can exist in multiple ways, and the details of how they occur usually matter. In this particular case, the problem was not going to bed, nor was it going to sleep (the girl went to bed before the adults did), but it involved her awaking during the night, usually after the adults had gone to bed. In this case I also inquired about sleeping arrangements and the layout of the bedrooms in the house, since such details sometimes prove important, although often they are not particularly significant. I discovered that although they had been living in the same house for quite a few years, they had recently done some remodeling, improving a space that had been an unused attic. They put a bedroom there which then became the girl's bedroom; the two women now shared a bedroom on the second floor. Further, the women had only recently become very explicit about the intimacy of their relationship. For years they had shared the house but had not shared a bedroom; now they were sharing a bedroom, and this was quite clear to the girl. So although they had been accustomed to using the word *lovers* to refer to their relationship, and the girl had been (for many years, by their account) aware of their relationship, it was only recently that this symbolic change had occurred. There was a sense, then, in which the girl had come to see more vividly that her mother was close to another adult, closer in some ways than she was to her daughter, or perhaps the girl felt that her special relationship with her mother was now in question. Her mother had someone else who was special.

Most children express an interest at some time during their childhood in sleeping in the same bed with their parents. Parents vary, of course, in how they handle this, but it is a rare family where this issue has not arisen in one form or another. This girl was too old to say openly that she wanted to sleep with her mother, and given the situation, expressing such a wish openly may have been too threatening anyway. But her sleep disturbance was probably a function of the recent changes in the house, the changes in sleeping arrangements (her "exile" to the third floor, and her mother having a bed partner in a very explicit and regular nightly way). I think the adults had some awareness of this when they came in to see me, and I think this is why they told me so forthrightly and quickly of their relationship. But their awareness was not explicit, and they had even made clear that they did not consider their intimate relationship related to the girl's sleep disturbance, since as they said they had been lovers for years and the girl had known this all along.

Of course, the fact that they were willing to admit that there might be a connection between the girl's sleep disturbance and their household arrangements did not necessarily mean that they could improve the girl's sleep, because they were not willing to go back to the previous arrangements. In this case, the girl needed to come to terms with what had happened, and I worked with her individually around this issue. In a couple of sessions, she was able to talk with me about all this and she began to sleep better as a result. But there was another concomitant part of the treatment in this case which involved the women.

The mother had a long history of feeling guilty about the unusual way in which she was raising her daughter. She felt guilty, first, that the girl did not have a father in the home and, second, that the girl had to realize that her mother was more interested in intimate relationships with another woman than with a man. This mother was probably intent on being an especially competent, good mother, even more so than is often the case with mothers who are separated from their husbands. She was an intelligent, aware woman who knew that her unusual lifestyle might create problems for her daughter, but she had been trying as hard as she could to reduce those problems to a minimum.

This mother had in common with many devoted parents an unusual sensitivity to her child's needs. She found tolerating her daughter's unhappiness very difficult, and ordinarily when her daughter expressed distress, she would respond, trying ideally to eliminate that distress. When her daughter awoke at night, the mother would hear her daughter; the daughter would seek out the mother and would express unhappiness— anxiety, tension, stress. Mother would try to alleviate that distress but without knowing exactly what to do.

Only part of the presenting problem when I met them was the girl's sleep disturbance; another considerable portion was the way in which the mother reacted to the disturbance. She overreacted, out of a general sense of guilt, and out of a determination to do as well by her child as was humanly possible. And in spite of being intelligent, sensitive, and aware, she had not been able to see how her child's sleep disturbance might be related to Mother's relationship to her lover. So although she was not uncomfortable talking about that rela-tionship, she did not think of talking about it in the context of her daughter's disturbed sleeping pattern. Once this con-nection (or possible connection) had been pointed out to her, she was quite capable of talking with her daughter about the situation. Further, with my support and encouragement, she was able to pull back somewhat from her overreacting mode; she was able to say more firmly that her daughter would have to figure out what to do about her sleep disturbance, and meanwhile I supported the girl in trying to handle it on her own. I put it to her that the whole situation would work better if she could take care of herself at night. If she woke up, she would try to go back to sleep; if she could not, she would turn on the light and read, or she would listen to the radio until she again felt sleepy.

This might be the same advice an adult insomniac would be given. But in this case, the aim was not so much to help the girl cope with her sleep disturbance as to help her be more independent, to work with the girl on the one hand and the mother and her lover on the other to promote more autonomy for both of them. The mother needed her time with her lover at night; the girl needed to see that and to allow that to happen, yet at the same time she probably needed to be able to talk about her jealousy, her wish that she was the only one her mother cared about, and to assert her feelings about the desirability of a more exclusive relationship with her mother.

This was one example of a case where a presenting problem involving a child turned out to involve a family (an unconventional family by ordinary standards, but where the essential dynamics were not very different from those in a more conventionally structured family). There may, in this case, be other issues for this girl as she develops into and through adolescence, issues relating to her sexual identity which might be more complicated for her than for other girls her age because of the special situation in her family. But at the time I met the family, these were not in the forefront. The girl was not precociously developed sexually; her interests and psychological development were more typical of those of a somewhat younger girl. In time, of course, she may return with more developmentally advanced issues, which will be dealt with as they arise. And as I will emphasize again and again, one of the reasons our short-term approach is possible is that we know that we will be available in the future if other problems arise. When one feels that all problems—those immediately evident as well as others that are latent in the presenting situation—need to be dealt with in one treatment or therapy, then there is more pressure to extend the meeting times, or perhaps to increase the frequency of meetings.

WHEN DAD WON'T COME

Generally when a child is referred to our child mental health department, our secretary calls the family and sets up an appointment for the child and the parents. We have many single parents in our population, and typically the parent who lives with the child will appear with the child for the first appointment. I always inquire about the other parent, and if the other parent lives nearby, I usually ask whether it would be possible for me to meet that person. It often happens that the parent who is with me, typically the mother, will tell me that the father will not come: "He's too busy," "He disapproves of my bringing Johnny here to see you," "He and I don't get along," or even sometimes, "He is not interested." I have made it a practice to ask for permission to call the other parent; usually the child is happy to have me try to talk to the absent parent, and usually the parent who is in my office is willing to allow me to try to contact the other parent and will give me the phone number to help me do so.

Many times the missing parent is happy to come. Nearly always the dad (for he is usually the parent who is not living with the child) is interested in his child, and nearly always he can find time, when asked by me, to come and talk about the child. In some of these cases, the mother was right in saying "He won't come" in the sense that if she had asked, he might well have said no. In other cases, the mother is mistaken; or she may not want the father there and so she says that he does not want to come. She may feel angry at him for abandoning the family, or for not contributing to the support of the children, or for not fulfilling what she sees as his obligations for sharing the burdens of child care. Whatever the reasons, she may be angry enough not to want to include him in the request for help for the child. But very few mothers will prevent me from trying to call the father, so I always ask for permission to try that.

Once I meet the father, it often becomes apparent that a substantial part of the child's problems are connected with the bad feeling and conflict that exists in the parents' relationship. The parents are quarreling and this affects the child. In these situations, the child usually obtains some comfort just from the fact that I am talking with both parents, even if that talk occurs in separate sessions and even though it does not bring the parents back together (often the child's fondest hope). Sometimes I am able to persuade the parents that the child's best interests would be served by their cooperating more, and sometimes they will even agree to meet with me in my office to discuss the child. I may be experienced by them as a fair referee, or as a safety net to keep things from getting out of control. Often I may feel as though the couple is not moving any closer together through this process. There may indeed be irreconcilable problems, but the child may benefit nonetheless from the knowledge that his parents are talking about him, and when I meet with the child I may be able to share with him my experiences with his parents and allow him an opportunity to talk about them to someone who has not taken sides, who is not inclined to see either one of them as right or wrong.

So when Dad won't come, my approach is to try to persuade him to come. And my experience is that it is a rare father who is so distrustful of therapists and so uninterested in his child that he won't come at least once. But this is not to say that this approach is a panacea; there are many marital situations that led to divorce because the two principals do in fact find negotiating together about anything almost impossible. And in such situations I am no more likely to prove an effective mediator than any of the other people—professional and social acquaintances—who have probably tried in the past with this same couple. And I have had my share of fathers come in who paint situations in terms that are completely opposed to those used by their ex-spouses. Hearing such parents talk about the child and the child's living situation is sometimes like hearing about two different children, so opposed and contradictory are their views. In many of these situations, getting to the bottom of the problem may be impossible.

Occasionally it helps in such situations to try and get other relatives to come to see me. I always ask if there are other family members, or others who live with either parent, and if possible, I try to meet them because they may add details that are helpful. They could be other siblings of the child, or new lovers of either parent, or grandparents who live in either household. But there are some situations where the best I can do is offer support to the child, making clear to the child that I can see what difficult situation she is in the midst of, and offering her whatever help is appropriate to her age and situation to cope with the parental battles.

DISCIPLINE

The word that is most often used by professionals for the topic of discipline is *limit setting*, but I find that the easiest way into the topic with most parents is to ask them about chores and household rules. Most parents disagree about some rules, and about enforcement of rules; most parents are not in complete agreement about what consequences are appropriate for which infractions of particular rules. Thus this is a topic that will lead almost any couple into an interesting discussion. When the discussion indicates that there is some disagreement between the parents, I usually inquire further. If parents have had a chance to become comfortable with me and if I have already spent one or two sessions getting to know their child, then usually the parents are willing to share with me details of the arguments they get into when they disagree about how to handle their child.

If the disagreements seem unusually intense, I ask whether they often find these discussions difficult when they have them at home. If they say yes, then I usually offer them the opportunity to have such discussions with me, and if possible, I link these discussions to the probability of their child's behavior improving. Naturally I will only say that if I have some evidence that the behavior is linked to the parental disagreements.

As I have said already, my view is that nearly all parents have intense disagreements about their child. But when they cannot resolve these disagreements on their own, when they cannot find their way through them to some sort of accommodation, then usually they have other areas in which they are at loggerheads as well, and nearly always they will be willing to look into these areas at least to some degree with me. Occasionally I encounter couples who refuse to allow our discussions to wander off the topic of the child or matters directly related to their child. In these cases, no matter how convinced I am that their own disagreements are directly related to the difficulties their child is having, I will not pursue the issue, since trying to persuade people to look at some issue they are not ready for almost never works very well. I know that they and the child will be back—to see the pediatrician if nothing else—and that I will hear if matters with their child do not improve. In the meantime, I will see what else is likely to be of help. This may mean providing services more directly to the child (individual treatment, or referral to a child's group if an appropriate one is starting soon), or it may mean staying in touch with the parents by phone or by occasional appointments in order to keep track of how things are going at home.

There are situations where I learn from talking with the child alone that he wishes his parents were able to keep their disagreements to themselves, or at least not put him in the middle. Children in separated families are of course especially prone to feeling caught in the middle between warring parents, but often parents do not realize the degree to which they are trying to persuade the child to take sides. Most parents will recognize that they should not ask their child to take sides (the few exceptions are obviously going to be difficult treatment cases), so that sometimes an effective intervention is to meet initially with the child and whichever parent has brought him, then to meet alone with the child once or twice, then to return to the parents and say to them that they should try to leave the child out of things. Such direct advice only works when the parents are relatively intact themselves, but my approach is to assume as much intactness of functioning as possible on the part of my patients. Sometimes expecting a higher level of functioning from them (than they ordinarily exhibit) is useful in helping them perform better; and when I am simply mistaken in my assumption that they will be able to use advice effectively, I find out rather quickly.

PARENTAL HOPES AND DREAMS

Couples and families have developmental stages, just as individual children and adults do, and both forms of development must be taken into account in working with children. That is, one must look at the individual development of the child and of each parent; and one must look at the developmental stage of the family. There are many many ways in which consideration of these intertwined issues becomes very complex, and there is a sense in which they are always more complex than we can ever know.

In our setting, I always ask for the charts for the parents as well as the child who is my identified patient. From their charts, I can learn their ages, and usually I get some sense of important parameters of their life. Each of our patients is asked to fill out a brief questionnaire which gives such information as level of education and employment. Usually there is additional information about the family, all of which helps orient me before I first meet them. But usually the kind of information that is most important from a psychodynamic point of view is not already in the chart, so I must find out from the parents their own position in their families of origin, for example, or the ways in which they feel that they are trying to improve, with their own child, on the upbringing they received from their own parents. Most people, it seems, have a sense of ways in which they are trying to do better—psychologically, not economically—by their children than their parents did by them.

Sometimes this becomes obvious very quickly. A parent comes in with a 14-year-old and the concern is suicide. The child cannot understand why the parent is so worried, but it seems that the child once made a remark which implied that he was considering the possibility of ending his life. The parent was sensitized to this remark (and frightened by it as well) because his own mother killed herself when he was a child, or even later when he was an adult. Of course, it is rare that a child *never* thinks about suicide. Part of growing up involves individuation; part of being an individual is recognizing that one is mortal; and part of grasping the complexity of that situation is thinking about death and inevitably about whether death will come upon one unexpectedly or whether one will rather choose to take control over when and how it occurs. In a case as obvious as this one, the parent is quite likely to admit very quickly that he is perhaps overreacting and he is likely to know perfectly well why this is so.

But there are many cases where the imbrications of parental and child motivations and experiences are harder to untangle, although they must always be taken into account. Having children is in one sense a perfectly straightforward, simple undertaking; but from a psychological point of view, the entire process is permeated with complexity. The feelings are very intense, or at any rate they certainly are in the population I have been seeing. Our population has many families of varying social and educational backgrounds, but they have in common a rather dramatic and emotionally laden interest in their children. Naturally, the families I see are a biased sample of the families in our society, since I only see families who are concerned about their children. We do not see the runaways, since they do not come into our Center; nor do we see the many children whose parents do not take very good care of them. By and large the parents we see are vitally interested in their children even when they are having difficulties.

What this means is that each child is surrounded by a network of complicated wishes and desires and feelings on the part of each parent. Nearly everything that the child undertakes is of crucial importance to one or the other parent. This is all seen in exaggerated form with a first baby whose every gurgle and burp are attended by lively interest; but some form of this process, however subdued and attenuated in comparison, continues right through the child's life. I once heard from a father who was worried about his daughter, and only later did I discover that his daughter was 34 years old and married with a child of her own. The father lived in the same community as the daughter; their lives were still intertwined on a weekly if not daily basis; and he was worried about his daughter's attitude toward him. This is a rare event for us: we have few men in their sixties calling about their children in their thirties, but it is quite obvious that most parents that age are still vitally interested in their children. There is something about the project of having a child which, in our culture, is surrounded with many layers of complicated feelings, one portion of which has to do with doing better by the child than one's own parents did by us. Other parts involve our hopes for the future and our rather peculiar expectation (viewed from outside our social system) that our children will do something for us, will provide something for us that no one else can provide. We have hopes that we want them to fulfill; we have wishes for ourselves that are frustrated, but we hope our child will be able to gratify those wishes, and through doing so, give us pleasure. We inflict on our children all manner of weird desires, and often we do not even realize we are doing this. Untangling this in a therapist's office is hard. But when parents come in with a child to say that something is not right, nearly always there lurks—usually rather close to the surface—a whole galaxy of thwarted desires, and peering into that world is not always pleasant.

The simplest form of this occurs when a parent says, "I wanted my child to be happy; I was not a happy child, so I desperately wanted to give my child happiness; and now my child is not happy and this is simply too terrible for me to bear. Thinking about this fills me with despair." The parent who pours this out, however haltingly and inarticulately, is not likely to be helped by any kind of simple focusing on the child and her problem. If the presenting problem has a specific aspect to it, then looking at that makes sense, but usually there is in addition a more general and unspecific aspect to the presentation. The parent says, "I can see that my child is not happy." We ask, "How do you see that? What are the signs?" and the answer is usually formulated in terms of what appear, on the surface, to be trivialities: "Oh, I can tell, he sits in his room all the time," or "He never is contented sitting still, he always has to be running around with his friends," or "He avoids me, he won't talk to me openly the way he used to when he was younger," or "He doesn't seem to have any interests, he seems to be drifting about in life, he has no focus."

In a few of these cases, there is in fact something to be worked on with the child directly, but often there needs to be—instead or additionally—work with the parent. For what is necessary is that the parent become more aware of the internal sense of failure, the way in which the parent wants more from life than life is providing, the way in which the parent sees the problem as having roots deep in her own childhood, the way in which she is using her own child to rectify her own life. Once a parent can see this, in however muted and veiled a form, then often the intensity of the complaints about the child abates. The gist of the problem is that the parent wants something from a child that the child cannot provide: a meaningful life, a redressing of life's wrongs, a fulfillment of the hopes and expectations that have been frustrated over the years.

Again, as I have mentioned before, this point is one that many parents will grant abstractly; and it is one which, once they can see its application to their own life, they are willing to admit is a problem. Most parents know the phrase that you can't live through your children, even though most of us as parents try to do so in ways of which we are ordinarily rather unaware. But often this awareness is not ferociously defended against, but simply somewhat out of focus, and bringing it into focus does not necessarily involve long, arduous, complicated treatment. The therapeutic process may involve shifting one's field and direction of vision, and this may not always be terribly complicated or require a long time to occur.

Sometimes this level of analysis—of the parent's unfulfilled dreams—must be complicated by the context: there are often two parents and they may have opposing dreams, and sometimes parents are not entirely aware of the ways in which some of their battles over the child are battles about whose unfulfilled wishes deserve primacy. In these cases, we can try to help the parents talk with one another about their own lives, what sense they make of them, what wishes they have for themselves. Sometimes it is useful to urge parents to do something for themselves, not something to make themselves feel momentary pleasure, but something to move them forward toward one of these lifelong goals. A father is worried about his son's school performance; it turns out the father dropped out of high school. In such a case it may be useful to discuss with father and son the possibility of the father taking courses toward a high-school degree. Even if the father refuses, the conversation may be useful for the son, and the father may come to have a better grasp of all those forces in his son that make learning problematical, since he may again experience similar forces within himself.

Another example of this common predicament is when the parents come in to discuss chaos in their household. They seem to be saying that the focus of all the problems is one particular boy, their 10-year-old who always seems to be at the center of whatever difficulty is occurring. More complaints follow; they are diffuse, but seem to center on sibling rivalries in their children, and impossible dinner situations. Everyone is always fighting, and there is never a meal without an explosion of anger. The parents report that they feel like leaving town if things do not improve. As the discussion progresses, a sense begins to emerge that part of the problem resides in the woman's expectation that dinner should be calm. In her family of origin, her father's explosive temper used to disrupt whatever semblance of calm might exist, and as her brothers became older, they too would become enraged and often there would be open fights at dinner. So she hears all fighting as a prelude to war, and her wish is for a dinner with no quarreling whatsoever. On the other hand, the father was actually more upset by the difficulty he had talking to his wife than he was by the fighting. He wanted time to talk to her after each of them came home from a busy day at work, and their chaotic family situation at dinner made talking with his wife impossible.

In this situation, how can we decide which way to move? There is no obvious answer, and in truth we could go any of several ways. One approach is to talk about anger and families in an effort to explore the mother's attitudes about anger in general. Does she tolerate anger better in other situations (other than at dinner)? How have they handled anger in each of their children over the years? How do she and her husband express their own anger at each other and at the children? The point here would be to move toward helping the mother see that some angry expression is not unusual, that her own childhood may have had fewer controls and safeguards on the expression of anger than is ideal, that now she might come to terms with the fact that her children became angry at times without trying to assimilate the present situation (which might not be very serious) to her own infantile past.

Another approach might be to look at the couple: how much intimacy do they have? and is the man's complaint about the dinner situation part of a more general situation in which the couple seldom has uninterrupted time for each other? Are the children to some degree being used by the parents to avoid greater intimacy (children and their problems are often used in this way of course). This situation can be explored at greater length and concrete suggestions made, if that appears likely to be helpful.

Thus chaos in the household needs to be addressed, but not necessarily in the way the parents address it. They say that their child is the cause of the chaos, so their implicit plea is that he or she be fixed. But other views of the situation are possible, and with a different point of view, different possibilities for action open up, some of which involve the parents more than the child. This is not to deny that the child is involved in the chaos, but just to say that doing something about it might be done more efficiently through work with the parents.

CONFLICT

There are many different ways to deal with any issue that creates conflict between parents and child. Two major approaches are (1) to talk with the parents about their own lives (what they do for pleasure, how much satisfaction they derive from their work or from their friends), and (2) to do what amounts to conflict mediation between parents (around the question of which rules to establish and how to enforce them) or between parents and children (working toward some form of contract in which the child agrees to do certain things in return for certain privileges, and the parents agree to provide certain things in exchange for cooperation from the child with regard to chores or homework or whatever). I will discuss each of these in turn.

Parent's Lives

There is nearly always a sense in which the parents who come into my office are living through their children. Not to do so at all would imply a degree of detachment and self-absorption which the parents who are worried enough about their children to bring them in to see me do not have. Yet it is also true that living through one's children is not an optimal strategy for raising children. It is, paradoxically, both necessary and a mistake, and most parents experience the fluctuations in their own involvement with their children as the years pass and children grow older. This is an unavoidable existential dilemma, to which each of us, as parents, must work out some solution and if we are lucky, we work out a solution with a companion who is close enough to the children to experience the same tugs and pulls. Essentially the solution lies in constructing a life of one's own. For if a parent has a life separate from that of bringing up the children, then the parent is usually free to shift some of the enormous energy which was originally poured into the baby, and redirect it toward other interests or people. And as the years pass, this becomes more important, for if the child is to grow up in our culture, she must learn to establish some sense of independence, which is made possible by the parents gradually letting go. Our American phrase is "cutting the apron strings," although it is not only the child and mother who need to let go; both parents are clearly implicated in the holding on, and both need to let go, regardless of who does the cooking.

Now in an age when more and more parents work, when there are fewer families with a full-time homemaker parent, saying that parents need to develop a life of their own outside the family may sound peculiar. After all, doesn't the mere fact of employment outside the home guarantee that the parents have a life outside the family? The answer, of course, is no, since a job per se does not guarantee a fulfilling life, and there are many parents who have a job to earn a living but whose emotional energy is still centered on their family and children. In fact, to a rather alarming extent surveys indicate that many people feel that the "most important thing" in their lives is their family. I am never sure what people really mean when they say that; I suspect they mean to point to such facts as the distress they would feel if their spouse or child died; they mean to say that one can more easily find a new job than a new family; they mean to indicate the wrenching effects of divorce on most people. But I think they do not mean that they would like a life in which only their family matters. Thus in a society where everyone is expected to be able to leave the family, each person needs interests outside the family circle.

This is the crucial point: that a parent will do better with children if there are other events of interest in the life space, if the horizon is broader than if one only wondered when the child will arrive home from school, or what grade the child will obtain on the next test, or whom the child is talking to on the phone. Naturally, this is not the whole story; many parents with fulfilling outside lives will still get into impossible tangles with their children; there are other factors of importance in any dynamic equation that lead to conflict. But the absorbing outside life is one part of the equation.

Part of what I mean here by an absorbing outside life would ordinarily include a job, but the more important part is a responsiveness to people and events other than one's children.[1] Having a job does not guarantee that; not having a job does not make it impossible. So a job is just one convenient (but at times misleading) indicator of what I am discussing here. What I ask parents is not so much whether they work as how they like their work, or what they do besides take care of children. In my office, I see both overinvolved mothers and fathers, and the overinvolvement does not flow simply from lack of employment, since most of the mothers and fathers I see are employed. But how they feel about their employment

---

[1] This topic is connected with class differences—the more resources of education and money available to someone when she is young, the greater her chances of being able to find such absorbing outside interests—but it is not simply a sociological matter since there are substantial individual differences within people of the same class in this regard.

varies tremendously, and sometimes parents can see that their overinvolvement in their child is connected with their lack of involvement with their occupation.

Another aspect of this whole situation has to do with personal involvements. When a couple comes in, I wonder how they feel about each other; when a single parent comes, I wonder what involvements with other people exist in his life. Several things matter here. First of all, a parent who finds another adult important, and who feels that the other adult respects and loves and cares about him, is in a better position when it comes to a battle with the children. The parent has more strength, and the parent has some place to go when things do not work out well with the child. That is, there is a way to get support for whatever failure is being experienced with the child. This is not to say that both adults need to agree with one another, but simply to say that there is an emotional connection between the adults which is sustaining for the parent, an emotional connection besides that with the child. This takes some of the pressure off the parent-child relationship.

Saying exactly how this occurs is difficult. Part of it has to do with self-esteem: if one leans heavily on children for self-esteem, one is doomed to feel bad since children do not always do what one wants; they are often rude or unaffectionate or plain defiant, and feeling like a failure is the easiest thing in the world when one makes self-esteem entirely contingent on being a parent. One needs other sources of self-esteem. Another part has to do with emotional responsiveness: children are very responsive and more so during the early years than later, but even at their most demonstrative, they seldom give one exactly what one wants the minute one wants it; and most of the time their responsiveness is not synchronized with the needs of the parent. So a parent is required to swallow some degree of neediness and take it elsewhere, and this is vastly easier when one has other people around who will meet one's needs, who will talk with you when you are lonely, who will hold you when you are sad. One of the common pathologies of parent-child relationships arises when the child needs to be a parent to the adult; but another common difficulty arises when the child needs to behave as an equal with the adult, when the adult needs a partner and relies on the child to be that partner. This places too much pressure on the child and inevitably leads to some form of trouble, although the trouble may not surface in behavior in childhood (and thus may not come to me in my office). Instead, the problems may surface years later as the child, now grown, tries to come to terms with various life dilemmas whose roots are in a childhood where she was required to be too grown up, too responsible, too mature, in order to cope with a childish, dependent, immature, or helpless parent. This is most striking when a parent has some debilitating disease or a crippling illness, but it occurs even in other less extreme situations.

Now all parents have an immature helpless side, so if they cannot express it with their children, what are they to do? The answer is: express it with their true equals, with people their own age. Ideally, this is with a living partner (who may or may not be a spouse and the other parent of the children), but even when this ideal is not attainable, there are surely other adults around somewhere who can play this role in the parent's life. And when I meet parents who seem not to have another such adult in their life, I often try to reflect with them on what this may mean for their child. Reflection in conversation with me is not a solution, but my aim is seldom to solve a life dilemma, but rather to help the parents become aware of the contours of the dilemma and then prepare for action in the real world to change the situation.

Understanding this whole issue often enables a clinician to see more clarity in a family than would otherwise emerge. Much of what appears to be incredibly intense conflict between parents and child has, in fact, this underlying dynamic. The parent feels rejected and hurt by the child and resents the child for not providing what is needed, namely, affection, support, comfort, respect. But instead of saying that, the parent nearly always says, "The child is impossible, she does not clean her room, her grades are terrible, she is rude, she never does anything helpful around the house."

The diagnostic key is partly the extremity of the parental statement (she *never* does what she is supposed to do, which is almost always an exaggeration) and partly hidden in the complaints, since what makes all these individual derelictions so painful for the parent is that they imply a lack of respect for the parent, a lack of obedience, a lack of responsiveness to the parent's sense of values. In sum, the parent is often saying, "This child is different from what I expected and wanted." And often the child feels this and expresses it to some degree, saying things like, "You don't love me" or "You never loved me" or "You love my sister more than you love me." Parents respond by denying the accusation, but that is usually beside the point. For the child is often saying what the parent thinks; the child accuses the parent of not loving her, but the parent feels the child does not love the parent. And love is somehow bound up with obedience, and similarity, and fidelity to parental values, although it is an unusual child who can be completely obedient or similar or faithful to the parents' ideals.

Furthermore, many adolescents who have been particularly close to their parents over the years of earlier childhood may need to be more hostile when they begin to break away; there is a sense in which whatever rudeness is occurring, whatever rebelliousness does happen, is a tribute to the closeness of the parent-child relationship. The child would not need to kick so hard if the ties did not bind so tightly. Sometimes parents benefit from simply discussing this aspect of the whole dilemma, so that saying to a parent who seems to be in total conflict with a child, "You must have been very close to her," will often produce dramatic effects. For generally the parent will then pour out a tale of woe about how close they used to be, how lately there seems to be this wall between them, and how the child just wants to talk with her friends, she won't even say hello when she comes home after school, she says she hates her mother and doesn't want to be seen with her when they go shopping together. Such statements, made by the child, are certainly extreme and may sound impossibly rude to an outsider, but they flow from what is nearly always a very close parent-child connection which is in the process of being broken by ordinary adolescent developmental processes.

Helping parents to see this as normal is one form of intervention. Many parents do not see why a child should ever
need to break away; indeed, if our whole society were set up
differently, there might not be the same intensity of need
which we often see expressed. Adolescence, that is, varies
from culture to culture.[2] And in our culture, we have fewer
bridging strategies (rituals, etc.) to help smooth the path from
childhood to adulthood than some other cultures. So part of
the intensity of rebellion and defiance which adolescents often
express is due to their need to invent their own way of breaking
away; there is no socially agreed upon time or ceremony that
will do this for them. Furthermore, parents may be more
involved with their children now than used to be the case,
so the emotional ties may be deeper or closer and this might
make breaking away harder.[3]

But in any case, the child's statements of independence,
and their frequent tone of rudeness and defiance, can be more
easily tolerated if the parent sees them first as part of a
developmental process (this is not to excuse the behavior; the
parent should still make clear she does not like it, but she
may expect it to continue anyway). And second, the parent is
in a better position if she has other sources of respect and
love; this makes the rejection from the child hurt less.

My interest in the parents is usually genuine, although there
are a few cases where I cannot manage to like the parents
enough to be interested; some parents are truly impossible,
and I do not succeed with them because they usually see that
I feel that way. When this happens and I am aware of it, I
will try to refer them to a colleague, and my colleagues refer
some of their cases to me for similar reasons. But generally
I am full of admiration for anyone who has managed to raise
a child up to adolescence, and I wonder always how they do
it, how they juggle their life responsibilities with the difficulties

---

[2] There is substantial literature on this topic in the field of anthropology; see, for
example, works by Mead, Whiting et al., Munroe, and many others since.
[3] This is a hypothesis which is hard to prove; for interesting ideas and facts about
this whole question, see works in the bibliography on the history of the family such
as those by Shorter and Laslett.

of raising a child. So I inquire and in the process find out about their jobs and what else they do in life. Then at some later point, I will refer to that knowledge. If I know they like to read, I'll suggest to them that they read a book instead of engaging their child in conflict, and I do this in a way that, first, emphasizes how unhappy they are with the struggle with their child and, second, suggests that there must be better ways to live: for example, Wouldn't you rather read a good book? This always sounds odd at first, since it seems to be irrelevant, but I want to try to help parents see that they are making choices and that perhaps there is a better choice to be made in this situation. The child may be choosing to be obnoxious, but the parent is choosing to respond to it, to become caught up in the resulting conflict; other choices are possible.

Parents nearly always want to return to talking about the child, how rude she is, how impossible she is. But I want to bring them back to seeing how they are choosing to focus on that. Of course, part of their choice is based in their own judgment that their child will be in trouble later in life if she continues to behave in this way. They are trying to help her, they will argue. Part of their choice derives from their offended sense of righteousness: a child should not behave in this way toward her parents. Part is a reaction to the child: if she stopped behaving like that, they would not have to talk about it. But I want them to see that all of this still adds up to a choice on their part. Their daughter is choosing to behave badly in their terms; they are choosing to react to it.

Now I am not going to advise them to ignore their daughter's behavior. I want them to continue to object to it, to indicate that they do not like it. But I want them to stop beating their heads against the wall, to stop feeling that they can control their daughter, because they cannot; she will do what she wants until she decides to stop. They need to continue to try to structure their household so their daughter will have an incentive to stop behaving in her rude, defiant way. But they need to have other ways to spend their time besides arguing with her.

All of this discussion with parents needs to occur over some length of time, since parents nearly always require time to assimilate this different way of looking at their family life. They will initially feel that they are being asked to ignore their child, and this will feel terrible. Or they will discover that what sounds like fairly straightforward advice is in fact very hard to put into effect. Or in an interesting way, they will discover that their child complains about their new stance; the child will often articulate what the parents are feeling, that this different way of relating feels distant and cold and uninvolved. When this happens, I then invite the parents to bring their child with them so we can discuss together the meaning of family closeness and the complicated question of whether there are other ways for them as a family to be close without fighting. Sometimes there is no other way, but even in this case, the fighting will have a new resonance or another dimension; it may be uncomfortable, but the family will perceive that it may be necessary.

Actually that is rarely a conclusion that parents will reach about their fighting with an adolescent child, although it does occur in couples' counseling; that is, many couples discover that fighting is a way of making contact, a form of vividly experienced living, and they realize that they get something important from it. But parents usually do not see their fighting with their children in this way. So more often they simply become more articulate about their need for closeness, and once they see that that is what they want, they discover that there are other ways to obtain it. Sadly the parents must often resign themselves to accepting whatever closeness their child will allow, since as I have said already, being close to parents is not the primary developmental task of adolescents, and a later form of closeness will become possible only if they first can break away enough to establish a separate base, a distinct sense of identity. This sounds vague and general but in practice it comes down to things like wearing different clothing than the parents would approve of, having inappropriate friends, liking strange music, and sleeping and eating at odd hours. So the components of a search for a distinct identity often have little or no grandeur, but they can nonetheless lead to very intense fighting.

CONFLICT MEDIATION

Another major approach to resolution of problems of conflict between parents and children involves conflict mediation. If this approach is to be successful, the child needs to be seen as a partner in the negotiation or as a participant with rights of her own. Many parents do not wish to accept this, so that mediation cannot really occur until parents have been convinced that they must accept this assumption. Typically parents enter my office saying, "Make her behave." From there we move, slowly, toward some idea of how we are going to treat this problem, but from the very first moment I am trying to lay the groundwork for seeing the child as an important partner in whatever happens. I make a point of introducing myself to the child. I give my card not only to the parents but also to the child. I have a difficult name and the point of the card is to make sure they know how to spell it, to give them something tangible, to make sure they have my phone number so they can call me if they have questions. I direct my attention to the child, and if the child will not talk, then I turn to the parents, but always with the explicit acknowledgment that I will return to the child often, to see if he has anything to add to what his parents are saying. So I treat the child with respect, no matter how sullen or withdrawn or hostile or grouchy the child seems.

I also assume that neither the child nor the parents are particularly happy with the way things are going, even though the parents are usually the ones who are vocal about this (they have called to set up the appointment). I ask the child how he thinks things could be better at home, and nearly always the child will say things would be better if his parents did not criticize him so much and if they gave him more freedom. Then we talk about what kinds of criticisms bother him, which ones seem excessive and which ones seem appropriate; I nearly always assume that the child will agree that some criticism is justified (many parents will tell me that their child will never accept any criticism, but that is seldom really the case). Then we talk about what sort of freedom matters, and again, although many parents think their child wants total freedom, in fact, most of the adolescents I see simply want a somewhat later curfew, or more respect and trust from their parents about how they spend their time. They never say that they want their parents to turn over the keys to the family car, to turn over the bank account, and to give up all their rights. Rather they recognize that the parents run the household, and they simply want a little more leeway for their own different view of how things should happen. This may come down to wanting the freedom to keep their room messy, or it may mean that they think being grounded for three months is excessive punishment for poor grades one quarter at school, or for being home late one night.

Once we have reached this point, then we are ready to begin the conflict mediation. We have essentially made clear that there are two sides (or more than two, if the parents have differing views, and if there are other family members whose opinion is important). Ideally, each side needs to say what is wanted. Both sides have to discuss what the consequences should be of failure to live up to the terms of whatever agreement is reached. In my experience, one seldom needs a written document specifying all this and signed by both parties. Simply the process of engaging in this discussion seems to be the crucial element of the treatment; once parents and child have sat down and been able to talk about these issues in a calm way, usually they are able to figure out how to proceed from there.

Typically parents who engage in this kind of discussion with their child in my office will return after a couple of weeks to discuss how things have not been working as well as they had hoped. We then go over the details: where has their family become stuck? What are the disagreements which occur? how often? with what result? Sometimes the parents come with their child for this discussion, sometimes without the child, but ordinarily this process of continuing consultation with me continues for a month or two, and then often we stop meeting, and have another meeting several months later to review how things have been going.

Some families do very well with this sort of procedure. They are able to sit and talk without becoming consumed with rage; they do not bolt from the office in anger; they are able to be specific about what they want; and they are able to give up some things in exchange for others. All of these are rather high-level functions, in the psychiatric phrase. That is, not everyone is capable of this sort of behavior, but when parents and child can do this, it can work beautifully in the sense of managing the conflict so it does not get out of hand. However, this process does not abolish conflict, and families need to understand that. Anger will still erupt; feelings will still be hurt; the child will still feel misunderstood and victimized; and the parents will still feel that their child is outrageous at times. But the mediation process may be able to keep all of this under control and make surviving with grace possible. And in many life situations, surviving with grace is more to the point than abolishing unhappiness or attaining bliss.

When this kind of conflict mediation does not work, then usually there is more going on than meets the eye. The parents may be in severe conflict themselves with one another; the character structures in any of the participants may be more pathological than was first apparent; there may be other features to the case (e.g., alcoholism in one or more of the parties which is not discussed openly, or abuse, etc.). Or the issue may be more like those I discussed earlier, of parents wanting more closeness than they are getting, of a child needing more room for maneuver than he is being given, and in this case parents need to talk to me about how to shift their thinking about their child in ways I have already discussed.

It is helpful to keep in mind that working with adolescents requires being able to remember being adolescent. Without memories of the developmental process, then being sympathetic with an adolescent is difficult. For example, parents are often in the position of saying: how could you be so stupid as to do "X" (whatever it may be that was outrageous, silly,

stupid, etc.)? But a therapist who can remember doing similarly silly things will have an easier time trying to persuade
the parents to take a more tolerant view, not of the act (which
may indeed have been silly) but of the person who did the
act (their child). Furthermore, an adolescent who reaches the
age of 18 or so without having done some stupid or silly
things is likely to do worse things later, so parents need to
keep that in mind. It is not an age when things should go
entirely smoothly; most parents know this and can do well
with being reminded of it.

For repetitive acts, clear-cut consequences make sense. If
the child is supposed to be home by a certain time, there
should be a consequence if he is late; otherwise the rule makes
no sense. The consequences may just be that the parent is
angry or hurt; or there may be in addition some punishment.
Negotiations with the child about the rules and the consequences are a good idea, and one role the therapist can play
is in helping this to happen. Naturally if an issue is non-
negotiable from the parents' point of view, then there is no
point in pretending to negotiate it.

Many of the conflicts between adolescents and parents involve work: the adolescent's studies, and the vague general
question of what the child will do later in life to support
herself. Having grown-up models who are appealing is vital
for this developmental task; it is hard to expect a 16-year-old
to slave away at studies if the goal is to turn into an adult
like Mom or Dad who are always tired from working too hard.
The other side of the work issue is boredom; learning to
handle boredom is a life issue, so adolescents may as well
spend some time wrestling with this while they are young,
rather than trying to be productive all the time (no matter
how much parents might prefer this latter stance).

MAINTAINING NEUTRALITY

Adolescents are old enough to be able to see their parents
from an outside perspective and yet are often young enough
to be unable to move out of the house or to make the psy-

chological break from the parents' sphere. Sometimes seeing a therapist can provide an adolescent with crucial support in this direction; the therapist can support the child's desire to justify himself against his parents and, by meeting with him, can bolster the adolescent's ability to see more clearly, to articulate what he thinks is happening, and thus to gain power in the struggle with his parents.

Of course, there are pitfalls inherent in taking too critical a posture with regard to an adolescent's parents. Well known in the literature on child abuse, for example, is the fact that even abused children are reluctant to join with an outside person in seeing parents as abusive or harmful. Nonetheless it is true that many children are able to see that their parents have negative features and are able to derive support from seeing that someone else sees those faults.

The fact that a therapist sees the faults of a parent does not inevitably mean that the therapist is trying to take the adolescent away from the parents. Once the adolescent is convinced that the therapist is both on the side of the child and yet adamant in seeing the parents as people with rights to their own characters, however strange that might be, then the adolescent is often quite able to join with the therapist in forging a new view of his parents, a view that incorporates both positive and negative features. And this work may involve a crucial part of maturation, of moving beyond the more childish tendency to see parents as either all good or all bad.

The negative side of this process is that it supports ambivalence. But there is an important sense in which ambivalence is inevitable, and not to be avoided; it constitutes a very healthy advance over purity and single-mindedness. And adolescents are often far too prone to be single-minded and inclined toward purity. This is not to say, however, that they cannot in some cases be helped to a more complex and realistic view of life. So one form that therapy with adolescents can take is individual work. This may be helpful even when a careful evaluation makes clear that a considerable part of the problem is the parental unwillingness to give the adolescent more responsibility for his own life.

All of this is delicate because the therapist has the unenviable task of trying to maintain an alliance both with the adolescent and with the parents. The therapist cannot afford to be seen by either side as having a favorite, and one of the inevitable pitfalls of this kind of work with adolescents and their families is that in some cases, either parents or child will see the therapist as favoring the other party. When this occurs, then the best solution is probably to refer the family to another therapist after pointing out the predicament and discussing it with the family. If one admits the predicament openly and moves actively toward making another referral, then the situation is less likely to deteriorate to the point where the family abandons treatment and leaves altogether.[4]

There are many cases which present as adolescent problems which are susceptible to more direct work with parents, however. Not all parents are unworkable! Some are indeed ready to hear someone else tell them what they themselves already suspect: for example, that this is just a phase and that the adolescent will grow out of whatever is occurring at the moment. Of course, the only way this suggestion will be accepted is if one has already spent some time getting to know the parents and the child. In that case, the advice flows from knowledge and the parents will often respect that knowledge. If one is too quick to say, within five or 10 minutes of the first contact with the parents, "This sounds like a phase, don't worry, he'll grow out of it," then the parents are much less likely to believe the therapist. Thus the prerequisite to all advice giving is the establishment of a relationship and this cannot be done in five or 10 minutes. But it can be done in less than a year or even less than a month. With many, many families, one or two sessions of an hour each is sufficient to establish enough of a relationship so that advice giving becomes a fruitful intervention. Obviously this is not true with

---

[4] The best way to be sympathetic to both sides in any typical adolescent-parent battle is to have experienced both sides personally, but I would not go so far as to recommend that all therapists who work with families of this sort go out and get an adolescent child.

all families; here I am discussing those families which are healthy enough to benefit from advice.

There are other situations where parents come in to discuss a difficult problem adolescent and it becomes apparent that a main part of the problem is a conflict between the couple about how to treat the adolescent. In such cases, direct work with the couple will be the treatment of choice. The adolescent needs to be involved only at the beginning, as part of the usual assessment; once the diagnosis of the couple's conflict has been made, then couples work can occur. The aim of the work would be to help the couple come to an awareness of their conflict (in some cases they may not even realize that they are in acute conflict); or if awareness already exists, then to help them come to some acceptable resolution of the conflict, or at least help them to see that expressing the conflict vividly and continuously is not helping their child. That is, in some cases, the conflict may be resolved in the sense that the couple will come to some accommodation or compromise position and agree to support one another in a way that had not been occurring previously. In other cases, they may be helped to see that the conflict springs from a basic core conflict that is not going to be resolved easily, but they may be able to agree to try to keep the conflict out of their day-to-day interactions with their child.

So conflict resolution may be one goal of couples treatment, and an increased ability to segregate the conflict so that it does not intrude on their relationship with their child may be another goal of couples treatment. There are many cases that present as a problem adolescent which turn out, rather quickly, to be a case of rather acute marital conflict whose focus appears to be an adolescent, but where in fact the real problem is the way the couple exists together. In these cases, more prolonged couples treatment may be recommended—for example, through a couples group or through a more prolonged contract for couples work where the focus is less the child and more the couple in all its aspects.

In the next chapter I will focus on our work with younger children in play therapy, and in addition consider other questions like the vexing one of when and under what circumstances hospitalization can be helpful; and I will review several examples of specific suggestions we make in response to parental requests for help.

8

More Practical
Applications

PLAY THERAPY

Play therapy is the name given to what is done in therapy with young children. This approach has evolved in part because children do not talk so readily about themselves as adults do (so the more conventional talking approach does not work so well), and in part because children's play substitutes for free association, thus opening up the unconscious for the therapist.

In my own work, play is important but necessarily less important than in long-term individual therapy for many of the same reasons that free association is less important. That is, just as short-term therapy with adults cannot encourage patients to feel as though they have all the time in the world to talk about whatever comes to mind—rather they are urged, generally, to focus more on some particular dilemma—so short-term therapy with children does not generally rely on long hours of watching a child play, or playing with a child, to bring buried things out into the open. Such long hours of free play between therapist and child are invaluable, but not always because it is the only or best way to help the child. The play is invaluable primarily because it provides the therapist a way to learn about children, both the individual child he is working with and children in general. Playing with a child for long hours offers a learning opportunity that is not easily found elsewhere, certainly not through books or lectures, a way of learning about developmental psychology and about people. The play opens up a kind of detailed and intimate understanding of the child's problems which is scarcely possible in one or two brief interviews, or from history taking from the adult caretakers.

There are certainly other benefits to the long-term form of play therapy—for example, the parents get a very clear sense that the therapist is involved with their child and takes the child very seriously; this in itself can be tremendously important in leading the parents to feel that someone else is sharing the burden of whatever is problematic in their child. But all of this is not to say that long hours of play therapy are absolutely necessary to help a particular child get better, however that may be defined. And it may well be that some of the goals of long-term play therapy are just as grandiose when applied to children as they are when applied to adults: for example, one such oft-repeated goal is that of reconstructing the child's character or reparenting the child (providing the child with the sort of parent he did not have but needed, as though this can be done in twice-a-week or five-times-a-week sessions which last only an hour each). That is, I am skeptical that even five hours a week spent with a child or an adult will do everything that is often hoped for, although there is no question that it does something.

Given these reservations about long-term play therapy, how then is play important in short-term therapy? Since play is a form of communication, from the child to us, we use play in that way also; through the play we set up a dialogue with the child, or at least that is our goal, although at first we may necessarily be content with observing the child's choice of toys and activities. Play, then, is an alternative to more verbal ways of becoming acquainted. Play is also expressive. Therefore, like other therapists, we look at a child's play to learn something about the child's feelings and about hidden conflicts, as well as about the defensive maneuvers used to contain those conflicts.

But just as important is the use we make of play in working with the parents, since part of the goal of our therapy is to improve the relationship between the parents and child. This means that we try to help the parents see the richness of a child's play, the expressive side of play, and the restorative side, since children often use play to "work things through" as therapists usually put it. Some adults have a gift for playing with children and seem to intuit the importance of play for the child, but many parents, no matter how good they are with children in caretaking ways, lack this ability. So they will benefit from some help from a therapist in this regard. The therapist can draw attention to the child's play, can encourage the parent to sit and observe it, can suggest new ways in which the parents can enter into the play which may help the child work through whatever conflicts are currently occurring.

So I try to use the child's play, starting in the very first session, when I am generally meeting with the child and the parents together to find out what the difficulty is which brings them to my office. I allude to it in talking to the parents, I try to use it to illustrate what we are talking about, I take it as evidence that the child is listening to what we are saying even though he may appear inattentive, and I may even point out the symbolic content of the play if it is relevant. The point of all this is to let the child know I am paying attention to him even when I am talking to his parents, and to help the parents see the play as a communication device and as a therapeutic device for the child. So if the child has picked up a puppet in the form of a whale and makes eating noises with it, I may explicitly say something about my sense that the child's play is showing the child's feelings about our conversation. If the child is not happy about the direction of the conversation and tells us that through his play, then I want to draw attention to this, not because we are going to stop the discussion for the sake of the child's immediate comfort, but to make clear that the child's play is serving as a mode of communication, which we want to take seriously and notice.

Or if the child's noises become louder, I may say that it's clear he doesn't like what we're talking about and he's trying to drown us out but that we need to continue regardless.

Another example might occur when the child, after hanging on to one of his parents and then venturing only a short distance away, retreats to his parents. Then I may comment on how it takes a while to get used to this new office with this stranger; having said this I will continue with whatever the parents and I were talking about, so as not to put pressure on the child to participate further in a dialogue with me, at least not right now. Later I will want to talk or play with the child, but not yet. Another function that noticing the child's play serves is that it lets the parents know I am attending to their child, taking him seriously, seeing him as an important participant in what we are doing. Parents nearly always appreciate this, although occasionally when they are of the "children should be seen and not heard" school, they may feel I am taking the child too seriously. If I sense this, I do not stop what I am doing, but I do comment on what I feel is their attitude, in order to see if I'm correct, and if I am, in order to make clear to them that I do not share this attitude. I need to persuade the parents that I am on their side, but I do not want to do so at the expense of my own principles. So if it seems necessary, I add something about how in here (in my office) we need to allow the child a voice, since after all he's why the family is here today.

What are other ways in which play is important in my work with families? When toddlers and slightly older children are proving difficult to handle—a common complaint from the parents we see, who are distressed by temper tantrums and oppositionality—one way to break whatever cycle is occurring between a parent and a child may be to diverge into play. Of course, for a parent to be able to do this means that the parent cannot be so caught up in the conflict that stepping back is impossible. Thinking of play at a moment of angry conflict is often difficult. But one possible way into play is through imagining being the child. When the child is crying and stamping her feet over some frustration, the parent can try to imagine what that feels like, and one way to do that is to enact it. So if the parent tries stamping his feet, and pouting, or yelling, he may get some sense of what the child's state is. And the child may be propelled into playing parent in this situation: "No, you can't have it, not now, maybe later, now stop asking for it, right *now*." If the child can enter into this form of play—a play in which the parent and child are changing roles momentarily—sometimes that will take the child out of the stuck position she has been in, wanting something and not getting it. Additionally, there is often a therapeutic benefit to the parent, separate from whatever benefit flows from the child calming down and ending the tantrum; that is, this sort of temporary regression involving behaving childishly can help the parent reexperience a part of himself and put him more in touch with both himself and his child.

Many parents fear that if they do this, they are descending to the level of the child and that some form of catastrophe will result. It is as though they feel there is a regulated order in the universe which is being disturbed. Very rigid people will be hard to dissuade from such a position, but most others seem to find it possible, at least occasionally, to try what I am suggesting. Some parents need the structure of a game in order to play with their child; others will benefit from modeling (the therapist can show them what he has in mind by doing it with their child in front of them). Although parents are indeed the authorities in the family and ought to be in charge, this does not mean they can never be childish, never relax, and never play with their children. And for most American families, this is not very complicated, since our cultural ideology permits or encourages quite a lot of such behavior with children. Other cultures have more fixed notions of the child belonging to a separate sphere or domain than we do, and for them, this would all be more difficult.

Parents also often need help seeing that an impulse expressed in fantasy or words or play is not the same as an impulse expressed in direct action. There are varying degrees of direct action, and fantasy is different from reality. Most children grasp this rather readily as they grow older. Many parents, however, seem to worry that an angry impulse expressed, for example, in play is the same as an angry pounding of another person. But this is not the case, and if parents can be helped to appreciate this, they may be able to help the child deal with his anger.

Forbidding play with guns, for example, is probably not the best way to reduce the amount of violence in the world, although many parents make this assumption, equating play involving guns with killing. So one of our therapeutic goals is to help parents appreciate the importance of play for the development of children and to realize the rich resources that play offers them as well: a way of communicating with their child, a way of understanding their child better, and a way of helping their child work through conflicts. Sometimes a simple example is very helpful, like the familiar childhood game of peek-a-boo. Most parents who have children who are more than a year or two old remember how delighted a young child can be with this very simple game. However, most parents who have not studied child development or psychology have no framework within which to understand why this game is so perennially appealing. So a short discussion of separation anxiety and its gradual mastery through the game may illuminate for the parents how a very complicated psychological life issue—of separation, and ultimately, of death—can be assimilated and appropriated or worked through in a game. If they find this farfetched, then I acknowledge that it does seem fanciful; I usually add, however, that we may need such fanciful theories to account for the oftentimes bizarre quality of human behavior. I may go on to say that children's play often seems hard to understand on the surface, but that its puzzling appearance may give way to some kind of organized clarity once one sees how the play is connected with developmental themes. Obviously only a small part of this would be said at any one time, but in general some of my work with families includes what is most easily understood as a pedagogical component in which I try to help them understand some of the developmental aspects of children's growth. All of this is work that can be done in a time-limited framework if the parents are relatively intact and motivated to try to make things different, to create changes at home.

Involving the Parents

Inherent in what I have been saying is an underlying principle, that therapeutic work with children often involves the parents, not just because parents have a sacred status, not out of any very sophisticated concept of the family system and the importance of the parents for all the children in the system, but rather out of a more ordinary appreciation of the fact that it is the parents who are on the scene with the child most of the time. No matter how much time a therapist spends with a child, it is still miniscule compared with the amount of time parents spend with a child. So if influence is going to be exerted, the parents are the logical ones to do it, and time spent persuading parents to try something new with the child will often go 10 times further toward ameliorating the situation than the same time spent alone with the child. The reasons for this are as simple as the one I just stated: the parents are there more, and they have more power and influence than the child does. So part of the work I do involves trying to help the parents see the usefulness of a different view of play, so that it will include much of what the young child does.

Take bedtime problems as an illustrative example. Many parents come in to talk about the difficulties they have putting their child to bed, or keeping him in bed once he is there. Several different things are needed here: the parents need to agree on some course of action, and they need a plan for implementing it. But besides that, they need in part a broader view of what is happening, which is best provided by altering the context within which they view the problem. For the essence of what is happening is not a management problem (although treating it as such may be important), but rather a developmental stage which is not circumscribed but will be repeated, with variations, again and again through childhood and adolescence. This may sound discouraging, since it seems to say that the problem will never go away, but the point is not that but rather that the child's behavior is natural, given her needs, given what is happening in her development. Naturally she tries to avoid going to bed, naturally she wants to get up in the middle of the night and see her parents, or to move to their bed and sleep with them. All this is to be expected; it would be odd if this sort of thing never happened. But just as naturally, the parents need their own privacy and sleep, so they cannot get up in the middle of the night and play with the child and they cannot let the child stay up until she falls asleep from exhaustion (although some parents find this a workable approach).

So what is happening here is a natural event, laden with conflict between the child's interests and the parents' interests. Early in the child's life, this is a straightforward power struggle, one which I happen to think the parents should win, although there are certainly some parents who do not agree (but then, they would not consult me about this matter to start with, since they would not see the child's desire to be up at night as a problem). So I think the child needs to be moved to the schedule that other people are on, a schedule that involves sleeping at night and being active during the day. This cycle may be based in a physical event (the rising and setting of the sun), but more important, it is how our society structures the sleep-waking cycle. Later in the child's life, however, the issue is more complicated; there is some component of a struggle for power, but there are other motives mixed in as well. Untangling them all can be very arduous. What are some of the other motives?

One motive may be the parents' desire to be close to the child; a related one may be their desire to be good to the child, to gratify his needs. Sometimes this desire is rooted in an inability to tolerate the child's unhappiness, which in turn arises from the parent's own very powerful sense that when he was young, no one paid any attention to his unhappiness. When motives such as these lead parents to allow a child to get them up at three in the morning to play, even though they need to get up at seven the next morning to go to work, then something is askew, and discussing the whole issue in a developmental framework may be helpful. That is, I try to make clear to the parents that the child naturally wants to see more of them, but that they have rights as well, and I support their sense that they are being good enough to the child; they need not feel the need to do even more for the child. Underneath this whole dilemma is often a terrible difficulty with saying no to a child and this difficulty in turn may be related to very complex parental issues of relationship to all authority. However, going into all that is usually not necessary, although sometimes it is worth discussing the general issue of how one asserts rights against others, for parents who have difficulty asserting their rights against their child often have parallel difficulty asserting rights in other contexts.

That is, any difficulty a parent has with a child may be simple lack of management techniques, but may also be a way of coping with the parent's own damaged psychological development, either a felt sense of deficient nurturing in his own background, or a still unresolved conflictual relationship with his own parents and with all authority figures. Keeping all this in mind is difficult and one of the challenges of any form of therapy with children and families.

How does play enter into all of this? A child who is having problems with bedtime or sleep will usually reveal through his play whether the main underlying issue is separation or instead, perhaps, a struggle for control. If a struggle for control is the main issue, then the play will ordinarily involve aggressive themes, and the child's manner of organizing the play will show his interest in having control over what happens; the therapist can check this by trying to intrude into the play, to change one or another element in the play (suggesting that a car be put here, or blocks go there). The child's way of receiving such suggestions may indicate whether a desire for control is a dominant theme. Or the play may instead feature puppets that move closer to one another, then further apart; or blocks that are pushed out of one area into another; or the child may make comments during the play which indicate a sensitivity to the issue of where the parent is ("Is she still in the waiting room?" "How do you know?" "What if she left?"). So it is not just the play that is being examined, but the structure of the play, the way the therapist is included or excluded from a role in the play, the comments that are made during the play, the way in which the play may be interrupted at some point when the child experiences a dangerous feeling (a sudden play disruption ordinarily indicates that some important affect is occurring).

Once the therapist has an indication of what the main issue is, then the parents can be told. If the parents see that the underlying issue is separation, for example, then they often have an easier time asserting themselves around the bedtime problem. At least, this is true with parents who are able to agree that tolerating separation is an important ability. There are some parents who think they and their child should never be separated, but that is not common.[1] So the play would be used as an illustrative example of the same issue which is inherent in the sleeping problem. Once parents can begin to connect things together, they often have an easier time figuring out what to do. A parent who thinks his child's midnight awakenings are due to an earache will take certain steps (calling the doctor, having the child's ears looked at) which would otherwise not occur. Similarly, a parent who sees the waking problem as a developmental stage having to do with separation will often figure out what needs to be done without much assistance.

Thus paying attention to play is central for a variety of reasons, although not necessarily the same reasons conventionally given in books on play therapy with children. The

---

[1] In my own practice I have encountered families from ethnic backgrounds in which separation is not seen as a vital part of development. I have seen couples who are having trouble with an adolescent child which appear to be separation problems; but I then find out that the parents live next door to their parents, or even in the same house with the older generation. In some cultures, this is normal, and to help such people see the importance of separation is probably impossible; the children are caught in a very real and probably inevitable conflict between the country they live in (the U.S.) and their parents' ethnic origins, whatever they may be.

conventional reason—that play is the preferred therapeutic mode for children—is not wrong, but needs to be supplemented in the ways I have been describing.

HOSPITALIZING CHILDREN

We rarely hospitalize children for psychiatric reasons, partly because we believe that removing the child from the family is almost never a viable way of addressing a problem. When a separation between parents and child is needed, there are better ways to effect it, ways that do not have medical concomitants, and that do not have such a powerful negative labeling effect (having been hospitalized psychiatrically is never a point in a person's favor in our society). Our experience is that hospitalization can in fact make working things out in the family even harder, and parents and child may often want to prolong a hospitalization because they discover that separation is indeed pleasant. Since hospitals are for illness, they should not be used simply to promote separation and individuation.

What *can* hospitals do? They can of course keep a child safe if there is some question of the child hurting himself. But they do this not through any mysterious agency, but through having people around to keep an eye on the child. When a trial of medication is indicated, they can also provide a controlled setting to make sure the child takes medication, and to do whatever tests are necessary to monitor the biological effects of the drug; and because there is constant ongoing observation of the children, they can make certain that any changes in the child's behavior or affect or demeanor are carefully noted.

Other than these two positive functions of psychiatric hospitalization, what others are there? The child's ordinary caretakers (whether parents or residential school) get some relief, if the child is very difficult to handle. Everyone who is worried about a child's safety can relax temporarily, since the chance of a child coming to harm in a hospital is very small compared with life on the outside. In some cases, where good observational data about a child are hard to come by, because the parents and school cannot provide it, a hospital will give an opportunity for gathering such information. That is, the hospital may answer the question of what this child is like, with the caveat that the child has been removed from his ordinary situation (home and school) and so may behave differently than usual. This is an expensive way of gathering such data, but sometimes there are no plausible alternatives.

On the other side of the ledger, there are various possible adverse aspects of psychiatric hospitalization for children, some of which I have already described. Parents are the usual caretakers of a child, and putting a child in a hospital almost always decreases their role, even when the hospital promotes family work and frequent visiting. When parents cannot take care of their child, then they need to say so, but a more lasting solution than hospitalization is necessary. A child who has been hospitalized often must live with that label and it is never a positive one. (However, sometimes hospitalization does serve a positive function in this regard in that it provides what appears to be an objective indicator of the seriousness of the problem. This may be important both for the child and the family. The fact that a child is in the hospital means that the family must confront the seriousness of the child's problem. Children do not go to the hospital for trivial reasons. For some families, this is the major positive aspect of the hospitalization.)

Another set of problems arises for our clinic because we do not have our own psychiatric hospital for children under 16. Thus when we want a child in the hospital, we must look for one in our area, and then turn the child over to the hospital. This always makes it harder for us to be in charge of the treatment, and often makes it impossible for us to do much more than stand by, watching what unfolds. Ideally we would have available such a hospital, as we already do for people ages 16 and over. We also have a day treatment center for those over 16. In these situations, we have control over what happens and we can use the hospitalization to focus on whichever clearly defined task we see as critical.

PARENTAL REQUESTS FOR HELP

When parents bring a child to us, their request may take
various forms, and nearly always there needs to be some
translating of their request, however it is worded, into terms
that make sense from our point of view. At one level, parents
are nearly always asking us to help their child become different, which usually means more like the child they want
him to be, or more amenable to the tasks of life, whether
those are school-imposed or have more to do with chores at
home. When this request is close to the surface, it can be
dealt with directly, that is, in terms of a discussion of how
the child is a separate person with her own needs and characteristics so that one cannot simply make her different in
any simple way. Her cooperation needs to be enlisted if she
is going to change, and in some cases parents can see that
very readily. In these cases, a shift has already occurred, from
the parent saying to us, "Do something to or for our daughter"
to "Let us see if our daughter wants to do something and
whether she will do it with you." Or we can talk about how
having a fully docile child who does everything appropriately
is not a very likely possibility nor, if possible, would it probably
be very appealing. If the parents agree to that, then a shift is
already underway from the initial position in which the parents
said, "Our child is not cooperative," to saying, "Our child is
not *always* cooperative," or "She is not cooperative about a
few things in particular which concern us immensely." If that
point can be reached, then often parents can work with their
child to define those areas where cooperation is greatly desired, leaving other areas more to the child's discretion and
autonomy. In these other areas, she can decide herself how
cooperative to be. All of this will occur in cases where the
presenting problems are not very deep, where there is not a
long chronic history, and where parental pathology is at a
minimum. This is the situation in not just a small number of
our cases, but neither is it the majority of our cases.

Sometimes parents say straight out that they consider their
child bad and they want him fixed so he is good again. Here

it is important to make a careful attempt to gather information about the child which goes beyond the presenting symptom, whatever that might be. The aim in doing this is to gain data that support the position that the child is not all bad, or not always bad with everyone in every situation (almost no one is, of course). Behind this is an attempt to move the parents away from seeing the problem as one of fixed character structure (which they want modified) to their seeing it as one of certain behaviors occurring in a certain situation which need to be modified. The point of this is that behavior is usually easier to modify than character structure. So if the parents call the boy a pathological liar, one needs to help them see that sometimes he tells the truth, or that he has not always been a pathological liar. Usually parents who care enough about their child to go to the trouble to set up an appointment with us and bring their child in have not entirely given up on their child, so that no matter how angry they may be, they are not totally convinced that their child is once and for all just plain bad. Occasionally there are family dynamics that necessitate that there be a bad child, and the patient in the office may have been selected; intervening in these cases is not always easy whether one is working briefly or long-term. Or parental pathology may be such that a rigid division of the world into good and evil is required, and the child is now in the evil spectrum. In such a case, no amount of just talking to parents is going to make much difference. But most cases are not so pathological. With some of these families, the difficulty may be that the right intervention has not been tried.

One of our tactics in such situations is to keep track of what has been tried, so as to keep trying new things. If couples work has already been done, then a family approach might be worth pursuing. Different family approaches can be tried (some more structural, some more strategic perhaps). The one-way mirror can be used, with an observing team (as Selvini Palazzoli does in Milan). Or individual work with the child or putting the child in a group might help. Sometimes switching to a different clinician will be effective, using the same modality of treatment that has already been tried and failed with a previous clinician. Or sometimes the family's developmental process will carry it forward to the point where the same intervention that was tried earlier with no success will now have a more powerful impact. The patient's medical chart will ordinarily allow a clinician to note what has been tried in the past, so that new approaches can be attempted. Of course, whatever approach is used must have some basis in the clinical situation as it has become known to the clinician; and ordinarily our clinicians consult with their clinical team before changing modalities in an effort to see what ideas other clinicians may have. But there are some families that will probably not be helped by any therapist, no matter how well-meaning or skillful the clinician may be. We, too, have our share of families who do not respond to interventions.

Once the parents will admit that the child is not all bad, then the question has shifted from Why is he bad? to Why does he do this bad thing at this particular time? This is often an easier question to answer. So when parents at first describe a child as a liar, the task of transforming the child into a truth-teller may be too overwhelming. But if it is a case of a child who tells a lie when he is scared, in particular when he is scared of what his parents may do to him, then some room for progress exists. The parents can be helped to see how their child is showing his good nature by having the decency to be scared of them; and sometimes they can be led to try new ways of disciplining their child which will not so terrify the child. Of course, usually what needs alteration is not just the discipline, but the tone and manner of the parents. So that becomes another direction the work takes: helping the parents see that it is possible to institute punishments for infractions of rules without loading the punishment down with all kinds of moral baggage, the point of which is all too often to convince the child that he has joined the side of the devils. Better to just give the punishment, whatever it is, and drop the matter, although for some parents this unfortunately seems to represent pandering to Evil and it does not sit well with them.

Some parents come in who are more sophisticated and will say that they want us to find out what is troubling their child and help him, on the assumption that their child would not be doing these bad things unless something were troubling him. Occasionally in these cases there really is something bothering the child, and he is willing to talk about it. Much more common is the child who says that the only thing troubling him is that his parents are always on his back.

To use our earlier example, the child may have a messy room, and despite repeated requests to pick it up, nothing improves. The parents come to see me and say that if their child were not troubled, he would be more responsive to their wishes. So I am supposed to discover what is truly troubling their child and do something about it. Here the shift that is needed is from the parents' definition of trouble (something the child does) to a view of the child as establishing his own sense of values, which may vary from those of the parents. He may want a messy room, and the mess may not reflect internal chaos or low self-esteem (as many parents will argue quite seriously). Or more frequently, he may not want to go to the trouble of cleaning, or he may not want to be like his parents who are always cleaning. But whatever the nature of the existing circumstances, the child can be seen as *doing something other than causing trouble*. That is, from the child's point of view, trouble is not the aim of his behavior. So if trouble is the result, that flows from the parents' way of perceiving the situation, and there needs perhaps to be some alteration in that. This is not to say—which many parents are afraid of—that the mess is the parents' fault. Rather this is to say that if they could relax about it or work with the child toward formulating some list of rules for frequency of cleanup of the mess (say once a week, so the room can be vacuumed), the trouble would disappear. Not the trouble of the messy room, but rather the trouble of the fight between parent and child which results from the interaction of the messy room with their values about cleanliness and order.

So the parental conception that the child has a problem that needs fixing needs to be modified, though the direction the modification takes in the therapy will hinge on the precise presenting circumstances. The point of this view is not to minimize the child's problems which may be real, but to make clear that they exist in a context which includes as a vital component the parental reaction to the problem. The child does something and the parents do something: that nexus is the problem. Usually they are not separate, independent acts but are rather exquisitely dependent on one another so that modifying one of them necessitates modifying the other. Neither is usefully seen as the original act, with the other being the reaction; rather each is a reaction to the other, and either one may be primary in any particular behavioral sequence, any fight or argument.

Here I am saying something that runs counter to much of what parents will insist to me when they tell me that if their child behaved (they mean behaved well, according to their views), there would be no trouble. This may in fact be true in one sense, but their conclusion is erroneous since they insist that they are just reacting to the child's behavior. He lies, so we get angry; if he did not lie, we would not get angry—this is the form their argument takes. But what if the anger and the lying are intimately bound together, not in a mystical sense which holds that each atom is part of all others, but rather in a psychological and sociological sense that human acts are interdependent? What if the boy lies partly because he is afraid of his parents' anger (and not because he is a sociopath who is destined for a life of crime)? When parents first hear this, they hear it as an attack on them, as though they are being told that it is their fault the boy lies. That is, they turn their original premise upside down and now say: because we are angry, he lies, so you are telling us not to get angry, and then the problem will vanish. But this is not the point at all, since this is the same overly simple analysis of human behavior which they came in to the office with, only turned the other way around. First they thought it was the child's fault; now they think I'm telling them it's their fault.

But the truth is much more complicated and hard to grasp: that both child and parent are bound together in a way that defies our common sense notions of human separateness and identity but which nonetheless needs to be accommodated in our view of how people behave. Ideally child and parents together need to be persuaded to look at matters in this way, although in reality it is often the parents who must take the responsibility of working from within this altered way of viewing reality. The parents do have more responsibility, since they are always older and usually more mature. So they have the right to make up the rules, but they have the equal responsibility to see how the rules affect the child and to alter the rules if the effects seem adverse. Notice I do not talk about abandoning the rules; children usually are quite agreeable to there being rules, though they may object to the specific form that the rules take or they may think there are too many rules. But children are not usually fighting for total freedom. They are usually much more moderate and simply wanting some autonomy, some say about what happens.

Most problems that arise at this juncture are connected with the parents' overinvolvement with the child. The parental dilemma is always the same: to provide care and protection, to be involved, and yet gradually to disengage, and again and again it seems that the parents who find the former not just easy but truly enjoyable have difficulty with the latter. Even worse, the child usually is accustomed to having an over-involved parent and may become upset if the situation changes.

Then apparently we have multiple goals in our encounters with patients. One aim is to help them with whatever problem they come to us with, and the variety of problems that people present with is truly amazing. Another goal, sometimes, is to shift their view of social reality, the social reality which they inhabit and which partly they have constructed, for that is my conviction. So achieving this goal is more complicated, since it requires that the parents and child all engage with me in considering their familial reality as a construction, and this is of course an odd notion for most people. Even when it is an intellectually plausible or appealing idea, it is still hard to grasp in the concrete praxis of one's daily life.

THE SOCIAL CONSTRUCTION OF REALITY

What is the best way to do this, to help the parents shift their view of reality, to help them see how their view of reality is a construction that may benefit from some modification?

There is no one way, of course, and what works with one family may not work with another. So the keys are persistence and flexibility: the persistence to keep trying when one thing does not work, the flexibility to try different things.

My own techniques begin with my attempt to make clear that I am attentive not just to the parents' view of things but to the child's view, and that I assume that the child's view will vary from that of the parents. Why is this important? Because it opens up a view of a reality of multiple perspectives. Mother has her view, father has his view, which although overlapping with mother's view will be different in some ways—and I will push for the differences, starting even in the very first interview—and the child has a still different view. For a few families this will be felt as an attempt to drive a wedge between family members, but most people will react by feeling that I am showing a respect and concern for their individuality; they will ordinarily not feel threatened at first, and will instead react by being more expansive. Nearly always people appreciate attention (this is after all one of the crucial fulcrums around which all our methods of therapy revolve, since we nearly always pay close attention to people, no matter what our various approaches may be), so a technique that involves paying alternating attention to various family members will generally be successful in the sense of drawing each person out, in involving each person in what is happening in the session.

I do not need to underscore the evident phenomenon of there being a variety of views in order to use it later in my effort to help the family see that we are dealing with a social construction which does not necessarily need to go on existing in its present form. I only need to point out, at relevant points, that we are dealing here with a situation but also with different views of a situation.[2]

Sometimes shifting a viewpoint is easier than changing something larger. For example, if a couple discovers that one strand

---

[2] Contemporary family therapy and various theoretical approaches in this field have emphasized this idea. See for example Bradford Keeney's *The Aesthetics of Change* (1983) or Lynn Hoffman's book on family therapy (1981).

in their recurrent marital conflict involves scenes arising out of the husband's feeling that the house is a mess and wanting it cleaned up, one level of response might involve taking just his point of view, not in the sense of sympathizing with his desire for cleanliness, but in the sense of saying to him, well, what can you do about this? Obviously there are several things he can do, one of which is to clean up the mess himself, or to ignore it, or to see it as an inevitable consequence of living a busy life in which there is too much to be done. Other activities may be higher on the list of priorities than cleaning up the kitchen. Feeding the children or preparing in the evening for the following day's work may both be more important than cleaning.

Notice that in this example the couple must first of all be able to recognize some pattern in their quarreling and acrimony. This in itself is often a complicated feat, one requiring substantial therapeutic work before it can be attained. The next step, in the above case, was to try to help the husband shift his perception of the situation. The original definition of the problem was: the house is messy. This was accurate, and there is no point in trying to persuade him that the house is not really messy. But the newer view of the situation is that he needs to do something himself, other than push his wife to clean the house.

OPENING NEW PERCEPTIONS OF THE SITUATION

It is worth noting here that there is very little focus on the husband's feelings of anger, irritation, and resentment. Much more attention is paid to the idea that he can do something about his feelings or about the situation that engenders his feelings. A different vista would open—not an irrelevant or trivial one, but one that we do not find helpful in our short-term work—were we to inquire, for example, about his feelings about his mother, or his feelings about the role division between the sexes and how his sense of that is rooted, perhaps, in his own childhood and the images he still carries around of what a real man or woman should be like. All of this might be explored in a different context than the one we provide, and people who come in explicitly saying they want to explore such issues are told sooner rather than later that we do not offer that particular service.

With couples who are agreed that cleaning the house is the wife's role, there is no point in trying to help the husband start cleaning the house. A different approach might be to ask him what he can do to get his wife to do what he wants done. This line of questioning is useful in most situations, since it shifts the responsibility for what happens off the bad person who is not doing her duty, and onto the moral person who wants the dutiful act carried out properly. How can he get his wife to clean? What can he do for her that will help her give him what he wants? You can say this to either member of almost any dyad about almost any complaint, and sometimes it is dramatically effective. If the woman is hurt that her husband does not greet her at the door in the evening with a smile and a kiss, the wife can be asked what she could do to get the husband to greet her in that way.

Humor

What other techniques are there for helping people shift their perceptions of a situation, to help them realize that they are important contributors to whatever the situation is? Another technique I find useful because it is consistent with my style is humor, the sort of humor that partly revolves around recognizing that there are different ways of looking at any given action or situation. Humor is a very complex phenomenon and my discussion of it here is confined to my attempt to show ways in which it is a useful device for liberating people from whatever constrained view of a situation they may already possess.

Humor can help bring into view the lighter side of what otherwise might be felt as an intolerably serious situation. Sometimes people sink or are pulled down into the negative aspects of their lives; the sadness, or guilt, or anger, or grief may feel insurmountable, and for some people, feeling that someone else knows the situation but is not overwhelmed by it is helpful. If humor can help convey this, then it may be useful, partly perhaps because humor may contain within it the seeds of a recognition that there is more to life than whatever the sadness or anger may contain. And often this is a very powerful suggestion which is better made implicitly, through humor, than explicitly. That is, telling someone who is very angry that by tomorrow they will have forgotten about the incident that enrages them may not be as effective as some attempt to find the humorous side of whatever has happened, and the humor may implicitly be saying the same thing—there is more to life than this moment of rage.

Humor may in effect create a small moment of time-out, or a minor key release from the bondage of whatever terrible fate seems to have enveloped one. By time-out, I am referring to what conventionally happens in sports contests when the action is very hot and one side wants a moment to recoup, to gather its forces before returning to the fray. The convention of being able to declare a time-out is very useful although life does not always oblige. Therapists who work with couples often suggest that a rule be instituted that a fight can be interrupted by either side declaring time-out; in part this suggestion is rooted in an awareness that events have a dynamic of their own and that if one can interrupt the dynamic before it goes too far, one may have saved a situation from deteriorating too horribly to be easily repaired. For such a convention to be useful, however, a fighting member of a couple must be able to step far enough outside the fight to realize that a time-out is needed. And the couple must be cooperative enough to agree on the rule, and to observe it when it is invoked. This is more than many fighting couples can manage. In sports contests, there are coaches and referees who can call time-outs from their perspective outside the immediate arena; similarly, a therapist may play this role for a couple until they are able to develop their own capacity to keep some observing part of themselves out of a fight, and thus are able themselves to call a time-out when it is needed.

Humor, then, allows patients to internalize whatever the point of view is which permits a humorous perspective, and that new somewhat external perspective may help them when they are becoming trapped by some situation. Not that the humor truly changes the situation. Humor does not cure anything, does not really solve anything. All it does is momentarily lift the people who are participating in the humor outside the situation they are in, so that for that moment they can see it from a different point of view. The advantage of humor over pedagogical observations—over lectures or interpretations or explicit advice given by the therapist—is that it is more subtle and ingratiating, and more difficult to fend off for many people.

A four-year-old who is being defiant may be pushing his parents into similar defiance, that is, into a similar assertion of their own individuality and rights. The boy becomes more extreme, and the parents reciprocate. What can happen is eventual mayhem, as the parents will probably have to resort to brute force and power to get their way. But if they can step back—can get some distance on the defiant four-year-old who is their son—then they can see him as a petty tyrant, perhaps, who is ludicrous in his vain attempts to impose his total will upon the recalcitrant world. A four-year-old is so small compared with his parents that his tyranny is in truth nothing to be afraid of, since it will lead nowhere. The world is too imperious for a four-year-old to bend it to his will, his efforts are as futile as those of the king who wants the oncoming tidal sea to roll back from the shore. Parents can be more helpful to a child who is being imperious if they can stop themselves from being sucked into the dynamic of ruler-and-ruled, of controller and controlled, and instead simply laugh at the spectacle.

Some parents will object that when they try humor with their children, the children complain, saying that their parents are laughing at them and are making fun; the child feels, report the parents, that she is not being taken seriously. Parents who report this usually feel deep in their bones that their child deserves to be taken very seriously all the time, and such parents need help, although humor may not in fact be the help that is needed. The problem in this situation is that serious attention is *not* always what is needed, and parents have to realize that. A parent who always laughs at his child will be destructive, but a parent who can never laugh at his child is equally corrosive of that child's development of a healthy autonomy, since giving intensely serious weight to everything a child does can lead to a form of narcissism which will be less and less appealing as a child grows older. The charming narcissism of young toddlers does not long endure.

So I am arguing that humor is a way of calling a time-out, and a way of lifting oneself out of what might otherwise seem an overwhelmingly distressing situation. One of the other important uses of humor is that it can bring people together. The way in which it does this is no more mysterious than any coming together, and almost any experience with significant affect connected to it can bring people together. In my own work, I sometimes use humor to build an alliance with someone who has otherwise remained on the periphery of a family session. In some cases a person on the periphery is there because she has perceptions that are not acceptable to the others in the room. If nonverbal cues exist that indicate this is happening, then sometimes I will reach out to such a person either by trying to articulate what she might be thinking, or by using humor as a way of bringing her into the mainstream of the conversation. Humor may be a technique which will be felt as less coercive than a more direct comment on the person's lack of participation.

An Anthropological Perspective

Another important way of helping people perceive that their problem is partly a social construction in which they are participating involves explicit remarks about our own socio-cultural milieu. Comments that begin with "in our culture" can be used, as when I may point out that not learning to read is only a problem in a culture that defines literacy as of huge importance. Peer pressure for adolescents is an immensely more aggravating problem in a culture that segregates children by age so that adolescents are all grouped together through the social mechanism of compulsory schooling. Having a child toilet trained by a young age is more important when the child is going to be in a school setting at a young age, where the teachers do not want to have to cope with many untrained children whose diapers needs changing. Independence training is more important in our society where parents are seldom with a child all day long, since many parents now work outside the home and so children need to learn to leave the family and home at an early age to go to school.

All these—and many more—are ways in which grasping what a child and family are experiencing hinges on an informed appreciation of the nature of our changing culture. Often all this is too much taken for granted and only becomes a focus when therapists meet a family from a different culture. But it should always be kept in mind, and pointing out when it is relevant is one way to help a family realize that what is being defined as a problem is not a diseased or crippled child but rather a child in interaction with a family and society in which certain forms of behavior are desirable and other forms of behavior less desirable. A boy who is daydreaming when the teacher calls on him is not necessarily a bad boy; his daydreams may be more interesting than what the teacher is saying and cultivating one's imagination can be important in life. However, daydreams can also be a way of retreating from life's demands, and if one is unable to cope with any of life's demands, there is a serious problem. More important, perhaps, a child who disobeys his parents sometimes is not necessarily a bad child, since society will not benefit from having only obedient people in it. Some disobedience is probably socially useful (in one perspective anyway). Our society is not an army in which hierarchy and instant, complete obedience need to be valued above all other virtues.

Many parents realize all this, and sometimes their consultations with us are intended only to allow them to articulate this point of view and then to check and see whether it makes sense to us. Sometimes it does make good sense. Other times, the parents are conducting an elaborate justification for behavior that is rather extreme, and maladaptive or self-destructive (the two are not the same, of course). Making these discriminations is not easy, but my point here is simply that the social context needs to be kept in mind in talking to parents about whatever is defined as a problem, and I often find that making explicit comments—such as those an anthropologist might make—about our society can be one way of helping the parents obtain some leverage on a situation, some way for them to lift themselves above the surface of a problematic situation.

THE IMPORTANCE OF THE SITUATIONAL CONTEXT

The point about the distinction between maladaptive and self-destructive behavior probably needs to be elaborated, since many parents confuse the two and since they are intertwined to a degree, which makes any neat separation of them impossible. Maladaptive behavior is behavior that does not suit a particular context. If one does not have any choice about the context—if one is in a situation and must stay there, all mobility being restricted—then maladaptive behavior will in all probability lead to suffering. But in our society, many people are not completely restricted to one situation. To start with, most of us inhabit more than one situation. I have a family, which is one situation, and a job, which is another. In addition, I have friends who do not belong to either my family or my job situations, so they provide an additional context for me. Further, I can change jobs and, in some sense, I can change families as well (at any rate, many people do so in our culture).

So adaptation has to be considered in light of the question "to what?" Parents sometimes worry that certain of their child's behaviors are so maladaptive that they are suitable for no purpose whatsoever, but that is seldom the case. I do not want to claim that it is impossible, but in my experience, it is very rare to find a child doing something that has no redeeming values, no germ of adaptation anywhere in it. Usually what parents mean is that the child is not adapting to the situation that they conceive as of crucial importance, namely, the family or the school. Then they often will make the inference that this lack of adaptation to a critical environment today implies a lack of ability to adapt to any environment ever in the foreseeable future. Usually this is a mistaken inference, although convincing parents of that is hard.

The idea of self-destructiveness is a separate idea, although parents often couple it with that of maladaptive behavior. Take poor grades as a good archetypal example. The child is getting poor grades in high school and the parents argue that this means the child is not going to get into college and will not be able to earn a living and is destroying his future. So the parents try to persuade or force the child to study, to get better grades. In fact, much of adolescent refusal—to study, to be neat, to wear the right clothes, etc.—is in the service of needs that are just as important as the parental needs for achievement and getting ahead, so often children who refuse certain tasks are in fact fighting for themselves, but in a way that their parents are unlikely to appreciate. But seeing into this tangled web is not simple, and of course there are some adolescents who are truly self-destructive, who are going to destroy themselves, and who are not likely to let their parents stand in their way. But such adolescents are not common, and most of those we see are instead engaged in a battle for their own survival which they are determined to win.

In summary, what is maladaptive today for the child may turn out to be highly adaptive tomorrow, if it succeeds in helping him build a more solid sense of himself and his capacities. Unfortunately, our schools provide a narrow vision of success; ordinarily there are only grades, sports, and popularity with peers as indices of success. Many adolescents have great difficulty connecting themselves with any of these socially accepted versions of success, so in desperation they may reach out for less acceptable means (drugs, etc.)[3]

---

[3] Edgar Friedenberg's analyses of this situation (e.g., in *The Vanishing Adolescent*, 1959) are still germane.

Doing anything about all this is hard, but a therapist can help parents to appreciate the dimensions of the problem. And sometimes a therapist can help the adolescent realize that the difficulties she is having in life are *not* a sign of bad character or of stubborn opposition to benign parental pressures, but rather arise out of a very complex situation, one part of which—the social situation presented by the school environment—is certainly out of her control. There are other ways to be valuable in life than getting good grades or playing sports well, or being popular among one's peers. In the long run, other things matter much more. If a therapist can help an adolescent see this, then that is a very positive accomplishment, even though seeing it will not change the total situation very much.

But it will change the situation in an important way, and comprehending how this occurs is one of the keys to the nature of short-term therapy. To understand this, we must see that *the situation* is constituted by a multiplicity of factors. To start with there are certain more-or-less objective social facts. In addition, there are motives that arise, in part, out of the past and that point into the future; there are perceptions of a situation and of people; and there are feelings. In addition, there is complexity in the interactions among all these, both within one person and between many people. Finally and most important, there is action, construed in the broadest possible sense.

In the example we have been considering, a girl is not doing as well as her parents desire. The girl has feelings about this situation, both about her poor grades and about the pressure her parents are putting on her as a result. She is trying to do something, although we may not be sure exactly what that is. She lives in a society in which grades do matter to some degree; that is, a record is kept which is relatively permanent, which eventually may be sent to colleges if she chooses to apply to colleges. About this last fact, she can do nothing except acknowledge it and try to take it into account.

What can be changed here? Many things, potentially, but a better question is: where shall we begin? Obviously the answer

depends on the evaluation of the case. If the evaluation indicates that this girl is searching for some personal sense of
what matters, and as part of her search is rejecting parental
definitions of what matters, then one place to begin to move
is in the direction of helping her find her own voice, her own
sense of herself. One way to do this is quite simply to talk to
her in a sympathetic way, indicating that her opinions matter.
Oddly enough, many parents who love their children fail to
do this because they become so enmeshed in the battle over
grades, and they become determined to *make* the child do
what is good for her (i.e., study more).

Another possibility is to encourage the girl to keep a journal,
or if she already does, to regard that as an important activity.
Here the therapist is implicitly helping the girl see that there
are many forms of important activity, that studying may be
one such form, but that writing for oneself is another. Parents
too often seem to convey, through their demeanor and attitude,
that there is only one important form of activity, that is,
studying. Thus they rail against what they call time wasted on
the phone with friends and will take away the phone as a
sanction, which they hope will force the child to study.

But with an adolescent, such punishments are almost never
successful; they do not usually help the child study more.
More often than not parents only succeed in making their
child feel attacked, and the child's response is often to attack
back with whatever (admittedly feeble) means are at her disposal. Ideally one rarely forces the child to do anything once
the child is in high school or even, I suspect, once the child
is beyond the age of eight or 10. Rather one tries to persuade
the child, and usually punishments are not the most effective
means, although they or the threat of them are sometimes a
helpful adjunct to other means of persuasion.

There are certain exceptional cases in which an adolescent
essentially does what many adults do, that is, asks others for
help doing something that is difficult. Just as an adult who is
trying to stop smoking or trying to diet may ask others for
assistance in this regard (may ask others not to offer cigarettes,
not to give a large portion of dessert, not to tempt with tasty

fattening foods), an adolescent will sometimes make clear that she needs help studying. So she will convey in a variety of ways that she wants her parents to help her stay off the phone. In such a case, the parents would want to answer the phone and take messages for their daughter. Or if the child is not being entirely explicit about what she wants, the parents can try various limits to see whether their child senses them as supportive. So a phone or television limit can be tried, if it is done in a way that makes obvious how the parents are trying to come to the support of their daughter's own desire to study.

THE CONFLICT OF DESIRE

But the crucial detail here concerns the desire to study. Whose desire is it? A child who wants to study is a very different case from a child whose parents want her to study. When wants collide, then conflict ensues, and the mistake that many parents of adolescents make is to disparage the legitimacy of the child's wants. The situation is further complicated by the frequent lability of the adolescent's desires. One day she wants one thing, another day something else. It is a rare adolescent who knows exactly what is wanted, and I would go further and argue that it is a rare person who knows exactly what is wanted. But adolescents are usually less adept than adults at covering up their fluctuations of desire and mood; they have less well developed characterological defenses, to use the jargon of our field; and they have less experience of knowing what happens when they pursue one thing rather than another. So they need to learn what happens when they pursue studying and then compare that with what happens when they pursue friends instead, or pursue daydreaming or watching television. Experimenting with different ways of living is one way children have of trying to figure out what they want to do later, and interfering with this process is fraught with peril, although many of the dangers may not appear until years later. Here I am referring to the difficulties some older adults encounter when they try to discover what they want when they are no longer 14 or 17 but 35 or 40. Parents may quake in dread as they watch their children experiment with different possibilities, but better to allow and support some degree of experimentation during adolescence than try to drive it underground altogether.

The Ambiguity and Fluctuation of Desires

There is a larger sense in which I think most people do not know clearly what they want, and the reasons for this lie hidden in both the complexity and fluctuations of our society and in the nature of human desires. This is not the place for an extended discussion, but essentially there are multiple facts which, when taken together, make clear that human wants or desires are a very complicated matter. One fact is that our society is relatively individualistic, which means that people are expected to pursue their own desires, are expected to *have* particular desires of their own. Another fact is that the variability of potential activities in our society is very large, many things are possible for those with resources, and many people (not all, of course) have resources of time and money and energy. All this choice and the relative scarcity of constraints (compared with other societies and other possible situations) place a very large burden on each individual. The burden is that choices are necessary every step of the way. Finally there is the fact that people do not appear—contrary to what Freud at times tried to argue—to have a fixed or finite set of motives. Rather people potentially have an immense variety of motives, which probably alter over the years and which almost never all work together in a coordinated, harmonious way. If only it were so simple as just sex and aggression, or approach and avoidance. But in fact there are numerous wants, and more are being created constantly, both through the machinations of our business and advertising industries and through other less commercial processes. For example, great artists may create new desires. Once one has heard Beethoven's late quartets, perhaps living without them is impossible. And it may be that many arts work in this way, that is, by creating needs for things that previously did not even exist. For example, when one falls in love, one develops new wants which did not exist formerly, for a particular other person, and all of life involves a similar dynamic. Wants arise and sometimes replace earlier ones, sometimes coexist in awkward balance with older wants. Learning to handle all this is difficult, and adolescents of course have difficulty doing so, and if they do not because they narrow their horizons, that is not necessarily a good thing, although it may be a convenient thing if their narrowed horizons happen to include goals of which the parents approve.

This situation—the one described, of a society that emphasizes individualism, and in which new wants are constantly being created—bears on adolescents with peculiar intensity in our society. Rarely is there a graceful way of handling all the pressure. So when parents attempt to simplify life and argue, for example, that the teenage child has just one job, to study, they are perhaps commendably trying to shrink life's complexity to a manageable domain, but it is rare that an adolescent will nod his head and say, yes, you are right, that's all that life is about. An adolescent who does that will sooner or later have to raise his head from this rather constricted point of view and see that there is a bigger world out there which must be taken into account.[4]

So one of the thrusts of short-term therapy involves helping people widen their horizons, helping them see that there is more to life than whatever relatively narrow conception of it they possess. Actually most people know that life is complex, so the problem is better stated as one of calling them back to their senses. They have abandoned a view of life as complex in favor of a constricted view of life as a battle, for example,

---

[4] Anyone who works in a college counseling center encounters such people, who have doggedly kept their eyes fixed on their studies during high school and then during the college years, fall apart—usually temporarily—as they try to figure out what does really matter to them. See for example William Perry's interesting book, *Forms of Intellectual and Moral Development in the College Years* (1970).

between the parents and the child over studying. This is never the whole story. Nor is toilet-training ever the whole story. So parents are often helped in a quite simple way when they can be effectively reminded that there is more to life than struggling with their child about his use of the phone or his toilet-training.

9

Conclusions

FOCUS AND RESPONSIBILITY

I have attempted to say something about an approach to intermittent, short-term therapy which has been found useful in a health maintenance setting that mandates limited mental health benefits. But the significance of this approach does not lie in keeping the limited benefit in mind, but rather in always thinking in terms of keeping a clear focus on the work of therapy and not letting things drift or waiting to see what unfolds in the course of time. I have attempted to review various factors that make this possible, primary among which are the activity of the therapist, and the cooperation of the patients who have at least some degree of positive sense about the organization of which we are a part. But what about the others, those who have no such positive sense, who come unwillingly to treatment, who are ambivalent at best about treatment, who are part of multiproblem families with no stable family members who might make sure that appointments are kept and homework carried out by the family members?

My answer would be simply that such patients are not well served in our system, but I would add furthermore that I think that they are not well served by any system that provides verbal therapy. Such families need much more than therapy, and what they need is rarely available through any mental

221

health setting, even those that routinely do outreach, since that is just one small piece of what is required. To take the example of a family headed by a woman, in which there has been a history of child abuse and multiple partners for the woman, we can scarcely pretend that holding appointments open for them, no matter how many times they come late or miss appointments altogether, is going to help them. Nor can we seriously think that simply going out to visit them in their own home will make a huge difference, although it could help. The whole enterprise of psychotherapy rests at bottom on the assumption of the patient being engaged in the endeavor. When the patient is reluctant to undertake the hard work, then nothing can happen. Naturally, with any patient, once a relationship has been established, then anything may be possible. So any action on the part of the therapist that helps create such a relationship will be likely to contain in it something that may be beneficial. (Of course, any relationship also contains within it the seeds of possible harm; no matter how we try above all else to avoid harm, we cannot avoid the snares that accompany the dependence inherent in any relationship—the dependence of the patient on the therapist, for example. More on this in a moment.)

In Chapter 1, I referred to an article by Eugene Gendlin (1986). He makes the critical point that one cannot provide therapy to someone who does not want it. Our good intentions as therapists are not enough, and although we all know this in one sense, we are reluctant to make this knowledge one of the grounding principles of our work. Our reasons may be several: perhaps a fear that if we do, people will be less likely to turn to us for help in their times of need; perhaps our reluctance to confess such a weakness (people hope we have more power, and in part we enjoy allowing this illusion to grow). We surely dislike feeling helpless, and one way to avoid the feeling is to believe we have the power to cure or help when in fact we do not.

But there still remains the question of how much therapy is enough for a particular problem or a particular patient. Unfortunately none of us knows the answer to this question. We can sometimes tell whether a patient is improving or not, but we have no way of knowing what the relationship is between that process and the therapy process that we are intending to make happen (in Gendlin's phrase). Of course, we do not ever really make therapy happen just by intending it; rather we try to engage the patient in the process, and if the patient becomes engaged, then something constructive may happen. But in our setting, all the therapists must struggle with the difficult question of whether more meetings or more effort expended on a patient or family will make a difference. Our difficulty is exacerbated by the community we live in, since other therapists who do not have to operate within our constraints would routinely offer more services than we do (i.e., more sessions) and although we may think that such offers do not necessarily lead to any more improvement in patients than what we offer, we nonetheless are left having to defend our position (which is still, after all, a minority position). But the best defense of our position—that brief, intermittent therapy will suffice for many people, is in the first place to admit that there are some people who are not going to improve just because the therapist tries to help them; second, to argue that some people need more than any system of care is going to be able to offer them (more resources, more money, more housekeeping help, etc.); and finally, to keep in mind always that a different approach, or a different provider applying a similar approach, may help the patient more than we are able to do. So we make an explicit part of our system the idea that not every therapist can necessarily provide therapy to every patient who comes his way.

CONSULTATION AND CONFLICT

To return to the topic of dependence, our approach to work with children and families relies in part on an understanding of the necessarily conflict-laden nature of dependence between parent and child in a culture which so overvalues autonomy and independence.[1] A considerable portion of our work con-

---

[1] See Albert Memni's (1984) interesting book on dependency for a discussion of some aspects of this situation.

sists of what we have called consultation to the parents about this issue; we believe that children and parents will inevitably have conflicts and that we can help parents understand why and help them develop better ways of handling the conflicts that do arise. Thus our perspective is informed not just by the usual knowledge of family therapy techniques and conventional ideas about individual psychotherapy, but by a more sociologically based perspective as well. Most problems benefit from being seen within a social context as well as a developmental context. So throughout the book I have drawn attention to ways in which a problem may be developmentally ordinary (a four-year-old having nightmares, for example), or may be sociologically quite ordinary (the orientation of adolescents to their peer culture, which leads to some of the difficulties most parents have with adolescents, is in large part a function of the age-segregation of children in our society). This is not to say that the conflict is not painful, just that what needs to be done is to develop a perspective that will show it as ordinary pain. Freud said this well when he said the aim of psychoanalysis is to transform neurotic misery into ordinary misery, but too often this remark is not taken seriously, but heard as a form of cynicism or jaded world-weariness. In fact, it is straightforward realism.

A SOCIOLOGICAL PERSPECTIVE

There is another side to the sociological perspective I have presented; namely, that all behavior—even the most disruptive and seemingly impulsive behavior of children who are apparently out of control—has its structured, organized aspects. Particularly in working with a nonhospital-based population as we do for the most part, we can emphasize the ways in which what the child is doing has a point. It is rarely blind impulsivity, even in very young children, assuming they have been living with socialized adults during their early years. We express this perspective in our work when we ask parents to reflect on what they think the child is doing. What is your idea or theory about the child's behavior? is the question to ask. Parents sometimes prefer to see their child as mad or bad, but this is almost never adequate; more often the parents we see are puzzled and will say they simply do not understand at all. So some of our work with families involves our pushing the parents toward a recognition of the organized aspects of their child's awful behavior. If the child cries at night and will not go to sleep, it may be colic and have to be endured until the child's intestinal system matures; but more often, especially in children over two, the crying is aimed at some goal, however inchoate. The crying is quite emphatically not designed to drive the parent crazy, no matter how much the parent may sometimes feel that is the case. The child may simply want his parent near him, all the time. Or the child who at age eight does not come home on time from playing down the block may be exploring his autonomy, trying to see what the limits of his power are. Or he may be responding to peer pressure to stay out, to disobey parents, to ignore the parental summons home. No matter what the child does, there is usually some organized aspect to it, and the organization of the child's behavior is often related to the organization of the parents' and family's behavior.[2]

For many parents, this is the major work of therapy: coming to see their child's misery or his miserable behavior as a part of life and not to be eradicated, even if it could be. Pain is part of life (ordinary pain); and in addition, there is no way to have a conflict-free dependence involving a human who has built-in pushes towards autonomy, especially in a culture where both sides of this conflict obtain immense support. There are extensive supports for autonomy as well as for dependence. Recognizing this, in part, is common sense, and as we said earlier, part of our form of therapy can be described as calling parents back to the common sense they abandoned

---

[2] A very interesting presentation of this point of view with regard to one variety of behavior which is conventionally regarded as impulsive and out of control is found in a book, *Drunken Comportment* by Craig MacAndrew and Robert Edgarton (1969). They make a very compelling argument that drunken behavior is organized within each society. This, of course, is a conventional anthropological argument about most behavior, but it is a form of argument that can be very helpful to psychotherapists, but with which very few are familiar.

in their pursuit of the project of having perfect children. (Some parents have little common sense to be recalled to, and for them no form of therapy seems likely to help very much, although one should nonetheless never stop trying.)

So far as the issue of dependence on the therapist goes, our system mostly avoids the more intense aspects of the patient's dependence on the therapist (although not always, and not with everyone) because the relationships between patient and therapist are less intense due to the intermittent, time-limited nature of the contacts. Patients ordinarily cannot call their provider directly, but must go through a receptionist (the person we call an area assistant). The presence of the area assistants serves as a dilution to the otherwise more intense relationship that can arise between patient and therapist. Naturally we do not force all patients to speak to the assistant if they really need to talk to us; but the ordinary arrangement suffices for most patients. Furthermore, patients are told immediately that although we provide round-the-clock coverage for all health issues, we do not expect that the patient will routinely be able to speak to their usual provider. Instead, in an emergency they will have to speak to whomever is available. This is a frustration, but one imposed by the reality of our—and their—life situation. Some of our patients nonetheless develop intense transferences to particular providers; there is no way to prevent this entirely, nor would we want to, for transference will necessarily occasionally arise in any therapy.

ACTION

One of the central concepts in this book is that of action, and the associated phenomenological view that action is necessary for each of us to see what we are, to explore our identities, to extend our horizons. As we move forward (this is a perceptual metaphor, but psychologically useful) we see things from different angles, and more and more unfolds before us (just as things behind us recede from view).

Action is the therapist's necessity to begin with; he must know what he is doing and must be active in pursuit of whatever will be helpful with a given family. Even listening is not a passive process, but rather full of activity. It must be informed listening, and "informed listening is an active rather than a passive process that requires the making and breaking of countless hypotheses as the material unfolds" (Spence, 1982, p. 151). It is well known that experienced clinicians are not likely to insist on a complete history with new patients; rather they "proceed to elicit specific data to confirm or refute the hypotheses under consideration" and "they ignore extraneous information while focusing their energies on the elicitation of data that are apt to make a difference in clinical management" (Lazare, 1979, p. 131). The clinician cannot go in a straight line and must always be alert to the associative clues presented by the patient. So the work involves listening with the third ear *and* keeping a mental eye on the focus. All this is very tiring, of course, and makes short-term therapy very demanding, but there is no avoiding this problem.

But action is more importantly what the patient must do in order to change, and almost any action will lead to change of some kind. *Do something different:* this is a very powerful piece of advice, and again, it is one that many people recognize in a common-sense way, as they discuss, for example, what they want to do on their vacation or what they want to cook for dinner or wear to a party. But few people think of applying this idea when they are encountering a problem in a relationship, although that is one place when it can be extremely useful. Family therapists have made the most out of this idea[3] but all of us can use it in our therapeutic work. Most conflicts that are discussed with me in my office have a choreography which is relatively rigid; the content may vary, but the form remains relatively constant as my patients in fact often tell me. What can be done? To start with, do almost any part of the sequence differently and see what happens. This is one of the action imperatives that we have discussed at some length in this book, and it is one that does not require a lengthy relationship with a therapist in order to occur. All that is

---

[3] See Keeney's (1983) book, or Hoffman's (1981), for many examples.

necessary is that the relationship be sufficiently solid so that what the therapist suggests is taken seriously by the patient and the family. Thus one of our principles is that knowledge flows from action, and variability of action will lead to greater knowledge.

AMBIGUITY

In therapy, we are of course always working with essentially ambiguous pieces of behavior which are "rich in meaning, the meanings often overlapping and not hierarchically arranged. By that I mean that no meaning is clearly foremost in importance—until indicated by us or by the patient" (Spence, 1982, p. 154). As I mentioned in Chapter 6, the patient selects certain aspects of his experience, and the therapist, in turn, selects certain parts of what he hears to construct a focus for his hypothesizing. The words which are used are crucial, since they have tremendous power, the power to make meanings for us and the patient. All of this is important in any therapy, but it takes on additional weight in working with children, since many parents come in asking us to find out for them what their child is really feeling, as though we can either read the child's mind or have powers of divination. But the problem is not that we cannot see into the child, but rather that the child, like most people, feels many things if not precisely simultaneously, than in rapid succession. The child really does feel both depressed at times and then elated; he really is angry sometimes and blissful other times. Children should be entitled to have moods like the rest of us; and parents need to be able to feel comfortable with enduring the kaleidoscopic feelings of their children.

But in a more complicated way, even the feelings that alternate are often ambiguous: uncertain, unclear, without definite outlines. And the child's difficulties in this realm are complicated by the fact of his immature development. He is, first, still in the process of discovering what he is like and of creating himself to some degree, so that enacting various roles and feelings is part of his exploratory attempts. Additionally, his linguistic development is immature, so that his ability to discuss what he is feeling is hampered still further by his smaller vocabulary. Keeping all this in mind is important for parents. He is just experimenting: parents may say that about a child who tries a drug, but they need to be able to say that about almost anything a child tries. Furthermore, the child's not being able to say something clearly to his parents about what he is feeling may not be reticence or fear or distrust, which the parents often construe as the child's need for someone to talk to outside the family, but honest confusion and inability to find the right words. These are difficulties all adults experience as well, but the child's problems in these areas are even more marked. So one part of our work is helping parents see all of this, which again is perhaps common sense, but about which parents often need reminding.

OUR SYSTEM

All of these ideas I have been discussing are important; when combined together with our system of care they make short-term therapy possible. The system involves a group practice; many patients who are for the most part actively seeking help; a medical setting within which the patients receive all their care; quick responsiveness to emergencies; round-the-clock emergency coverage; and a limited mental health benefit. Within such a setting, the therapist can use the ideas I have been discussing in such a way that limited periods of therapeutic work interspersed with other periods of no active work (during which the patient may nonetheless be thinking about and integrating what had occurred during the period of active treatment) make sense.

However, we still have the problem of needing to coexist with other systems of care which are different. This inevitably means there are conflicts between us and agencies such as hospitals and schools and courts, all of which often go from the initial identification of a child with a problem to the conclusion that long-term treatment is the only possible answer. What this has meant for our system is a long, slow process of gradually educating those in other agencies in our community about our methods of treatment. Their view originally was probably that we were not providing adequate care, and their usual interpretation of this was probably that we were neglectful in an attempt to save money. We hope that gradually we are persuading them that this is an oversimplified and erroneous view. However, anyone who attempts short-term, intermittent therapy must keep in mind that others will at least be initially bewildered.

A DEVELOPMENTAL PERSPECTIVE

Earlier we alluded to the way in which we look at people and their problems from a developmental point of view. This includes seeing therapy as a developmental process. To begin with, a person may not be ready for therapy when she presents herself for the first time with a problem. Patients are always ready for a solution and often will ask for exactly that: a solution to their pain. But therapy is something slightly different from a solution, and some people need time to appreciate this; and part of that time need not necessarily involve active treatment, but instead can involve a period of waiting and thinking things over, with the knowledge that the therapist will be available when the patient is ready to resume.

Second, therapy has a developmental process of its own. Describing what needs to happen is complicated, but the actual meetings between therapist and patient are only the outward manifestations of the crucial process. What must occur is some shift in the patient's way of viewing things, or way of thinking about and experiencing life events. Such alterations usually occur naturally in the course of daily life (without any intervention). This is the central fact to keep in mind: developmental change occurs continuously, even in adults. Shifts in experience are a natural event. Believing this is of critical importance to any therapist who wants to try methods of treatment such as I have been describing in this book. For only when one believes this can one conscientiously plan to treat people without seeing them frequently. If one does not believe this, then one is inclined to assume that face-to-face meetings and active therapy are critical for the process of change and improvement in the patient, and once one assumes that, then one is moving toward a treatment plan involving frequent sessions.

If one sees people as changing naturally in the ordinary course of events—and this is another aspect of our developmental perspective—then one sees intervention by a therapist as an unusual event. So when an intervention appears necessary, our assumption is that all we are doing is assisting in helping someone who is stuck move forward once again, in what is ordinarily a naturally occurring process. Our assumption, furthermore, is that the necessary work that the patient is doing does not occur only in the therapist's office. The patient is working things through, reflecting, and thinking about things continuously; the actual meetings help this process and perhaps get it going again when it has come to a halt, but they are not the only curative factor.

If such reflective work is not occurring during the in-between times, then even frequent face-to-face therapy sessions are not likely to have much impact. All therapists know this, although there are many reasons why acknowledging this and making it a constitutive part of the treatment plan are not common. But once one does build on this idea in constructing a method of treatment, there is no reason why a therapy cannot consist of two or three sessions spaced fairly close together, and then a period of a month or two of no meetings, and then a resumption of active treatment (office meetings). Or the plan can involve almost any conceivable combination of actual meetings and periods of fewer meetings.

Exactly how a treatment plan is worked out depends on the individual patient. But in using this approach with any patient, the therapist must frequently look closely at the question of whether the patient is working. We ask much more quickly (than one might in private practice): Is anything happening? Shall we stop for now for a month, then meet again? The general question is: How is the patient using this time?

Another way to look at this is to wonder whether there is any way that the patient can obtain outside the office what she is getting in the office, however that may be described. Many couples use time in the office as a chance to talk to one another; thus many therapists who work with such couples will ask whether there is any way the couple can arrange to talk to one another without coming to the office. Can they schedule meetings with each other even though the therapist will not be there? Many couples will say that that sounds peculiar but they will nonetheless admit that they ought to be able to arrange it.

Patients in individual treatment may experience the dialogue that occurs in the office as life-sustaining and may feel that there is no substitute for this dialogue in their everyday life; but internal dialogue occurs constantly in most people and to some degree the therapist may become an internalized voice for the patient, so that even when the therapist is not physically present, his psychological presence may be felt by the patient. We therapists engage in dialogue and find that this helps clarify experience; but this finding only makes sense if we see experience—as I have described it in this book— as inevitably ambiguous to some degree. If experience were always clear-cut, then periods of confusion would be rare events; and therapists would have much less scope for influence, since part of their power derives from the power of words used in dialogue to shape experience. Finding a story to tell, finding an interpretation to use for what has happened, is part of what happens in therapy; but this is an infinitely subtle and complex process, and nowhere as simple as finding the right interpretation and then giving it to the patient, who then has insight and is enlightened. Rather there is a process, and although this process involves the therapist in a critical way, the main part of the work needs to be done by the patient, and patients vary in how ready they are for this work. Thus they may either not be ready for therapy (even though they are suffering), or they may be able to do some of the work on their own without regular and frequent meetings with the therapist.

PROBLEMS WITH OUR APPROACH

The approach I have been describing leads then to alternating periods of what we can call active and inactive treatment. Some telephone work can occur simultaneously, during which the therapist and patient can check with each other about whether they are pursuing the best course of treatment. To work in this way is only possible of course when there is an unending supply of patients; if a therapist is in private practice, he may not have enough patients available to allow each one to come and go on an irregular schedule. And this approach will only work when the patient is inclined to feel taken care of by the system; for the patient who feels abused by the system, or who feels the system neglects her, this approach will not work, since the context within which the treatment occurs will be different in an important way (will be different in the sense that the patient feels it differently). Thus we always have some patients who feel we are not taking care of them, not taking their problems seriously, not giving them the treatment they need and deserve. Such patients might not improve with more frequent and regular meetings either, but they would perhaps feel less abused and this in itself would make a possibly powerful difference. As we pointed out earlier, for some patients, an unending supply of attention may be the prerequisite to any possibility of change, and with such patients, we are not going to be very successful.

An important constituent of our approach is our effort to persuade the patients, either explicitly or tacitly, that our treatment plan is going to be effective. There is no way to do this very quickly, except with the very few patients who are directed to a particular therapist by the recommendations of many of their friends; or who trust their primary doctor so much that they assume that any specialist to whom he refers them will be wonderful. Such patients are predisposed to accept whatever the therapist says very quickly. But most of our patients are not in these categories. Thus we need to educate them about our view of therapy. Some of this is explicitly pedagogical (we tell them how we work). But most of it is implicit in the way in which we book their appointments, and in the ways in which we talk to them in the office. Giving homework, to take a very simple example, is a tacit way of saying to the patient that she must do something at home to keep the treatment going. This is also a way of saying that the work is not just to be done in the office in the therapist's presence.

We run particular dangers in using our approach unselectively with everyone, since we have no good ways to discriminate those patients for whom this approach is ideal from those for whom it is probably not the best treatment method. For example, we tend to rely in part on the patient in deciding when to see the patient next; if the patient is inclined to want to work on her own for a while, we are predisposed by the forces inherent in our system (which has many patients who want help) to believe the patient. Thus we surely overlook some proportion of patients who are simply fleeing treatment. As I have pointed out earlier, we have some built-in safeguards insofar as all our patients continue to see their primary care providers, and thus need to come into our building and are engaged to some degree with others who will ask them about their psychiatric situation, or who may inquire whether the patient is still suffering whatever it was that led her to seek out treatment in the first place. But some patients may disguise all their problems, fearing that their doctor will send them back to the therapist, and we have no way of knowing which patients these may be. Thus we recognize that we miss some patients with our approach. Some who are fleeing treatment we might miss anyway with any approach; but others may be discouraged by the amount of responsibility our approach puts on them. Some almost certainly need longer than we can usually give them to enter into the introductory phase of treatment (building an alliance with the therapist). And some, of course, will not be able to handle the structure: the need to book appointments ahead of time, to go through area assistants in booking appointments, to be punctual, to deal with area assistants when checking in, to talk with strangers during emergency off-hours consultations. But to point this out is to say the obvious: no approach works for everyone.

In conclusion, the therapeutic methods described herein, although developed in an HMO, are pertinent to any setting where resources are limited. They provide a different way of doing time-limited therapy and expand on the ideas which are well known in discussions of brief therapy. Our methods provide a broader and perhaps more useful approach, which has considerable flexibility and is not limited in its value to a small group of patients. As has been made clear, there are some patients for whom our approach will not work, but it is not a large proportion of those who come seeking services. So we can use our approach without the restrictions that other proponents of brief therapy sometimes find necessary.

Bibliography

Berne, E. (1964). *Games people play*. New York: Grove Press.

Bettelheim, B. (1969). *The children of the dream*. New York: Macmillan.

Bettelheim, B. (1976). *The uses of enchantment*. New York: Knopf.

Brownmiller, S. (1975). *Against our will*. New York: Simon & Schuster.

Budman, S. (Ed.) (1981). *Forms of brief therapy*. New York: Guilford Press.

Davanloo, H. (Ed.) (1978). *Basic principles and techniques in short-term dynamic psychotherapy*. New York: Spectrum Publications.

Dennison, G. (1969). *The lives of children*. New York: Random House.

Dubos, R. (1961). *The mirage of health*. New York: Anchor.

Ferenczi, S. (1951). The further development of an active therapy in psychoanalysis. In *Further contributions to the therapy and technique of psychoanalysis*. New York: Basic Books.

Ferenczi, S., & Rank, O. (1925). *The development of psychoanalysis*. New York: Nervous and Mental Disease Publishing Company.

Frank, J. (1961). *Persuasion and healing*. Baltimore, MD: Johns Hopkins University Press.

Freud, S. (1909). Analysis of a phobia in a five year old boy. *Standard Edition, 10*. London: Hogarth Press, 1957.

Friedenberg, E. (1959). *The vanishing adolescent*. Boston: Beacon Press.

Friedenberg, E. (1965). *Coming of age in America*. New York: Random House.

Gardner, R. W., Holzman, P.S., Klein, G. S., Linton, H. B., & Spence, D. P. (1959). Cognitive control: A study of individual consistencies in cognitive behavior. *Psychological Issues, I* (whole No. 4).

Gendlin, E. (1962). *Experiencing and the creation of meaning*. New York: Free Press.

Gendlin, E. (1981). *Focusing*. New York: Bantam Books.

Gendlin, E. (1986). What comes after traditional psychotherapy research. *American Psychologist, 41*, 131–136.

Ginott, H. (1969). *Between parent and teenager*. New York: Macmillan.

Ginott, H. (1971). *Between parent and child*. New York: Macmillan.

Guthrie, G. D. (1967). Changes in cognitive functioning under stress. Doctoral dissertation, Clark University, Worcester, MA.

Haley, J. (1973). *Uncommon therapy*. New York: Norton.

Hoffman, L. (1981). *Foundations of family therapy*. New York: Basic Books.

Keeney, B. (1983). *Aesthetics of change*. New York: Guilford Press.

237

Laing, R. (1967). *The politics of experience.* Baltimore: Penguin.

Laing, R. (1965). *The divided self.* Baltimore: Pelican.

Lazare, A. (1979). Hypothesis testing in the clinical interview. In Lazare, A. (Ed.), *Outpatient psychiatry: Diagnosis and treatment.* Baltimore: Williams & Wilkins.

Laslett, P. (Ed.) (1972). *Household and family in past time.* Cambridge, MA: Cambridge University Press.

Leary, M. R., & Maddox, J. E. (1987). Progress toward a viable interface between social and clinical-counseling psychology. *American Psychologist, 42*(10), 904–911.

MacAndrew, C., & Edgarton, R. (1969). *Drunken comportment.* Chicago: Aldine.

Macmurray, J. (1957). *The self as agent.* London: Faber & Faber.

Macmurray, J. (1961). *Persons in relation.* London: Faber & Faber.

Malan, D. H. (1963). *A study of brief psychotherapy.* New York: Plenum.

Malan, D. H. (1976). *The frontier of brief psychotherapy.* New York: Plenum.

Mann, J. (1978). *Time-limited psychotherapy.* Cambridge, MA: Harvard University Press.

Mead, M. (1928). *Coming of age in Samoa.* New York: William Morrow.

Mead, M. (1930). *Growing up in New Guinea.* New York: William Morrow.

Memni, A. (1984). *Dependence.* Boston: Beacon Press.

Miller, A. (1981). *Prisoners of childhood.* New York: Basic Books.

Miller, A. (1983). *For your own good.* New York: Farrar, Straus & Giroux.

Mishler, E. (1986). *Research interviewing: Context and narrative.* Cambridge, MA: Harvard University Press.

Munroe, R., Munroe, R., & Whiting, B. (Eds.), (1981). *Handbook of cross-cultural human development.* New York: Garland STM Press.

Palmer, R. (1969). *Hermeneutics.* Chicago: Northwestern University Press.

Perry, W. (1970). *Forms of intellectual and ethical development in the college years.* New York: Holt, Rinehart & Winston.

Redl, F., & Wineman, D. (1952). *Controls from within.* New York: Free Press.

Riesman, D., Glazer, N., & Denney, R. (1955). *The lonely crowd.* Garden City, NY: Doubleday.

Rosen, S. (Ed.) (1982). *My voice will go with you: The teaching tales of Milton H. Erickson.* New York: Norton.

Santostefano, S. (1962). Miniature situations test as a way of interviewing children. *Merrill-Palmer Quarterly, 8,* 261–269.

Santostefano, S. (1965). Construct validity of the miniature situations test, I. *Journal of Clinical Psychology, 21,* 418–421.

Santostefano, S. (1978). *A biodevelopmental approach to clinical child psychology.* New York: John Wiley.

Santostefano, S., & Wilson, G. (1968). Construct validity of the miniature situations test, II. *Journal of Clinical Psychology, 24,* 355–358.

Schafer, R. (1954). *Psychoanalytic interpretation in Rorschach testing.* New York: Grune & Stratton.

Selvini Palazzoli, M., Boscolo, L., Cecchin, G., & Prata, G. (1978). *Paradox and counterparadox.* New York: Jason Aronson.

Shorter, E. (1975). *The making of the modern family.* New York: Basic Books.

Sifneos, P. (1964). *Ascent from chaos.* Cambridge, MA: Harvard University Press.

Sifneos, P. (1972). *Short-term psychotherapy and emotional crisis.* Cambridge, MA: Harvard University Press.

Sifneos, P. (1979). *Short-term dynamic psychotherapy: Evaluation, technique.* New York: Plenum.

Spence, D. (1982). *Narrative truth and historical truth: Meaning and interpretation in psychoanalysis.* New York: Norton.

Sterba, R. (1951). A case of brief psychotherapy by Sigmund Freud. *Psychoanalytic Review, 38,* 75–80.

Tomm, K. (1984). One perspective on the Milan systemic approach, Parts I and II. *Journal of Marital and Family Therapy, 10* (2 & 3), 113–125, 253–271.

Weary, G., & Mirels, H. L. (Eds.) (1982). *Integrations of clinical and social psychology.* New York: Oxford University Press.

Whiting, J., Kluckhorn, C., & Anthony, A. (1958). The function of male initiation ceremonies at puberty. In E. E. Maccoby, T. Newcomb, & E. Hartley (Eds.), *Readings in social psychology.* New York: Henry Holt.

Whiting, B., & Whiting, J. (1975). *Children of six cultures.* Cambridge, MA: Harvard University Press.

Winnicott, D. (1964). *The child, the family, and the outside world.* New York: Penguin.

Winnicott, D. (1965). *Maturational processes and the facilitating environment: Studies in the theory of emotional development.* New York: International Universities Press.

Winnicott, D. (1971). *Therapeutic consultations in child psychiatry.* New York: Basic Books.

Index

241